Men, Addiction, an

CW00971839

In the substance abuse and addiction treatment realm, males outnumber females two to one. While gender issues are seen as a key element of women's treatment, the acknowledgement that males are "gendered beings" who have lived lives full of male-specific developmental challenges is often overlooked. This text takes a developmental life-span approach to examine the neurobiological and psychosocial factors associated with substance use disorders for males, specifically in relation to emotional growth and awareness, and how these areas, in turn, affect the development of healthy relationships. Theoretical concepts from the field of interpersonal neurobiology, the psychology of boys and men, and the substance abuse and addiction literature are interwoven with practical clinical examples to help elucidate how the notion of fostering emotional development can strengthen the treatment and recovery processes with boys and men. Relevant case examples are included that illustrate work with males of all ages and address a variety of factors associated with culture, ethnicity, race, religion, and sexual orientation. Mental health practitioners will find this a valuable guide to understanding male development in relation to substance use and abuse and to providing more comprehensive, gender-responsive counseling and assessment practices.

Mark S. Woodford, PhD, is an Associate Professor and Chairperson of the Department of Counselor Education at The College of New Jersey.

The Routledge Series on Counseling and Psychotherapy with Boys and Men

SERIES EDITOR

Mark S. Kiselica
The College of New Jersey

ADVISORY BOARD

VOLUMES IN THIS SERIES

Men, Addiction, and Intimacy

Strengthening Recovery
by Fostering the Emotional
Development of Boys and Men

Mark S. Woodford

Routledge
Taylor & Francis Group

NEW YORK AND LONDON

First published 2012
by Routledge
711 Third Avenue, New York, NY 10017

Simultaneously published in the UK
by Routledge
27 Church Road, Hove, East Sussex BN3 2FA

Routledge is an imprint of the Taylor & Francis Group, an informa business

Library of Congress Cataloging in Publication Data
Woodford, Mark S.
    Men, addiction, and intimacy : strengthening recovery by fostering the
    emotional development of boys and men / Mark S. Woodford.
        p. cm.
    Includes bibliographical references and index.
    1. Men. 2. Substance abuse—Patients—Counseling of. 3. Emotions. I. Title.
    HQ1090.W66 2012
    362.29'186—dc23
    2012001658

ISBN: 978-0-415-87099-3 (hbk)
ISBN: 978-0-415-87100-6 (pbk)
ISBN: 978-0-203-86979-6 (ebk)

Typeset in Berling
by EvS Communication Networx, Inc.

Contents

Series Editor's Foreword

In 1997, Terrance Real, a family therapist, published a deeply moving book, *I Don't Want to Talk About It: Overcoming the Secret Legacy of Male Depression*. Drawing from his own painful experiences and those of men he had counseled professionally, Real argued that many of the problems experienced by men, including depression and substance abuse, are linked to the male socialization process. Real stated that boys are "greatly encouraged [by their families and society] to develop their public, assertive selves, but they are systematically pushed away from the full exercise of emotional expressiveness and the skills for making and appreciating deep connection" (p. 23). The more brutally a boy is pushed in this direction, Real continued, the more likely he will hide and deaden his feelings of vulnerability through compulsive drinking, drugging, womanizing, and workaholism, and externalize his pain through explosions of rage and abusive behaviors that isolate him from true intimate contact with others. To help troubled men counter these strong socialization forces and overcome their hidden pain, Real recommended that we show compassion to men, empathize with the shame and fear they have about being vulnerable, help them to recognize the wounded child within them, and teach them how to be emotionally expressive and experience true intimacy.

Several psychologists stated a similar point of view in the groundbreaking book, *The New Psychology of Men*. For example, in his chapter calling for a reconstruction of masculinity, Levant (1995) argued that we must help men to shed outdated notions of masculinity emphasizing that it is shameful for men to express tenderness and vulnerability. In another chapter of the book, Brooks and Silverstein (1995) pointed out that many of the major ills of our society, such as substance abuse, are predominately male problems, which, they argued, are linked to the male socialization process. All three authors stated that we must show empathy for men who are raised to conform to constricted notions of masculinity, understand the price that men and society bear for the problems associated with male gender role conflicts, and practice a gender-sensitive approach to therapy that helps boys and men to embrace less restrictive forms of masculinity. In his more recent work, Levant (2001) added that we must teach men the language of emotions and how to use emotional expression to form deeper personal connections with others.

Since the publication of *I Don't Want to Talk About It* and *A New Psychology of Men*, the field of addictions studies and treatment has also recognized the importance of gender as a factor in understanding and treating substance abuse. *In Principles of Drug Addiction and Treatment: A Research-Based Guide*, the National Institute on Drug Abuse (NIDA; 2009) stated:

> Gender-related drug abuse treatment should attend not only to biological differences but also to social and environmental factors, all of which can influence the motivations for drug use, the reasons for seeking treatment, the types of treatments that are most effective, and the consequences of not receiving treatment. (p. 20)

The NIDA (2009) also noted that effective treatment of alcohol and drug abuse must include an understanding of the impact of substances on the brain. The NIDA (2009) stated that substance abuse:

> affects multiple brain circuits, including those involved in reward and motivation, learning and memory, and inhibitory control over behavior. Some individuals are more vulnerable than others to becoming addicted, depending on genetic makeup, age of exposure to drugs, other environmental influences, *and the interplay of all these factors* [italics added]. (p. v)

When I conceived the *Routledge Series on Counseling and Psychotherapy with Boys and Men*, I realized that the series would not be complete unless it included a book addressing the complicated interplay of these factors in the development and treatment of substance abuse in boys and men, and written by a scholar who has the ability to integrate the literature on substance abuse, counseling, men and masculinity, developmental psychology, the psychology of emotions, and neurobiology. To find that scholar, all I had to do was walk down the hall from my office at work and pitch my idea to my good colleague, Dr. Mark Woodford, associate professor and chairperson of the Department of Counselor Education at The College of New Jersey (TCNJ). It turns out that Dr. Woodford, a master addiction counselor and an authority on substance abuse counseling who had skillfully revamped our substance abuse counseling curriculum at TCNJ, was already toying with writing the exact book that I had in mind. After working as an addictions and dual diagnosis counselor at the Colonial Hospital and Recovery Center in Newport News, Virginia, and at Rehabilitation and Health, Inc., in East Boston, Massachusetts, and then conducting investigations into the recovery process among undergraduate students struggling with drug and alcohol abuse, Dr. Woodford became intrigued by the manifestation of substance abuse in boys and men. He kindly volunteered to write a seminal chapter (Woodford, 2008) regarding his thoughts on the topic for the first book on this series, *Counseling Troubled Boys*. That chapter became the foundation for his current project, *Men, Addiction, and Intimacy: Strengthening Recovery by Fostering the Emotional Development of Boys and Men*, which is the latest addition to the series. It is truly a remarkable volume.

Writing with an accessible and compassionate voice, Dr. Woodford explains in *Men, Addiction, and Intimacy* that boys and men are "gendered beings" who are raised with societal expectations about what it means to be a man. Males who are taught very constricted, traditional notions of masculinity tend to grow up believing that they should be tough, avoid the expression of tender emotions that could make them appear vulnerable to others, and not ask for help when they are in distress. Dr. Woodford further explains how these ideas of manhood can play a role in male substance abuse and addictive behaviors, which in turn can affect the development of the brain and erode important emotional bonds that men have with others. Thus, gender-sensitive counseling with boys and men who have substance abuse problems involves understanding the client's male socialization experiences, teaching him about the how the brain works, and fostering his emotional awareness and communications and his connections with others as he moves on the path to recovery. Dr. Woodford also demonstrates how to tie this male-friendly approach into theories and strategies of substance abuse counseling through a series of case studies with five different age groups of males, spanning the early adolescent years (ages 12–18 years) through older adulthood (ages 60 years and above). Thus, he offers us a gender-informed, interdisciplinary, life-span developmental approach to substance abuse counseling with men.

I am grateful to Dr. Woodford for his masterful, integrative book, which will inform the helping professions for many years into the future, and I am honored to have his comprehensive book as a volume in this series.

Mark S. Kiselica

REFERENCES

Brooks, G., & Silverstein, L. B. (1995). The dark side of masculinity: An interactive systems model. In R. F. Levant & W. S. Pollack (Eds.), *A new psychology of men* (pp. 280–324). New York: Basic Books.

Levant, R. F. (1995). Toward a reconstruction of masculinity. In R. F. Levant & W. S. Pollack (Eds.), *A new psychology of men* (pp. 280–333). New York: Basic Books.

Levant, R. F. (2001). Desperately seeking language: Understanding, assessing and treating normative male alexithymia. In G. R. Brooks & G. Good (Eds.), *The new handbook of counseling and psychotherapy for men* (Vol. 1, pp. 424–443). San Francisco: Jossey-Bass.

Real, T. (1997). *I don't want to talk about it: Overcoming the secret legacy of male depression*. New York: Fireside.

Woodford, M. S. (2008). Moving beyond "drinking like a man": Tailoring substance abuse counseling strategies to meet the needs of boys. In M. S. Kiselica, M. Englar-Carlson, & A. M. Horne (Eds.), *Counseling troubled boys: A guidebook for practitioners* (pp. 219–242). New York: Routledge.

Preface

Pleasure- or stimulus-seeking and self-destructive motives are indeed apparent in addictions, but in my opinion they are more often by-products of or are secondary to problems in self-regulation in which the capacities for managing feelings, self-esteem, relationships, and self-care loom large.

—Khantzian (1999, p. 44)

Imagine a man waking up to find a storm raging inside his body and mind. Like a sailor on a stormy sea, he tries to secure himself to something solid. Yet the elements of the storm push and pull him like a tug-of-war. At best, this man has been taught how to stand and respond to the waves of sensations in his body, the images in his mind, and the thoughts and feelings that arise as the tremendous forces of his "storm" surge and subside. From a flexible, yet solid stance, he is wholly aware of the impact of the storm on his mental, emotional, and bodily states. And there is recognition, as well as a sense of knowing from experience, that this storm will pass. At worst, he does not have the skills to respond and becomes overwhelmed by the push and pull of the mental and emotional elements of the storm. At this point, our proverbial man is in a state of crisis. Feeling off-balance, he may grasp for whatever he can hold onto in order to gain a sense of stability in his body and his mind. Importantly, his inability to respond well to these crises can have an immensely detrimental effect on his life and the lives of others, especially when the way that he chooses to find a sense of balance in the storm is through the use of substances of abuse or through engaging in addictive behaviors. These adaptive responses act only as temporary solutions, often exacerbating the challenges of his emotional and mental life.

When the mental and emotional storms of life hit, we want to be able to feel as if we can stand upright on our own two feet without being swept away. Learning the skill of being aware of one's internal states is the first step in finding balance and stability in recovery, which in turn can aid in managing the emotions that often come within the significant relationships in our lives. Being able to tolerate the intensity of these elements depends largely upon the ability to focus one's attention; that is, "to use awareness to create choice and change" even in the midst of chaos (Siegel, 2010, p. 80). This intentional behavior of focusing attention on these internal states of body and mind is the essence of *self-regulation*—having the ability to find that sense of balance when internal and external forces are pulling and pushing us in different directions.

Having the ability to be with ourselves in order to self-regulate our emotional states is intimately connected to having the ability to be with others. However, the notion of self-regulation, that a "self" can self-regulate, carries with it an individualistic connotation that says: "I can regulate myself without anyone's help." This idea of a self that regulates in isolation is an enticingly deceptive thought—one that can be a recipe for emotional and psychological distress in and of itself, especially when the way that one chooses to find a sense of balance in the storms of life is through the use of substances of abuse or through engaging in addictive behaviors. Interestingly, this stance parallels the traditional male role norm of "self-reliance" (Levant et al., 1992), as well as the adult avoidance attachment style that has been characterized as "compulsive self-reliance" (Mikulincer & Shaver, 2007). The assessment process in substance abuse and addiction treatment can include gaining an understanding of how these types of gender and developmental factors might play a role in a client's history of self-regulation in times of crises, particularly in relationship to the significant others in his life.

For our familiar man, the waves of sensations in the body, the images in the mind, and the thoughts and feelings that arise are the internal elements of his storm. How they have come to be a part of his experience will vary greatly depending on the external elements of his social, cultural, economic, and political background. Perhaps more importantly, how these elements manifest themselves as behaviors in his life will be deeply rooted in the complex interplay of his internal development as a boy and man and in his socialization processes related to his gender, culture, ethnicity, race, religion, nationality, and sexual orientation, as well as the socioeconomic status of his family of origin and the geographic region in which he was raised. These elements are the *context* of his mental, emotional, and relational life. They are the complex sociocultural, developmental influences that have shaped who he is as a human being. And they will affect how he will choose to behave when he is overwhelmed by emotional or psychic pain from states of stress, anxiety, shame, fear, or panic. Will he choose to process his thoughts and feelings internally—or at all? Will he ask for help? Will he try to avoid the pain and discomfort by using substances of abuse or engaging in addictive behaviors? How will he frame these challenges when confronted with them? Will he take responsibility for them? Or will he blame them on others? Will he say that they are a by-product of his career successes, failures, or some combination of these that he will call "stress" in his life? Rather than saying that he is having feelings or emotions, will he say that something is "bothering" him? Or will he say that he is "just not sleeping well right now" or that he is simply distracted, frustrated, or agitated by his work? Each boy and man will have a story to tell about what these elements are, how they came to be a part of his experience, and how he has dealt with them in the past. What he chooses to share—and when and with whom he chooses to share it—will depend greatly on how these factors have influenced his development as a male.

GENDER MATTERS

Interestingly, at the turn of the 21st century, if one searched through some of the best-selling substance abuse and addiction counseling textbooks in the field looking for instruction related to gender and addiction, one would likely find that most chapters dedicated to gender are centered primarily on women's issues in treatment—and for good reason. Women's issues traditionally have been overlooked in the medical and mental health fields, including the substance abuse treatment field, until developments in feminist thinking, gender studies, and psychology and counseling brought much-needed attention to women-specific issues in addiction treatment (Brady, Back, & Greenfield, 2009; CSAT, 2009). For example, women-specific treatment programs focus on addressing the stigma that women face when they decide to seek help through addiction treatment. They emphasize self/relational issues, as well as treating trauma related to domestic violence and abuse (Covington, 2000; Grella, 2008). These gender-responsive programs have been influenced largely by research on women's issues (Covington, 2008) and emphasize the importance of addressing contextual and developmental factors throughout the assessment and treatment process through the use of "relational-cultural theory" (Jordan, Kaplan, Miller, Stiver, & Surrey, 1991).

In documenting the history of the addiction treatment field and the recovery movements in the United States, White (1998) emphasized the importance of remembering the "lessons from those who have gone before us" and reminded us to "respect the struggles of those who have delivered the field into your hands ... respect (with a hopeful but healthy skepticism) the emerging addiction science ... and respect the power of forces you cannot fully understand to be present in the treatment process" (White, 1998, p. 342). Women's and men's studies have taught us that gender-related forces have a significant impact on our lives, i.e., that gender matters. How we develop a sense of who we are as human beings is intimately connected to our gender socialization processes.

By respecting what we have learned from gender studies, we can tailor our counseling strategies to fit with the gender- and culturally-specific characteristics of clients and their families. This requires the cultivation of a *gender-responsive mindset*. This mindset is fostered for mental health professionals in much the same way that multicultural counseling competencies are developed. Through a process of training, education, and self-reflection, counselors can begin to understand the importance and relevance of attending to both gender and ethno-cultural factors in their counseling and prevention practices. With knowledge, substance abuse professionals can more easily recognize the gender-specific developmental challenges that their clients are facing and then tailor the services that they are offering in a more contextually-sensitive way.

In terms of women-sensitive approaches, there have been great strides in raising awareness about the need to increase the availability of resources that provide guidance for how to address the specific needs of women in substance abuse treatment (Brady, Back, & Greenfield, 2009; Briggs & Pepperell, 2009; CSAT, 2009; Straussner & Brown, 2002). With a few exceptions (e.g., Covington, Griffin, & Dauer, 2011; Griffin, 2009; Isenhart, 2001; Straussner & Zelvin, 1997), the same cannot be said about the field in terms of resources that increase awareness and knowledge with regard to males as being gendered beings (Kilmartin, 2007) in the substance abuse prevention and treatment realms.

Yet studies in men and masculinity related to counseling and psychotherapy with boys and men (Brooks, 2010; Brooks & Good, 2001a, b; Horne & Kiselica, 1999) have brought recognition in the mental health professions that gender-responsive prevention and intervention strategies are needed. This research has highlighted "the notion that being a man matters to the extent that masculinity is a focal organizing principle for all aspects of a man's life" (Englar-Carlson, Stevens, & Scholz, 2010, p. 222). Having an understanding about the male-specific issues that have been identified in the psychology of boys and men (e.g., the challenges of building rapport or assessing the full impact of the modeling/enforcement of male-ness in a man's culture) can inform the initial phases of treatment and enhance the delivery of evidence-based substance abuse and addiction counseling practices.

DEVELOPMENT MATTERS

In *Addiction and Change*, DiClemente (2003) discusses several categories of models of addiction that include: social/environment models; genetic/physiological models; personality/intrapsychic models; coping/social learning models; compulsive/excessive behavior models; and an integrative biopsychosocial model. He describes the development of addiction as being "a personal journey through an intentional change process that is influenced at various points by the host of factors identified in these etiological models" (p. 20). Importantly, he writes that "implicit in the concept of human behavior change is a *developmental perspective*" [italics added for emphasis], and that "change in humans takes place over time, at different points in the life cycle, and, most often, involves a sequence of events" (2003, p. 20).

No matter what the developmental level of the client, we can cultivate a mindset that helps us to see the multiple influences and complexities of the personal, social, political, economic, and cultural forces that push and pull our clients in their environment. As we begin to see our clients' developmental continuum within the context of their lives, we can both look back and see ahead to how these boys—and younger and older men alike—were raised to think and to feel as they do and how these contextual and developmental forces have and will affect their decisions about substance use as they move forward with their lives in recovery.

Most professionals who have worked with adults who are suffering from substance abuse and addiction can recall instances where they were listening to their clients tell stories that tragically reflected what could be termed as "missed opportunities." As they listen, they hear crisis points in their client's lives where prevention or early intervention for the substance abuse problems could have changed the course of their client's lives. Even though prevention programming at the universal, selective, or indicated levels (Hogan, Gabrielsen, Luna, & Grothaus, 2003) will not be a specific focus of this book, developing a preventative mindset will be at the forefront of the discussion about the effects of interventions on the multiple systems of influence in a male's life— his family, friends, and co-workers. Because addiction can progress to unpredictable depths, it is safe to assume that we may always be at a point where further harm can be prevented. In this way, any intervention along the developmental continuum, whether preventative or rehabilitative, can be seen as reducing harm for the client and for all those with whom they will come in contact.

In addition to the etiological models of addiction mentioned above by DiClemente, there are several neurobiological theories of addiction that will be drawn upon when discussing brain development (chapter 2) and self-regulation and emotional intimacy (chapter 3) from a developmental perspective, namely theories of addiction related to: the dopamine/reward (mesolimbic) system; executive functioning (prefrontal cortex); processes of relapse (related to the functioning of the amygdala and the prefrontal cortex); reward/stress systems (mesolimbic and hypothalamus-pituitary-adrenal); and cellular synaptic plasticity (Erickson, 2007; Koob & Le Moal, 2006). In light of research in these areas, it has become evident that substance abuse and addiction professionals need to have at least a rudimentary understanding about neuroanatomy, especially in relation to the neurocircuitry of motivation and reward, and the effects of substances of abuse on the executive functioning of the brain. Although this book is primarily focused on processes associated with working with males, readers will gain knowledge about the basic structures and function of the brain that may also be useful in working with women in substance abuse treatment.

Neurobiological addiction research is often focused specifically on understanding "how drugs act on individual nerve cells as well as large groups of nerve cells in the central nervous system" (Erickson, 2007, p. xi), and most addiction education related to neurobiology focuses on how drugs of abuse affect the actions specific to neurotransmitter systems in the brain. However, as we learn more about the effects of drugs of abuse on the brain, we can broaden this discussion by taking an interdisciplinary, developmental approach that includes research on relational studies and the connections between the brain, body, and mind in relation to addiction. For example, the interdisciplinary field of inquiry called "interpersonal neurobiology" (IPNB) (Siegel, 2001, 2010) provides the scientific underpinning for understanding how our body and mind are connected and develop through our relationships with others. As Cozolino states: "How the connections occur, what impact they have on us, and how relationships change the architecture and functioning of the brain are the essential questions of interpersonal neurobiology" (Cozolino, 2006, p. 19). Most importantly for our purposes here, writings from the field of interpersonal neurobiology will provide a language for educating ourselves—and our clients—about brain-body development and its connection to our ability to recover our emotional, mental, and relational health after the storms of substance abuse and addiction have left their mark on our lives.

A GENDER-RESPONSIVE, DEVELOPMENTALLY-INFORMED APPROACH

Multiple research and clinical disciplines are involved in understanding the etiology and treatment of alcohol and other drug abuse as well as its impact on individuals, families, and society. The gender-responsive approach outlined in these pages represents a synthesis of concepts and ideas from several emerging fields of research related to gender, substance abuse and addiction, and human development across the lifespan. Chapter 1 provides a foundation for understanding why gender and emotional development matter in substance abuse counseling with males. Chapter 2 focuses on educating boys and men about substance abuse and its effects on the developing brain. Chapter 3 offers a process for strengthening recovery in boys and men by nurturing their emotional awareness and affective communication processes; that is, fostering their capacity for emotional intimacy in recovery. These three foundational chapters provide the theoretical concepts that will be interwoven with practical case examples to help elucidate how the notion of fostering emotional development can strengthen the treatment and recovery processes with boys and men.

At the heart of this book is the notion that addiction counselors have an imperative to "adapt counseling strategies to the individual characteristics of the client, including but not limited to, disability, gender, sexual orientation, developmental level, culture, ethnicity, age, and health status" (CSAT, 2006, p. 73). These contextual elements affect one's (a) current life situation, (b) beliefs and attitudes, (c) interpersonal relationships, (d) social systems, and (e) enduring personal characteristics (DiClemente, 2003). A male-responsive approach that seeks to engage boys and men at the point where they are in their change process will take into account these contextual factors as they are manifested both in their current sociocultural environments, as well as in the influences of their past developmental gender socialization processes. Understanding these contextual challenges will help us to see more clearly the context of change; that is, the areas of functioning in a client's life that either complement or complicate change. The complex interplay of these contextual factors can be best described in developmental case studies, which are found in chapters 4 through 8.

These case studies illustrate work with males in a variety of practice settings, show a continuum of substance-related challenges, and address a combination of factors associated with gender, culture, ethnicity, race, religion, and sexual orientation. Additionally, the case studies demonstrate how developmentally appropriate gender-responsive counseling practices can be delivered for five different age groups of males: early adolescent males, ages 12 to 18 (chapter 4), later adolescent males, ages 18 to 24 (chapter 5), males in early adulthood, ages 24 to 34 (chapter 6), males in middle adulthood, ages 34 to 60 (chapter 7), and older adult males, ages 60 and above (chapter 8).

The case studies are intended to be practitioner friendly and lead the reader directly into the case in the way that a basic psychosocial case presentation might unfold in a treatment team meeting when difficult cases are being presented to the team by a staff member for consultation and supervision. The format for the case presentations mirrors the domain areas that are found in the Comprehensive Adolescent Severity Inventory (CASI) (Meyers et al., 1999) for adolescents and the Addiction Severity Index (ASI) (McLellan, Luborsky, O'Brien, & Woody, 1980) for adults. The case studies are designed to show how a developmentally informed, gender-responsive assessment can augment basic information that is gathered through the standard psychosocial assessment process. For example, gathering information about the client's developmental attachment history and male socialization processes (by using exercises like those outlined in Appendices B through E) can augment the standard information that is gathered about "family/social relationships" in the ASI for adults or "peer relationships" in the CASI for adolescents in order to enhance our understanding about the client's current relationship patterns and challenges in treatment.

Readers may notice that each case study begins with the word "Imagine." This word asks the reader to switch their thinking into the realm of possibility and envision how a developmentally informed, gender-responsive approach might unfold with these cases that are placed in a context with a diagnosis, a brief patient placement discussion, and a description of the treatment setting. Even though the case studies are written in the past tense, the clients in the case study narratives are fictional. And although they may have different mental and emotional aspects or have a compilation of qualities of actual people with whom the author has known, any similarities to specific clients that the author has worked with are purely coincidental.

Importantly, this gender-responsive approach that attends to the emotional development of boys and men is not a new theory or set of techniques that can be seen as separate and apart from evidence-based practices in the substance abuse and addiction treatment field. Rather we will see in the developmental case studies how fostering the emotional development of boys and men can strengthen, enhance and augment the treatment approaches that are most common in the field today: for example, motivational enhancement, cognitive-behavioral strategies, and twelve-step facilitation, as well as psychodynamic and systemic approaches.

COMING TO TERMS WITH TERMINOLOGY

To conclude, several brief caveats are provided related to the choice of terminology in the book. First, as the *Diagnostic and Statistical Manual of Mental Disorders* (*DSM*; APA, 2000) continues to change over time, differing opinions remain about the best way to name these substance-related challenges that people may face in their lives (Juhnke & Hage-dorn, 2006). Subsequently, for the purposes of including the broad developmental spectrum of the boys and men that may arrive in a substance abuse professional's office, the terms "substance use," "substance abuse," and "addiction" are used throughout the book. These terms serve to name and describe these challenging phenomena, rather than unequivocally define (or provide criteria for) them.

From a developmental perspective, these terms represent a continuum that moves from problematic use of substances (substance abuse) to a potentially degenerative process that, if left unchecked, can grow progressively worse over time and severely limit—and cause harm to—one's life. When this process of using substances in a detrimental way reaches a stage where it becomes the central organizing feature of a person's life, then it will be referred to as an "addiction." Even though the terms "substance abuse" and "addiction" are used here as a type of short-hand representing a continuum for any number of substance use disorders in which these boys and men may be diagnosed, the developmental case study chapters will provide specific diagnoses where appropriate, including co-occurring disorder diagnoses in some cases.

Second, an additional challenge related to terminology is choosing what to call the people with whom we are working and how best to describe what it is that we are doing with them. Depending upon our professional background, we may be more accustomed to using the terms "consumers," "patients," "students," or "clients," for example. For this book on substance abuse and addiction counseling, the term "client" is used to describe the boys and men who may be referred for professional help due to problems resulting from their substance use. This decision is based on the guidance of a national curriculum committee composed of a multidisciplinary panel of experts in the addiction field who helped to create a technical assistance publication (TAP 21), *Addiction Counseling Competencies: The Knowledge, Skills, and Attitudes of Professional Practice,* that is "intended to provide guidance for the professional treatment of substance use disorders" (CSAT, 2006, p. 1). Practice Dimension VI in TAP 21 is aptly named "Client, Family, and Community Education" (CSAT, 2006).

Furthermore, in TAP 21, Practice Dimension V describes elements of counseling with individuals, groups, families, couples, and significant others. Even though there are many words that could be used to describe these therapeutic practices, such as "treatment," "psychotherapy," "remediation," or "therapeutic interventions," the term "counseling" is used in most cases throughout this book to describe the "collaborative process that facilitates the client's progress toward mutually determined treatment goals and objectives" (CSAT, 2006, p. 101).

Lastly, a major emphasis in this book is on helping men to strengthen their *recovery* from substance use disorders. Public perception, media messages, and professional definitions of the term "recovery" vary greatly. For example, when we say that someone is "in recovery," do we mean that they are in *remission* from their substance use disorder, that they have reached some *resolution* about their substance abuse and have made changes in their life, or that they are simply practicing *abstinence* from their drug of choice (Laudet, 2007; White, 2007)?

For our purposes here, we will use the initial definition that was developed by a group of researchers, policymakers, treatment providers, and recovery advocates "as a starting point for open communication and improved understanding about this important concept" (The Betty Ford Institute Consensus Panel, 2007, p. 222). By their definition, "recovery from substance dependence is a voluntarily maintained lifestyle characterized by sobriety, personal health, and citizenship" (p. 222). Furthermore, the term "sobriety" in this definition "refers to abstinence from alcohol and all other non-prescribed drugs," *personal health* refers to "improved quality of personal life," and "citizenship" refers to "living with regard and respect for those around you" (p. 222). Therefore, "strengthening recovery" from this standpoint would mean both reducing lapses/relapses and helping men to build a quality of life "worth living" that starts in treatment and transitions into a sustainable, healthy lifestyle—both individually and relationally. From a gender-responsive perspective, when we work with males in treatment, we can (a) understand traditional and contemporary aspects of male socialization process in order to "meet men where they are" (e.g., if they are emotionally restricted or have an anti-therapy mindset) and (b) address the potential male-specific barriers that can hinder the development of both the intrapersonal (self-awareness) and the interpersonal (other awareness) aspects of their lives.

REFERENCES

American Psychiatric Association. (2000). *Diagnostic and statistical manual of mental disorders* (4th ed., text rev.). Washington, DC: Author.

Betty Ford Institute Consensus Panel. (2007). What is recovery? A working definition from the Betty Ford Institute. *Journal of Substance Abuse Treatment, 33,* 221–228.

Brady, K. T., Back, S. E., & Greenfield, S. F. (Eds.). (2009). *Women and addiction: A comprehensive handbook.* New York: Guilford Press.

Briggs, C.A., & Pepperell, J. L. (2009). *Women, girls and addiction: Celebrating the feminine in counseling, treatment and recovery.* New York: Routledge.

Brooks, G. R. (2010). *Beyond the crisis of masculinity: A transtheoretical model of male-friendly therapy.* Washington, DC: American Psychological Association.

Brooks, G. R., & Good, G. E. (Eds.). (2001a). *The new handbook of psychotherapy and counseling men: A comprehensive guide to settings, problems, and treatment approaches* (Vol. 1). San Francisco: Jossey-Bass.

Brooks, G. R., & Good, G. E. (Eds.). (2001b). *The new handbook of psychotherapy and counseling men: A comprehensive guide to settings, problems, and treatment approaches* (Vol. 2). San Francisco: Jossey-Bass.

Center for Substance Abuse Treatment. (2006). *Addiction counseling competencies: The knowledge, skills, and attitudes of professional practice.* Technical Assistance Publication (TAP) Series 21. DHHS Publication No. (SMA) 02-3625. Rockville, MD: Substance Abuse and Mental Health Services Administration.

Center for Substance Abuse Treatment. (2009). *Substance abuse treatment: Addressing the specific needs of women.* Treatment Improvement Protocol (TIP) Series 51. HHS Publication Protocol No. (SMA) 09-4426. Rockville, MD: Substance Abuse and Mental Health Services Administration.

Covington, S. S. (2000). Helping women recover: A comprehensive treatment model. *Alcohol Treatment Quarterly, 18*(3). 99–111.

Covington, S. S. (2008). *Helping women recover: A program for treating addiction.* San Francisco: Jossey-Bass.

Covington, S. S., Griffin, D., & Dauer, R. (2011). *Helping men recover: A program for treating addiction.* San Francisco: Jossey-Bass.

Cozolino, L. (2006). *The human science of human relationships: Attachment and the developing social brain.* New York: Norton.

DiClemente, C.C. (2003). *Addiction and change: How addictions develop and addicted people recover.* New York: Guilford Press.

Englar-Carlson, M., Stevens, M. A., & Scholz, R. (2010). Psychotherapy with men. In J. Chrisler & D. McCreary (Eds.), *Handbook of gender research in psychology (volume 2)* (pp. 221–252). New York: Springer.

Erickson, C. K. (2007). *The science of addiction: From neurobiology to treatment.* New York: Norton.

Grella, C. E. (November, 2008). Generic to gender-responsive treatment: Changes in social policies, treatment services, and outcomes for women in substance abuse treatment. *Journal of Psychoactive Drugs, 40*(4), 181–197.

Griffin, D. (2009). *A man's way through the twelve steps.* Center City, MN: Hazelden.

Hogan, J. A., Gabrielsen, K. R., Luna, N., & Grothaus, D. (2003). *Substance abuse prevention: The intersection of science and practice.* Upper Saddle River, NJ: Pearson Education.

Horne, A. M., & Kiselica, M. S. (Eds.). (1999). *Handbook of counseling boys and adolescent males: A practitioner's guide.* Thousand Oaks, CA: Sage.

Isenhart, C. (2001). Treating substance abuse in men. In G. R. Brooks & G. E. Good (Eds.), *The new handbook of psychotherapy and counseling with men: A comprehensive guide to settings, problems, and treatment approaches* (pp. 246–262). San Francisco: Jossey-Bass.

Jordan, J. V., Kaplan, A. G., Miller, J. B., Stiver, I. P., & Surrey, J. L. (1991). *Women's growth* in connection: Writings from the Stone Center. New York: Guilford.

Juhnke, G. A., & Hagedorn, W. B. (2006). *Counseling addicted families: An integrated assessment and treatment model.* New York: Routledge.

Khantzian, E. J. (1999). Self-regulation and self-medication factors in alcoholism and the addictions: Similarities and differences. In J. Lilienfeld & J. Oxford (Eds.), *The languages of addiction* (pp. 44–65). New York: St. Martin's Press.

Kilmartin, C. (2007). *The masculine self* (3rd ed.). Cornwall-on-Hudson, NY: Sloan.

Koob, G. F., & Le Moal, M. (2006). *Neurobiology of addiction.* London: Elsevier.

Laudet, A. B. (2007). What does recovery mean to you? Lessons from the recovery experience for research and practice. *Journal of Substance Abuse Treatment, 33,* 243–256.

Levant, R. F., Hirsch, L., Celentano, E., Cozza, T., Hill, S., MacEachern, M., et al. (1992). The male role: An investigation of norms and stereotypes. *Journal of Mental Health Counseling, 14,* 325–337.

McLellan, A. T., Luborsky, L., O'Brien, C. P., & Woody, G. E. (1980). An improved diagnostic instrument for substance abuse patients: The Addiction Severity Index. *Journal of Nervous & Mental Diseases, 168,* 26–33.

Meyers, K., Hagan, T. A., Zanis, D., Webb, A., Frantz, J., Ring-Kurtz, S., Rutherford, M., & McLellan, A. T. (1999). Critical issues in adolescent substance use assessment. *Drug and Alcohol Dependence, 55,* 235–246.

Mikulincer, M., & Shaver, P. R. (2007). *Attachment in adulthood: Structures, dynamics, and* change. New York: Guilford Press.

National Institute of Drug Abuse. (2009). *Principles of Drug Addiction Treatment: A Research Based Guide* (2nd ed.). (NIH Publication No. 09-4180). Washington, DC: U.S. Department of Health and Human Services.

Siegel, D. J. (2001). *The developing mind: How relationships and the brain interact to shape who we are.* New York: Guilford Press.

Siegel, D. J. (2010). Mindsight: The new science of personal transformation. New York: Random House.

Straussner, S.L.A., & Brown, S. (Eds.). (2002). *The handbook of addiction treatment for women.* San Francisco: Jossey-Bass.

Straussner, S. L. A., & Zelvin, E. (Eds.). (1997). *Gender and addictions: Men and women in treatment.* New York: Jason Aronson.

White, W. L. (1998). *Slaying the dragon: The history of addiction treatment and recovery.* Bloomington, IN: Chestnut Health Systems/Lighthouse Institute.

White, W. L. (2007). Addiction recovery: Its definitions and conceptual boundaries. *Journal of Substance Abuse Treatment, 33,* 229–241.

Acknowledgments

My acknowledgments for this book begin and end with my wife, Dr. Jennifer Sparks. Jen's thoughts and feelings, her life example of living as a truth-teller in conscious relationships, and her love, thoughtfulness, and encouragement over the years echo throughout these pages. Quite simply, this book would not have been written without her inspiration and presence in my life. And for that, I am eternally grateful.

To my daughters, Hana and Hyatt Sparks-Woodford, I thank you for your love and encouragement and for sharing your play space with me when I needed it. I am so fortunate to have you as my daughters. To my parents, Macklyn and Calvin Woodford, my siblings, Patricia, Jimmy, Kathy, and Stuart (by birth) and Jim, Vickie, and Teresa (by marriage), and all of my nieces and nephews, I thank you for your love, support, and encouragement over the years. You all continue to teach me about dedication to family. And I deeply appreciate your steady presence in my life. To my in-laws, Judy and Mitch Mensch, thank you for teaching me about the importance of celebrating and living life to the fullest. With this book project complete, I am enjoying more time to do just that with you and all of my family.

I am also fortunate to have a network of friends and colleagues who have supported me during the writing of this book. At The College of New Jersey (TCNJ), I would like to thank Charleen Alderfer, Marion Cavallaro, Sandy Gibson, Marcia Grimaldi, Joe Hadge, Stephanie Jacobs, Angela Peterson, Nancy Scott, MaryLou Ramsey, Atsuko Seto, and Bob Watts. I want to especially thank my friend and colleague Mark Kiselica at TCNJ for inviting me to include this book project as part of the Routledge Series on Counseling Boys and Men, as well as Dana Bliss at Routledge for his patience and support along the way. You both have given me tremendous guidance and care throughout this project. A special thank you also goes to Barbara Andrew for her support, encouragement, and presence. Thanks for tolerating my seemingly endless need to find just the right metaphor to describe what is most important in life.

Additionally, there are multiple other individuals that I have known over the years too numerous to thank here individually who deserve my collective expression of gratitude. They are my clients who have demonstrated the courage to change in the face of fear, anxiety, and shame. And my friends, colleagues, and students from the College of New Jersey, the College of William and Mary, the University of Virginia, and the Yardley Friends Meeting. Thank you for your kinship and collaboration over the years.

Lastly, writing this book has been a deeply personal journey for me. In many ways, I have both painfully and joyfully learned about the importance of relationships, emotional awareness and expression, and intimacy; which brings me back to my gratitude for my wife, Jen—to whom I dedicate this book. Much of what I have learned has come through our discussions and lived experiences in relationship with one another. Jen inspires me. And I will be forever grateful for her courage, patience, and perseverance in relating to me with profound emotional integrity and intimacy. Thank you from the bottom of my heart.

1

Substance Abuse Counseling with Boys and Men

Gender and Development Matters

First the man took a drink. Then the drink took a drink. Then the drink took the man.

—Chinese Proverb

Common sense will tell you that the progression described in this proverb does not happen to every man who "takes a drink." However, there are men for whom the wisdom of this ancient saying, in its simplicity, captures the essence of their lived experiences. As they reflect back upon their own personal process of initiation and use of substances, they can see how the consequences of their substance abuse have left them feeling that somehow "the drink took the man" that they had hoped to be. And yet who is this "man" that they had hoped to become?

Even though it is not a common occurrence that men openly discuss what it means to "be a man" in society, most boys and men have an implicit sense of how they are expected to act as males in their culture. Whether it is conscious or not, males know from their gender socialization process as boys and men—that is, through the influence of family members, peers, and the media—that there are certain ways of being that are more "masculine" than others. Importantly, there are physical, social, and emotional consequences for males who rigidly subscribe to and act out (or outside) of traditional male gender roles (e.g., emotional restrictiveness and an intense emphasis on self-reliance and success, power, and competition), such as physical health problems, depression, anxiety, stress, and mental health issues (O'Neil, 2006), including substance use disorders.

The acknowledgement that males are "gendered beings" who have lived lives full of male-specific developmental challenges is having a positive influence on the way that counseling and psychotherapy is being conceptualized with boys (Horne & Kiselica, 1999; Kiselica, Englar-Carlson, & Horne, 2008) and men (Brooks, 2010; Brooks & Good, 2001a, b; Levant & Pollack, 1995; Pollack & Levant, 1998). Mental health professionals and the clients they serve can benefit greatly from seeing boys and men as being more than simply "generic human beings" (Kilmartin, 2007, p. xi). Nowhere is this statement truer than in the substance abuse and addiction treatment realm where the number of males outnumbers females two to one.

SUBSTANCE ABUSE COUNSELING WITH MALES: GENDER MATTERS

The 2008 National Survey on Drug Use and Health indicated that males (age 12 or older) were twice as likely to be classified with substance abuse and dependence as females and more than twice as likely as females to receive treatment for an alcohol and/or illicit drug use problem in the last year (Substance Abuse and Mental Health Services Administration, Office of Applied Studies, 2009a). Similarly, the Substance Abuse and Mental Health Services Administration's (SAMHSA) Treatment Episode Data Set (TEDS) indicated that twice as many males were admitted for substance abuse treatment than females in 2007 (Substance Abuse and Mental Health Services Administration, Office of Applied Studies, 2009b). Of particular concern is the subpopulation of adolescent male substance abusers. The Monitoring The Future study, a national survey conducted annually of secondary students, found that adolescent males were more likely than females to drink large quantities of alcohol in a single sitting, were more involved with illicit drug use than adolescent females (in most categories of illicit drug use), and reported higher rates of frequent use than females, resulting in significant costs to themselves and to society (Johnston, O'Malley, Bachman, & Schulenberg, 2010). Additionally, findings gathered by SAMHSA regarding adolescent admissions rates for substance abuse treatment services indicated that school-age adolescent admissions were 70% more likely to be males than females (Substance Abuse and Mental Health Services Administration, Office of Applied Studies, 2009c). Arguably more disturbing are the rates of substance abuse reported among later adolescent males (ages 18 to 25). This group, moving through the transition phase from late adolescence into young adulthood, has the highest rates of substance abuse among all age groups in the United States (Park, Mulye, Adams, Brindis, & Irwin, 2006). These statistics further indicate that males (and particularly adolescent males) tend to abuse substances at a higher rate and with greater consequences than females (Johnston, O'Malley, Bachman, & Schulenberg, 2006) and that this trend appears to continue into adulthood for males across the lifespan (Office of Applied Studies, 2004).

With higher numbers of males being admitted into substance abuse treatment programs, one might make the basic assumption that there must be a genetic and/or environmental causal link between being male and the development of substance use disorders in boys and men. However, making an assertion that male socialization processes somehow explain substance abuse and addiction in men would be both overly simplistic and inaccurate (and not the purpose of this book). Rather, pointing to the fact that two thirds of the individuals in treatment for substance abuse and addiction are males serves a more practical purpose. That is, if we know from the psychology of boys and men that male gender roles are "a salient organizing variable of client's lives and experiences" (Englar-Carlson, 2006, p. 28), then highlighting the salient features of the male socialization process can help us to identify how traditional male gender roles (and the resultant behaviors that we can observe in treatment) might be either barriers to effective treatment or, as appropriate, resources for successful treatment and recovery. Importantly, understanding how the male socialization process may affect boys and men's willingness to receive help for their substance abuse issues will increase our ability to have empathy, understanding, and nonjudgmental acceptance (key factors in the healing process) as our male clients struggle with ambivalent thoughts, feelings, and behaviors related to asking for help from others.

For example, men's literature related to gender role conflict (O'Neil, 2008; O'Neil, Good, & Holmes, 1995; O'Neil, Helm, Gable, David, & Wrightsman, 1986;) and gender role strain (Pleck, 1981) highlights the potential that boys and men may be struggling to live out traditional male role norms such as avoidance of femininity, restrictive emotionality, seeking achievement and status, self-reliance, aggression, fear and hatred of homosexuals, and non-relational attitudes towards sexuality (Levant et al., 1992). Gender role strain occurs when males find that they cannot live up to the gender role expectations (stereotypes, rigid standards, and norms) of their ethno-cultural background. Similarly, the concept of gender role conflict (O'Neil, 1981) entails a broad look at the behavioral, cognitive, and emotional problems that arise in various situational contexts, such as when males:

> (a) deviate from or violate gender role norms (Pleck, 1981); (b) try to meet or fail to meet gender role norms of masculinity; (c) experience discrepancies between their real and ideal self-concepts, based on gender role stereotypes (Garnets & Pleck, 1979); (d) personally devalue, restrict, or violate themselves (O'Neil, Good, & Holmes, 1995); (e) experience personal devaluations, restrictions, or violations from others; and (f) personally devalue, restrict, or violate others because of gender role stereotypes. (O'Neil et al., 1995; Englar-Carlson, 2006, p. 19)

As boys and men will come into treatment from a variety of ethno-cultural backgrounds and differing developmental levels across the lifespan, these male-specific challenges will have great variability within each individual client's lived experiences. Specific examples of how these male socialization processes play out in the substance abuse assessment and treatment process are provided throughout the developmental case studies in chapters 4 through 8.

Of particular importance are the emotional and relational issues and challenges that these males will face as they enter substance abuse counseling and proceed through treatment and into recovery. For example, imagine how the following gender role patterns might play out in an addiction treatment setting for men: (a) having an emphasis on success, power, and competition; (b) restrictive emotionality; (c) restrictive affectionate behavior between men; and (d) conflicts between work and family relations (O'Neil et al., 1986; as cited in Englar-Carlson, 2006). These internalized gender-based expectations would have an effect on a man's receptivity to the counseling process. Will he be pre-occupied with comparing himself to other men? If he is approached by another man in a physically affectionate way, how will he respond (e.g., with anger, disgust, or shame)? Will he have a desire to understand the impact of his emotional life (e.g., his mood and general affective states) on his relationships, specifically his choices about emotional expression around others (and especially around other boys and men)? Additionally, the combination of the traditional male value of intense self-reliance with the often mandated status of substance abuse sets the stage for a "perfect storm" of prohibitions about asking for help in general and specifically in seeking out help in a counseling setting to address substance-related challenges.

Substance abuse counseling clients rarely arrive in treatment with an eager enthusiasm to change. At best, they are often ambivalent about changing their behaviors (Miller & Rollnick, 2002). Having mixed feelings and/or ambivalent thoughts about whether they need to be in the counseling process at that point in their lives leaves them sitting on the proverbial fence. And, at worst, they are adamant that they do not belong in treatment. Perhaps their attendance has been legally mandated by the court system, or it may be the case that they have been challenged by doctors, family members, and/or a boss to take a look at their drinking or drug use. If they have been told that they had "better get help" for their problem "or there will be consequences," then we are faced with the dual challenge of mandated status in counseling (Wallace, 2005) plus the possibility that gender-based messages have contributed to a negative attitude about seeking professional help (Englar-Carlson, 2006). Without understanding how boys and men may choose to face these challenges (based on their individual male socialization processes and their particular early life histories), we may be left baffled by either an intense anger (fight), chronic silence (freeze), and/

or potential early departure from treatment (flight) in the initial phase of counseling.

The substance abuse professional trained in contemporary addiction counseling strategies will recognize their client's bewilderment and/or their ambivalence about being in counseling as characteristic of either the pre-contemplation stage of change (not seeing a problem) or the contemplation stage of change (seeing a problem and considering whether to act) (Prochaska, DiClemente, & Norcross, 1992). Seeing these stages of change from a heuristic perspective, the professional will very likely choose to use some version of motivational enhancement strategies, or specifically motivation interviewing (MI), to try to elicit intrinsic motivation from their clients to make changes in their behavior. A detailed description about MI principles and practices is beyond the scope of this book; however, there are several excellent resources available on this approach (Miller & Rollnick, 2002; Naar-King & Suarez, 2011; SAMHSA, 2002). Importantly, there is evidence that MI enhances the potential for individuals to engage in the substance abuse treatment process.

Rapport-building with boys and men in the initial phases of counseling can be enhanced by using motivational interviewing strategies that are contextually appropriate and meet each client where he is in terms of his stage of change. For example, the MI approach at the pre-contemplation stage emphasizes normalizing ambivalence and raising awareness about the client's substance-using patterns by providing personalized feedback from any relevant assessment findings, by exploring the pros and cons of substance use, and by offering factual information about the risks of substance use (SAMHSA, 2002). In providing these opportunities for client self-exploration and information gathering, counselors can use a decisional balance worksheet (to examine the costs and benefits of changing or not) and begin to observe any discrepancies between their client's and other people's perceptions about their behaviors. Importantly, this process should enlighten both counselor and client about how the client's personal values and experiences have influenced his decision to make changes in his life. What internal and external pressures, for example, might he identify as weighing heavily upon his past and future decisions about change?

Additionally, in the spirit of meeting these male clients at the stage they are in during this initial rapport-building phase, the MI strategies of emphasizing a client's autonomy, responsibility, and self-efficacy for change (Miller & Rollnick, 2002) can work in tandem with traditional male socialization processes related to being self-reliant, such as using one's own resources to overcome adversity (Kiselica, 2011). Although this may seem contrary to an approach that hopes to foster emotional development and an appreciation for the importance of interpersonal processes (e.g., asking for help) in recovery, this is an instance where we may be able to use a traditional gender expectation as a means to an end in engaging a male in exploring his personal values in relation to changing his behaviors in this beginning phase of the treatment process. Alternatively, in this same instance, it may be the case that gender role strain related to living out the value of self-reliance may make it difficult for this man to have a sense of self-efficacy, because his hope and his belief in himself as a man that he can change may have dwindled long before he entered treatment, particularly if he has had repeated "failures" at addressing his substance abuse issues. A gender-responsive approach would recognize both of these possibilities and respond unequivocally with the MI principles of expressing empathy, avoiding argumentation, and rolling with resistance (Miller & Rollnick, 2002). As we will see in chapter 2, these processes of therapeutic engagement change brain connectivity patterns and encourage new neural connections between the emotional (e.g., amygdala) and the executive (prefrontal cortex) areas in the brain, which in turn enhances capacity for self-regulation. Importantly, as we work in a male-responsive way, we can develop empathy for how this man may be viewing himself as inseparable from his behaviors that occurred while he was under the influence of alcohol and other drugs. For example, the consequences of these behaviors, including how he may see himself as a man, and how others view his behaviors as fitting their expectations of him as a man, are likely to be inextricably linked to the reasons that propelled him into treatment. Similar examples of how MI strategies can match male-specific needs in the rapport-building phase of treatment are provided in the developmental case study chapters that follow in the latter half of the book.

In summary, the psychology of boys and men (Brooks & Good, 2001a, b) emphasizes the sociocultural and developmental influences on males. In addition to outlining various mental health challenges that men face, such as alcohol and drug abuse, depression, anxiety and stress, and anti-social behavior and violence (Brooks & Good, 2001a; Cochran, 2005), this literature has taught us that developmental factors related to the male socialization process have an impact on how we can provide counseling service for males. With knowledge specific to male development (e.g., gender role conflict; O'Neil, Good, & Holmes, 1995), we can cultivate greater empathy and, in turn, be more effective in engaging males who may be reluctant to seek professional help in counseling (Vogel, Wade, Wester, Larson, & Hackler, 2007). Having a basic understanding of male-specific developmental issues provides an evidence base for our clinical work with boys and men (Cochran, 2005) at each phase of the counseling process; not only at the engagement, rapport-building, and assessment phase of treatment, but also in strengthening long-term stability and recovery from substance abuse. Importantly, as we will see in chapter 2, with increased understanding and empathy, we can deepen our level of responsiveness to our male client's developmental and emotional needs, which will ultimately create a counseling environment that will be essential to building the regulatory structures in the brain that can help to make relapse less likely in the short- and long-term.

SUBSTANCE ABUSE COUNSELING WITH
MALES: DEVELOPMENT MATTERS

Neuroscientists, physiologists, developmental researchers, and clinicians in the emerging field of interpersonal neurobiology (Cozolino, 2006; Siegel, 1999) have contributed a key conception about human development as it relates to mental health; namely, that our sense of well-being throughout our lifespan is mutually influenced by (a) our biological "hardware" (the body-brain connections), (b) our mental "software" (the mind and the sense of self), and (c) our relationships, specifically those that involve meaningful and emotional attachments to others. These relational connections help to give us both a sense of self and a sense of belonging (Siegel, 2001, 2010).

The term "interpersonal neurobiology" (IPNB) was introduced in 1999 by Daniel Siegel in his seminal book *The Developing Mind* (1999). IPNB is an emerging interdisciplinary field that bridges biological and social sciences and includes concepts from writings on attachment, genetics, comparative anatomy, psychoanalysis, constructivism, and evolutionary studies (Cozolino, 2006). Although deeply rooted in neurobiology, IPNB is not a "branch of neuroscience," but rather a field that is an "open forum for all ways of understanding reality, the human mind, and well-being" (Siegel, 2010, p. 279). Most importantly, it explores the connections between the development of the human brain, the mind, and our relationships, all of which are "fundamentally three dimensions of one reality" (Siegel, 2010, p. 58). The "one reality" of human development is that we are essentially "built" by the ways in which our neurophysiology is shaped through our social experiences.

In combination with related theories from the field of human development (such as attachment theory, cognitive developmental theory, psychosocial theory, social learning theory, and social role theory), interpersonal neurobiology can provide a foundational knowledge base for conceptualizing the impact of male socialization processes, specifically related to emotional development in boys and men. This integrative understanding will help us to better educate our male clients across the lifespan about (a) how important relationships are to their overall health and well-being and (b) how to monitor and modulate their emotional states and modify their behaviors (Siegel, 2010) to increase their chances to find stability (and much more) within themselves and in their relationships with others in recovery. This process is the foundation for fostering emotional development that is described in this book.

The Centrality of Emotions

"How are you doing?" Even though this question is frequently used as a common (almost mindless) greeting between strangers and intimate partners alike, it is an important question to ask yourself when you are trying to find a sense of stability in your life in recovery. And although the question refers to the action of "doing," at its core it is asking about a state of being and, more specifically, about one's emotional state of being. That is, we often greet people with a question that is inherently about feelings states. Whether we acknowledge it or not, emotions are central to our day-to-day lives. Additionally, emotions and related emotional processes (e.g., emotional regulation, emotional connections in relationships, emotionally meaningful events, etc.) are essential to our physical, social, and cognitive development across the lifespan. Likewise, emotional development is crucial to an emergent and integrated sense of self that is capable of regulating emotions and connecting to others in a vital way. What this "integrated self" will look like in boys and men will vary greatly depending on their socio-cultural and developmental influences, including the expectations, roles, and relationships that are common to their developmental life stages.

Being a developmentally informed, gender-responsive professional requires that one be able to discern between what qualities are unique to the individual (e.g., persistent emotional and behavioral characteristics related to temperament that show up early in life) and what characteristics are part of common themes related to their gender, ethno-cultural background, and developmental level (e.g., gender role expectations about masculinity and femininity, normative perceptions of emotionality, or perceived risks of substance abusing behaviors). Examples of this ability to move "from the specific to the general and back again" (Hughes, 2009, p. 283) to see the individual variability across developmental processes are provided in the case study chapters found in the latter half of the book. However, to start to understand emotional development in a more general way, we need to take a look back at the earliest appearance of this process along the long road to emotional maturity from birth into adulthood. To do this, we begin with the interplay between attachment and affective regulatory systems and early socialization processes, specifically the communication patterns that emerge between infants, children, and adolescents and their primary caregivers that either strengthen or dampen emotional development. And although this book is designed to help substance abuse professionals to foster emotional development in boys and men, these same processes are clearly at work in the social and emotional development of all human beings—male or female.

Early Socialization, Attachment, and Emotional Development

The earliest experiences of our lives, specifically those related to the infant-caregiver affective communication system, set the stage for our emotional development. As new emotions emerge in infancy, a "feed-back-regulated control system, which primarily operates as an affective process," develops with the goal of an "interpersonal state, such as *inti-*

macy, connectedness, sociality, oneness, love, attachment" (emphasis added; Tronick, 2007, p. 178). The affective communication system that develops through this process in infancy will have an influence on a toddler's and an older child's cognitive interpretations of internal and external events, which, in turn, will affect an adolescent's developing abilities to recognize and regulate emotions and to communicate effectively with others. Each developmental life stage builds upon prior stages. For the emotional development of a child, the support, acceptance, and responsivity of caregivers can be the foundation upon which they build their personal ideologies, define their life roles, and choose their careers or occupations "without feeling shame, guilt, or remorse for having violated other people's expectations" (Mikulincer & Shaver, 2007, p. 234).

In their seminal book on attachment in adulthood, Mario Mikulincer and Phillip Shaver have compiled over 25 years of research describing the key role that attachment systems play in our development as human beings throughout our lifespan (Mikulincer & Shaver, 2007). Related to survival and socialization, they describe the affective messages of infants (e.g., vocalizations and proximity seeking, such as clinging to a caregiver) as having an evolutionary advantage. That is, by seeking proximity to supportive attachment figures, infants are "more likely to survive and eventually reproduce, causing genes that fostered proximity seeking and other attachment behaviors in times of danger to be selected for and passed on to subsequent generations" (Mikulincer & Shaver, 2007, p. 11). Subsequently, there are hormonal systems (e.g., neuropeptides, stress hormones, etc.) that come into alignment between an infant and its caregiver (particularly between a mother and child; e.g., oxytocin, vasopressin, and cortisol) that are triggered by infant affective expressions.

In the first ten weeks of life, babies will coo and cry to convey affective messages to their caregivers that help to ensure their survival as human beings (Newman & Newman, 2012). By approximately six months of age, infants have "the capacity to experience and express at least seven primary emotions, that is, joy, interest, sadness, anger, fear, surprise, and distress" (Tronick, 2007, p. 179). On a very basic level, this is the beginning of a lifelong process of expressing emotions as a part of our social engagement with others. These initial affective messages cue our caregivers to respond to what is going on inside our developing bodies and minds. The interpersonal experiences that result from these cues and caregiver responses (or non-responses) are integral to the development of the neural circuitry that are involved with creating meaning, regulating bodily states and emotions, organizing memories, and communicating effectively with others across the lifespan (Siegel, 2001).

In the best case scenario, emotional attunement and resonance between a child and caregiver enhances bonding and attachment, which in turn helps not only to ensure the survival of the infant but also to foster the emotional development of the child. If this context is relatively stable across time, a child is very likely to develop a secure attachment with his or her caregivers. The developmental result of these positive social interactions is a felt sense of security that has many emotional and behavioral implications, not the least of which is that one learns that having an autonomous sense of self and having a sense of connection and reliance on others are not mutually exclusive. With an attachment relationship functioning well, "a person can devote attention to matters other than self-protection; being well cared for, he can appreciate the feeling of being loved and valued; in some circumstances, he can take risks, being confident that help is readily available" (Mikulincer & Shaver, 2007, p. 14).

In parallel fashion, to foster the emotional development of our adolescent and adult clients, we can cultivate our capacity for responsiveness in order to attune with our clients' emotional and developmental needs and respond to what those needs are without requiring that our clients be someone that they are not in order to meet our needs. Importantly (and similarly to parenting), as substance abuse professionals, we are not able to be emotionally responsive to our clients all of the time. However, as with the behavior of securely attaching parents, responsivity includes seeing when we have "missed the mark" in our responses to our client's emotional needs and initiating repair. Interestingly, this process of missing the mark (rupture) and accurate empathy (repair) builds the neural circuitry for emotional regulation and resilience (Badenoch, 2008).

Alternatively, from the perspective of mutual regulation in an affective communication system, if there is a pattern of "persistent and chronic interactive failure" relationally between child and caregiver, then "the infant is forced to disengage from people and things because the infant has to devote too much regulatory capacity to controlling the negative affect he or she is experiencing" (Main, 1981; as cited in Tronick, 2007, p. 174). Tronick (2007) adds that: "Eventually and paradoxically, to the extent that these self-directed regulatory behaviors are successful in controlling the negative affect and containing its disruptive effects, the infant begins to deploy them automatically, inflexibly, and indiscriminately" (p. 174). Over time and with repeated experiences (i.e., repeated states of being), "the infant gives up attempting to appreciate the nature of the immediate situation and instead approaches new situations already withdrawn and biased to act inappropriately," which "severely constricts the infant's engagement with the world, future options, and even autonomy ..." (p. 175).

There are several important points to remember with this latter worst case scenario. Firstly, as was mentioned, no caregivers are able to provide the attuned and resonant affective communication style that is conducive to a child's emotional development all of the time. Rather, there will be points in time when a caregiver's own emotional resources are "tapped out" and their exhaustion (or possibly their larger mental health challenges, including substance abuse) can compromise their ability to respond sensitively to their child or adolescent's emotional and behavioral expressions. In these circumstances (and, indeed, in most relational contexts, including a therapeutic relationship in counseling), it is the timing and the quality of our efforts at repairing the attachment relationships that hold the greatest sway in returning the subjective experiences of a child and caregiver back to relational congruence.

Second, great individual variability exists in the ways in which infants and children respond to their caregivers. For example, observe any childcare or preschool facility and you will see differences in the temperaments of the children as they play, specifically related to their style of behavior (e.g., activity level, emotionality, sociability, attention, and inhibition). These "temperament dimensions" have both genetic and epigenetic (e.g., attachment and affective communication styles) contributions; they are "the building blocks on which self-regulation develops" (Wills & Ainette, 2010, p. 131). Recognition of these differences will help caregivers to respond more effectively to the individual needs of their child.

Third, caregivers will vary in their knowledge about, and sensitivity to, emotional expressions and behaviors in infants, children, and adolescents. For example, some caregivers will be more attuned to an infant's bids for proximity and connection. Others will be more comfortable attending to an adolescent's developmental needs. Importantly, expectations about appropriate affective communication styles between child and caregiver will differ depending upon the caregiver's socialization processes related to their ethno-cultural and family histories, as well as the match of the gender of the child and the caregiver. Therefore, when considering the developmental influences related to a client's relational expectations and sense of identity, it is important to factor in the gender roles and relationship histories from their family of origin (e.g., father-daughter and mother-son interactions) as well as their significant social influences, particularly their relationships with their peers.

Lastly, and perhaps most importantly, the attachment literature has expanded from being primarily a theory of child development and has shed light on the adult mind with "its goals and strategies for attaining particular life outcomes, and its strong propensity for forming close relationships with other embodied minds and symbolic figures, such as past relationships, religious deities, and cultural groups" (Mikulincer & Shaver, 2007, p. 4). One of the hopeful perspectives that has come out of this literature is that individuals who may have had childhoods that would have been likely to produce insecure attachment styles as adults were able to find what has been called "earned secure attachments" by having had "a significant emotional relationship with a close friend, romantic partner, or *therapist*, which has allowed them to develop out of an insecure status into a secure/autonomous" status (emphasis added; Siegel, 2001, p. 91).

The significant interactions in these relationships help to form "working models" of attachment that allow "a person to predict future interactions with the relationship partner and adjust proximity-seeking attempts without having to rethink each one," and, as a consequence, "repeated attachment-related interactions result in increasingly stable mental representations of self, partner, and relationships" (Mikulincer & Shaver, 2007, p. 23). Importantly, these models include:

> autobiographical, episodic memories (concrete memories of specific interactions with attachment figures), beliefs and attitudes concerning oneself and relationship partners, generic declarative knowledge about attachment relationships and interactions (e.g., the belief that roman- tic love as portrayed in movies does not exist in real life), and proce- dural knowledge about how to regulate emotions and behave effectively in close relationships. (Collins & Read, 1994; as cited in Mikulincer & Shaver, 2007, p. 23)

Siegel (2010) explains that we develop mental working models for "me," "you," and "we," what he calls "Me-Maps," "You-Maps," and "We-Maps." These working models are not static but rather are dynamic mental representations that are shaped by the interactions between our present life experiences and our implicit (procedural) and explicit (autobiographical) memory systems. We will discuss the development of—and the importance of bringing attention to—these mental repre- sentations in more detail by referring to them as "me-," "you-," and "we- states of mind" in the developmental case studies in the latter portion of the book.

States of Mind Become Traits of Mine

"States of mind" are dynamic and are influenced by our physiologi- cal experiences and our mental interpretations of internal and exter- nal events. For example, think about the word "traffic." How does this word affect your emotional and mental state of mind? If you focus your attention on how you feel when you are sitting in traffic versus when you are relaxing in your favorite chair at home, you will have a felt sense about how our states of mind can be affected by the context of our lives. Either of these states of mind (created by thinking about "traf- fic" or "sitting in your comfortable chair at home") has an embodied, emotional quality associated with it. If you can clearly imagine yourself being stuck in heavy traffic, you may feel tense and easily agitated, with your heart racing and your breathing shallow and constricted. Alterna- tively, if you can imagine yourself in your favorite comfortable chair, you may feel relaxed and calm, as you breathe deeply and enjoy the quiet of your home. Yet someone else may have a completely opposite emotional experience in these situations. They may enjoy the challenge of navigating their car through a busy, traffic-filled city; they have the trait of being emotionally energized while driving. And yet they may feel uneasy and tense sitting in a chair in the quiet of their home. These emotional reactions tell us about how an individual's (brain-mind-body) systems process information, in this case related to the word "traffic" or "sitting at home in your comfortable chair."

Importantly, if we delve into the stories of our lives that come into our awareness as we process our experiences of being in traffic versus being in a quiet home, it will give us clues about how our "states of mind" become "traits of mine" over time. That is, the experiences in our lives that cause certain repeated states of mind strengthen the development of neural nets that create implicit and explicit memories, as well as patterned responses of behaviors, emotions, and thoughts—traits— that are automatically triggered when one enters a particular state of mind. The same process is involved with how our states of mind related to our gender socialization and our attachment histories have helped to create our personal characteristics; that is, our individual physiological and mental reactions that are associated with our felt sense of self and our conditioned responses to emotional and relational challenges in various situational contexts.

For example, in terms of interpersonal and emotional processes in general—and attachment dynamics in particular—early life experiences between child and caregiver will accumulate in our implicit memory systems over time; this, in turn, reflects the patterns that have been created in our neural circuitry related to regulating emotions, making meaning, and communicating well with others. This affective neural circuitry is integral to how we process information in our developing mind. As Siegel (2001) writes: "We can learn, note similarities and differences, make generalizations, categorize, associate, analyze, and create new combinations of information within the intricate firing patterns of our brains" (p. 162). Subsequently, the desires and beliefs that we hear as well as the embodied conditioned responses that we see as our clients tell the stories of their male socialization and attachment histories emanate from the neuronal firing patterns that have been affected by their developmental life experiences which have accrued over time.

Through a process of repeated neural firing patterns, the brain establishes a set of symbols or codes that serve as *mental representations* that have sensory, perceptual, conceptual (or categorical) and linguistic components (Siegel, 2001). And as our life experiences become more complex,

> the mind creates connections among the various elements of representations, ranging from sensations and images to concepts and words. The connections among the layers of neural activity weave a fabric of subjective life: They enable us to feel, behave, think, plan, and communicate. (Siegel, 2001, pp. 204–205)

Therefore, if we pay attention to the sensory, perceptual, conceptual, and linguistic components that are coming up for our clients as they tell the stories of their lives, then we can see (especially in the attachment system and the attachment styles that arise with different people in various contexts) how central a role emotions and their regulation play in the creation of their mental representations of themselves and others. Similarly, as we will see in chapters 2 and 3, clients can learn within the context of the therapeutic relationship how to increase their self-awareness (and their awareness of themselves in relationship to others) by paying attention to the sensations in their bodies and the images, feelings, and thoughts that arise into their awareness in treatment (Siegel, 2010), a process that will serve them well in the different settings and situational contexts that they will encounter in their lives in recovery.

The process of understanding oneself in a more intimate way sets the stage for understanding others more intimately; a process which, in turn, can lead to the development of supportive, emotionally connected relationships in recovery. As clients strengthen the "muscles of their mind" (and the related neural circuitry of self-awareness) by repeatedly monitoring their states of being (body and mind) in various relational contexts, they can begin to build an ability not only to see and feel their own "me state of mind" (intimacy with themselves), but also to see and feel others' states of being (i.e., "you states of mind") and gain a larger sense of the important relationships ("we states of mind") in their lives. With the increased self- and other-awareness that is nurtured in an emotionally responsive therapeutic relationship, clients can learn to (a) monitor their states of mind and body—their "self-states" (Siegel, 2001), (b) modulate their emotional states in a flexible and adaptable way, and (c) modify their behaviors in relation to self and others. Importantly, this process is the essence of how one attains emotional maturity as a relatively stable self-trait over time and, as a consequence, is able to have mature intimate relationships with others in recovery.

Socialization Processes, Substance Abuse, and the Continuity of Self-States

As human beings, we are essentially "built" by the interactions of our neurophysiology and our social experiences. We are social animals. Our sense of self, our identity, our self-concept, our ideals and values, and even our capacity for self-observation develop through interactions with other human beings. From a relatively simplistic developmental perspective, infants, children, adolescents, and adults alike all have increasingly complex affective regulatory and communication styles that affect their sense of self and how they act in relationship to the world, "and for all of them, the working of the communicative process— its degree of interactive coordination and affective reparation—is what is critical to their outcome" (Tronick, 2007, p. 176).

Similarly, we learn how to learn from other people; that is, we observe what others are giving their attention to in the environment as well as inside themselves, and we give value to what the significant people in our lives value. Most importantly for fostering emotional development in boys and men, human beings learn from each other how to understand their emotional experiences and how to express and communicate emotions with one another. It is in the interpersonal realms of child-to-caregiver, peer-to-peer, and significant other-to-significant other that we "grow up" learning about relationships, intimacy, and the capacity for having both a sense of self and a sense of mutuality with others. Likewise, it is in a socially supportive therapeutic environment that clients can learn (and re-learn) how to experience and strengthen both a coherent sense of self and an increased capacity for relating to others in a healthy and intimate way. Responsive interpersonal interactions in counseling, as well as in self-help support groups and recovery-oriented communities, can be both the impetus and the means for facilitating this process for re-learning about one's own social and emotional challenges.

For example, as clients begin to pay attention to their states of being—their "self-states" in various contexts—they will notice that the "people, places, and things" (to borrow a phrase from the self-help recovery movement) in which they encounter on a daily (and moment-to-moment) basis have an effect on their sense of self, their general affective mood, and their perceptions. In fact, they may notice that they have "specialized self-states" that arise in various relational contexts, such as a private, inner self-state versus a public, outer self-state, and any number of other selves, such as our "sexual, affiliative, status-seeking, survival-oriented, and intellectual selves" (Siegel, 2001, pp. 230–231). It may be difficult to grasp how we could have multiple "parts" to our "selves." However, as we have moved in and out of social situations over our lifetime, we have attempted to "achieve our goals by assessing situations and applying our internal rules to interactions with the environment," which creates specialized, efficient selves that can function in various relational contexts; and, therefore, "the idea of a unitary, continuous 'self' is actually an illusion our minds attempt to create" (p. 229).

The natural question then arises: If a unitary self is an illusion, then how can we have any sense of congruency or continuity in our sense of self over time? Siegel proposes the answer that

> *basic states of mind are clustered into specialized selves, which are enduring states of mind that have a repeating pattern of activity across time.* These specialized selves or self-states each have relatively specialized and somewhat independent modes of processing information and achieving goals. Each person has many such interdependent and yet distinct processes, which exist over time with a sense of continuity that creates the experience of mind. (2001, p. 231)

The challenge then is to find a sense of coherence through integrating our self-states across time. This process is particularly heightened in the developmental level of adolescence, which is characterized by the psychosocial task of "identity versus role confusion" (Erikson, 1963) and the "search for a consistent understanding of oneself" (Berger, 2010, p. 348). One can see why substance abuse (which can shift a person's states of mind rapidly) in early adolescence is associated with a higher risk for mental and emotional challenges at later developmental levels.

We can extend this developmental challenge to say that the "challenge in recovery" will include the search for a sense of coherence in our self-states in various relational contexts when we are not under the influence of alcohol of other drugs. For that reason, the proposition in this book is that the states of mind that are created through (a) substance abusing, addictive behaviors, and their relational consequences, (b) gender role conflict and strain, and (c) early life experiences that include persistent and chronic relational failure are each problematic in their own way and when combined only serve to compound the challenge of finding a coherent sense of self in recovery that is able to relate to others in an emotionally mature and intimate way.

Subsequently, we may find our clients wondering who they are and how they will function when they are not under the influence of alcohol or other drugs: "How do I have sex when I'm sober?" "How do I function in my job as a business man when I have always done business over drinks?" "How do I unwind after a tough day at work without having a beer with the guys (or smoking a bowl)?" "How can I continue to be a part of my _____ (men's club, sports team, group of friends, etc.) and not drink"? "What do I do when my _____ (wife, partner, significant other) is nagging the crap out of me?" Each of these questions speaks to a state of mind that will need to be recognized and responded to in an emotionally mature way, i.e., by monitoring bodily sensations and thought processes, modulating emotional states of mind, and modifying behaviors accordingly (e.g., seeking out the support of trusted others).

One last point about socialization processes, substance abuse, and coherent self-states needs to be emphasized. That is, because both addiction and gender role conflict often leave boys and men who enter treatment with an injured, vulnerable, and fragmented sense of self (that may be masked with a male "bravado" of invulnerability), it is within the consistent, trusting, and empathic therapeutic relationship that they will find a "nurturing, mirroring, and holding environment that can contain and manage negative, destructive impulses" (Flores, 2004, p. 83) to act out against themselves and others in treatment. Healthy relationships will continue to be essential as these males move into their recovery environments. As Philip Flores indicates in his book, *Addiction as an Attachment Disorder* (2004), "the absence of continued satisfying relationships in the substance abusers' lives always leaves them with an internal feeling of emptiness and a susceptibility to search for external sources for gratification" (p. 84).

Therefore, in terms of strengthening recovery related to our clients' "continuity of self-states" in various relational contexts, boys and men will need to explore their "me states of mind" in substance abuse counseling by:

1. Understanding where they are developmentally "stuck" (particularly in relation to their emotional development),
2. Becoming aware of where they have "adaptive specialized selves without a sense of authenticity," and
3. Noticing where they may be "filled with intense and unresolved conflicts across self-states." (Siegel, 2001, p. 231)

Additionally, for the boys and men who are trying to find not only a sense of stability in recovery, but also serenity, joy, and meaning in their lives and in their intimate relationships, fostering emotional development will include teaching them to pay attention to others' states of being ("you states of mind") and to their relationships ("we states of mind") by:

1. Being aware of their state of mind and their patterns of affective arousal (particularly physiological responses) in various relational contexts,
2. Recognizing their own (and others') affective communication styles, especially in relation to their experiences in their family of origin, and their male socialization processes (peer, family, and cultural influences),
3. Monitoring their goals and expected outcomes in communicating with others, particularly their notions of success or failure in affective communication,
4. Modifying their behaviors in relation to "emotional reparation during their reiterated daily exchanges with others" (Tronick, 2007, p. 174), and
5. Understanding (at least on a very basic level) the neurobiological, social, and emotional impact that substance abuse and addiction have on their states of mind and relationships across time.

In chapter 2, we will begin to examine the ways in which we can educate boys and men about the neurobiological and social impact of substance abuse and addiction, especially in relation to emotional growth and awareness, and how these areas in turn can affect the development of healthy relationships in recovery.

2

Educating Boys and Men about Substance Abuse and the Developing Brain

The overall insights from brain science suggest that how we focus our attention activates certain neural circuits ... coupled with emotional engagement, a sense of novelty, and optimal attentional arousal, teaching with reflection can utilize these prime conditions for building new connections in the brain.

—Daniel Siegel, 2007, p. 262

EDUCATING BOYS AND MEN ABOUT
BRAIN DEVELOPMENT

Psychoeducation is an approach that is often used in substance abuse treatment (Valesquez, Maurer, Crouch, & DiClemente, 2001) to teach relevant information related to the counseling process. The information may be primarily content-laden, for instance focusing on the biopsychosocial effects of substances on individual and families, or a combination of content and process, such as teaching content related to relapse, stress, and relationships and then practicing relapse prevention skills, relaxation techniques, and social skills training, respectively. This didactic approach may include experiential exercises, such as role plays or demonstrations that help to reinforce new ways of thinking and behaving. In the initial phases of the counseling process, psychoeducation may be primarily focused on engaging clients' reflective processes, raising awareness, and trying to instill hope for change.

In keeping with the motivational enhancement strategies discussed in chapter 1, it is helpful in the dialogue that occurs in this process to think about exploring how clients make meaning out of the events that have brought them into treatment and to elicit their perceptions about the challenges that they face in the situational and relational contexts of their lives. The counseling process itself may be an unfamiliar experience for males, and using interactive, stimulating hands-on demonstrations, activities, and stories in the beginning phases of treatment can be helpful to engage boys and men in the process. In designing a psychoeducational activity that will help to raise awareness, consider the notion that males tend to navigate more towards modes of "doing" than "being" (Rabinowitz & Cochran, 2002). For example, in groups, physical activities and storytelling can keep boys engaged in the psychoeducational process (Mortola, Hiton, & Grant, 2008).

Importantly, there are two modes of processing information related to the right and left hemispheres of the brain that affect change through the interpersonal dialogue that occurs during the psychoeducational process (Badenoch, 2008; Siegal & Hartzell, 2003). Firstly, the left-brain mode of processing tracks the linear, logical, and literal aspects of the content of the psychoeducational "story," as it moves in a sequence from beginning to middle to end. Well-crafted psychoeducational activities that engage left-brain modes of processing information will use common-sense, matter-of-fact stories to provide much needed (logical, literal, and linear) structure for males who are struggling to "make sense of things" in treatment and to find meaning and emotional stability in early recovery.

However, it is the right-brain mode of functioning that perceives and processes the nonlinear, holistic, and imaginative aspects of the psychoeducational experience, e.g., the visual, spatial, and nonverbal information that is conveyed through the speaker's tone of voice, facial expressions, and body language. Importantly, it is the implicit, attachment-based right-brain to right-brain relational connections (Badenoch, 2008; Schore, 2003) between counselor and client (as well as between client-to-client in group and family counseling settings) that also provide much needed emotional stability while engaging and building the neural circuitry and related capacity for self- and mutual-regulation in recovery.

Using the Brain in Your Hand

We can use a psychoeducational tool (such as "The Brain in the Palm of Your Hand" that is described below; Siegel & Hartzell, 2003) to reflect upon and explain more concretely how intertwined the processes of thinking, feeling, and behaving are in our brains and bodies. Because of what has been noted about males related to emotional expression and potential fears about the counseling process itself, leading with a psychoeducational discussion about thought processes may be helpful in the initial phase of treatment (rather than leading with a discussion from the onset about the importance of understanding one's emotions as an aspect of treatment and recovery, even though this will be very evident as their recovery progresses). Additionally, through this demonstration we can discuss how substances of abuse, when used repeatedly, can biochemically saturate areas of the brain that play a central role in decisional processes. In this way, we can show how over time one can "lose their mind on drugs" and, as a consequence, develop an unstable and often incoherent sense of self that thinks and acts "crazy" in various relational contexts. Ultimately, we will be able to show how the same neural pathways in the mid-brain that are involved in addictive processes are also associated with emotions, self-regulation, and emotional development.

Oftentimes, the terms "brain" and "mind" are used interchangeably. Making a clearer distinction between the two can help us to understand how the hard-wiring of the brain (i.e., the structural neural circuitry in the gray and white matter in our heads) functions to create the mind (i.e., the flow of energy and information in the brain; Siegel, 2001), which in turn can both affect and be affected by our relationships. In a best-case scenario, a "triangle of well-being" (i.e., brain, mind, and relationships) will emerge in the psychoeducational demonstration that elucidates how a coherent mind in recovery affects our ability to have empathic relationships, both of which are grounded in the physical reality of neural integration (Siegel, 2007) and in the embodied brain (Fogel, 2009).

Neuroscience can be heady (pun intended). Yet when basic brain science is presented to clients in a way that connects to their experiences, understanding these concepts can be extremely beneficial. Several writers in the field of interpersonal neurobiology have provided descriptions of a pedagogical tool that can be used to explain how the physical features of the brain (structures of the brain) work to organize the mind and shape the flow of energy and information (functions of the brain) in and between individuals. By using "The Brain in the Palm of Your Hand" (Badenoch, 2008; Siegel, 2007; Siegel & Hartzell, 2003), we can draw clients in with a story and a demonstration about the basic mechanics of the brain, and we can include a discussion of why knowing about the brain in relation to the use of substances of abuse can be helpful in finding a sense of stability and serenity in recovery. In order to demonstrate this model with individuals or in groups large or small, all we need are our hands and knowledge about various areas of the brain, how they interact with one another, and particularly how substances of abuse affect this process. The remainder of this chapter provides basic knowledge for this activity.

To help engage individuals as active participants in the demonstration, it is often helpful to ask your clients to mimic what you are doing and to create their own hand model for their brain. It is important to have a sense of humor and to know that even neuroscientists do not have all of the answers to how the brain works to create the mind. Humor can be a useful tool to engage boys and men (Kiselica, Englar-Carson, & Horne, 2008; Sweet, 2006). And, as questions will certainly arise during this activity, knowing what you know and explaining how much we do not yet know about this complex process will help to keep things in perspective.

Although specific structures of the brain will be discussed in this section, it will be helpful in a demonstration to males in treatment to use language that you feel will connect with the audience's experiences. For example, to keep it simple, less technical and perhaps broader descriptive language can be used to discuss these neural processes, such as calling the brainstem "our reptilian brain" (or "an alligator") that "eats without thinking" or describing our limbic region as the "center of our wants and needs" related to food, sex, companionship, and survival. Make sure to check in periodically with your clients to see how they understand what you are saying. Having a flexible and adaptable mindset will help you find the right language, metaphors (Robert & Kelly, 2010), and examples to connect the material to the audience.

Additionally, although this demonstration is primarily focused on the single individual's brain, body, and mind, it should be repeatedly emphasized throughout the discussion how interrelated this intrapersonal system is to the interpersonal relationships that we have in life. What we are doing in this exercise is providing the foundational knowledge base for clients to understand how substance abuse and addiction affect their brains in relation to having the ability to regulate one's emotions when dealing with the storms of life. Furthermore, this knowledge-base will be instrumental in understanding how to develop basic intrapersonal skills to help with self-regulation in recovery. For example, intrapersonal awareness is central to developing such relapse prevention skills as: identifying triggers, managing stress/emotions, managing thoughts, and managing cravings and urges. We will discuss the brain structures that are central to developing both intrapersonal and interpersonal knowledge, awareness, and skills (e.g., effective communication, effective refusals and assertiveness training, managing criticism, etc.) that will be the foundation for building relationships and social support systems in recovery (Daley & Marlatt, 2006).

To begin "The Brain in the Palm of Your Hand" demonstration, hold your hand in the air as if you are waving. Then fold your thumb onto the palm of your hand and fold your other four fingers over the top of your thumb. You should be forming a fist with your thumb on the inside of your other four fingers. Your hand is now a simple representation of your brain. You can also use both hands held together to demonstrate the left- and right-hemispheres of the brain and how they function in relation to emotional regulation. For now, however, we will use the one-hand model to represent an entire brain structure.

With your other hand, you can point to your wrist as representing the spinal cord leading down into the body. Then point to the three main areas of what is called the "triune brain" (MacLean, 1990; as cited in Cozolino, 2006). They are (a) the *brainstem* in the palm of your hand (which, from an evolutionary standpoint, represents our connection to reptiles) that is associated with maintaining homeostasis related to our basic bodily functions, (b) the *limbic region* represented by the thumb (which is often referred to as our older mammalian brain) that is associated with basic drives and emotions, and (c) the *cortex* represented by the four fingers that overlay the thumb (also called the neomammalian brain or neocortex because, from a phylogenetic standpoint, it is the "newest" part of our brain). The cortex allows us to be conscious, to have ideas, and to reflect on and communicate about abstract concepts (Siegel, 2010)—like the notion of our triune brain. In essence, the cortex allows us to reflect upon ourselves, a process that includes "at least three essential elements: receptivity, self-observation, and reflexivity (awareness of awareness)" (Siegel, 2007, p. 334). Importantly, it is the connectivity and the neurochemical communication between the prefrontal area of the cortex and the limbic region that gives us the capacity for self-regulation and response flexibility, which are keys to relapse prevention.

Over leaps of evolutionary time, these three parts of our brain have evolved together to the extent that there are "no clear delineations between layers ... all three layers are linked together in complex vertical neural networks, thereby allowing the whole brain to coordinate everything from simple motor movements to complex abstract functions" (Cozolino, 2006, p. 25). If you lift your fingers off your thumb, you can show how closely connected these three areas are in that the cortex wraps around and is connected to the limbic region, which sits adjacent to and is connected with the brainstem. As you talk about how each of these areas function, you can show how their structural proximity aids in electrochemical communication; as they are linked structurally, they are able to quickly share information between their differentiated parts. We will look at some examples of how this communication works shortly.

While describing "The Brain in the Palm of Your Hand," an important piece of the story of the mechanics of the brain needs to be emphasized: namely that the brain is not an isolated organ but rather is an embodied part of the central nervous system. As Siegel writes in the preface to Ogden, Minton, and Pain's *Trauma and the Body* (2006):

> Though some interpretations of neuroscience think of the 'single skulled brain' as the source of all that is mental, this restricted view misses the scientifically established reality that most brains live in a body and are part of a social world of other brains. (Ogden, Minton, & Pain, 2006, pp. xv–xvi)

Furthermore, even though we will discuss the structures within the brain as being separate and distinct, they are connected to one another in systemic ways that are not easily teased apart. To paraphrase Thomas Merton, no brain structure, nor neural or hormonal system, nor brain itself is "an island." Therefore, when we feel something stirring in us, it is not just something "in our head." Rather, it is our full body and brain connection responding to something such as sensations in the body, images in the mind, thoughts, and feelings (Siegel, 2010) that are happening in response to some internal or external stimuli. For that reason, when we feel fear or stress, we cannot identify the one single neural and hormonal structure in the brain that is responsible for that feeling. Instead, there are neuroendocrine systems in our body and brain related to fear and stress that are intimately connected to our relationships with others that, in turn, are connected to our patterns of behavior, such as eating, sleeping, and sexuality. These interconnected systems are complex and dynamic (Fogel, 2009).

At this point in the demonstration, it is helpful to show the central position of the thumb in our "Brain in the Palm of Your Hand" model. Remember that the thumb represents the limbic region that is related to affective arousal and appraisal, emotions and feeling states, and emotional regulation. In its central location, the limbic region has multiple structural connections and functions that are related to our affective states of mind and that help us to evaluate and respond to situations, to form relationships, and to create memories (just to name a few key connections). Let us use an analogy to demonstrate how central the limbic region is (when connected to the prefrontal cortex) to our decisional processes and our emotional reactivity or responsiveness in various situational and relational contexts.

Putting Reactivity in Context: The Doorbell Analogy

Imagine that you are in your home and the doorbell rings. The sound of the doorbell is the external stimulus that travels through the central nervous system (CNS) to the brain for evaluation and response. Let us think of this sound as sending a ripple of energy and information (Siegel, 2001) that travels through the CNS and the spinal cord to arrive at the brain stem. The brain stem is involved in maintaining stability and homeostasis in terms of heart rate, respiration, blood pressure, body temperature, body fluids, and body weight (Fogel, 2009), and it affects whether we are alert or sleepy, as well as being instrumental in our fight-flight-freeze response system (Siegel, 2007).

When the doorbell rings, there are a range of responses that can occur sub-cortically at this point, meaning that the body may react before the cortex has an opportunity to consciously reflect upon the stimulus and inform the actions that follow. The sub-cortical areas—the brainstem alone or in concert with the limbic region—may motivate the body to move before we have a chance to think about what we are doing (in our neo-cortex). We may be wondering why our heart rate and breathing changed so rapidly "for no reason." This happens because evolutionary forces created a quick response system that would move us away from a threat as fast as possible and then allow us to process the meaning of the danger (and perhaps how to prevent it in the future) once we are free and clear from risk. This reactive system works because the brainstem receives input from the body and, in concert with the limbic system, can mobilize us when we are faced with an immediate threat.

Returning to the ringing doorbell analogy, we have to provide some context to this situation in order to understand how the limbic system might respond to this stimulus. As we explained, the limbic region is essentially an affective system. When aroused, it will begin to attribute a basic value of "positive" or "negative" to the sound of the doorbell ringing, called the "hedonic tone of the feeling" (Fogel, 2009, p. 57). If, for example, we were expecting our close friend or loved one to arrive at our home at any moment, and we heard the doorbell ring, then our immediate bodily response (including our brainstem and limbic response) might be positive; we would move quickly to answer the door and welcome our guest into our home. According to Siegel (2007), the limbic system is involved with feelings of attachment to caregivers, the encoding of autobiographical memories, and the "appraisal of meaning and the creation of affect, and our inner sensation of emotion" (p. 34). When we feel motivated at the level of our "basic needs for survival and for affiliation and meaning" (p. 35), then the chances are good that our limbic system has been activated. Therefore, upon opening the door, we would very likely experience feelings of pleasure and satisfaction, as the limbic and higher cortical regions are engaged in attuning to and resonating with our guests, as well as building memories and stronger affectional and mental representations (Siegel, 2001) of our friend or loved one in our brain.

With repeated experiences such as these, we build the neural circuitry that would associate a ringing doorbell with positive feelings and memories. These emotional experiences cause clusters of neurons to "fire" together (i.e., communicate through electrochemical means) in the limbic system. Over time, this process can change the structure of the brain by ingraining the neural circuitry into neural nets that would respond similarly to related stimuli in the future. In this way, our personal history creates expectations and predictions about our future. Because our brains change in response to our personal experiences, even identical twins that are formed from the same combination of sperm and egg will not have identical brains in terms of structure and function because of their context-dependent lived experiences (Cozolino, 2006).

This context-dependent process works at the neurological level to change brain structure when clusters of neurons fire together. Neurons are the nerve cells in the brain and other areas of the central nervous system that communicate with each other through the use of neurotransmitters, which "stimulates each neuron to survive, grow, and be sculpted by experience" (Cozolino, 2006, p. 4). The magnitude of these neural connections is mind-blowing. Our brains have an estimated one-hundred billion neurons, where each neuron connects to approximately ten thousand other neurons, making for approximately one-million billion neuronal connections in the brain (Siegel, 2001). Therefore, when we say "clusters of neurons are firing together," we are talking about an immense number of neurons communicating with each other through electro-chemical means.

Taking our doorbell analogy further, imagine the brain as a house with an electrical system that allows us to have a doorbell that rings and to be able to turn on the lights when we enter a room. When we build a house, we wire the house so that the electricity can flow through the wires and into the doorbell or the lights so that, when we push a button or flip a switch, energy will travel through the wires to the doorbell or the light bulb. In using this crude analogy in relation to our minds, the "wires" are the neural circuitry that allow for the flow of energy and information through our brain. You can continue to use the "Brain in the Palm of Your Hand" model by pointing to the sides of the hand where the ears would receive the energy of the sound waves that are then transformed into electrochemical "currents" that travel to various parts of the brain and body (e.g., the brainstem and the limbic region, and the musculoskeletal system).

When internal or external stimuli are detected, a chain reaction in our central nervous system is triggered. As you are describing this, it is helpful to remember to emphasize the word *trigger* because this is the language used in relapse prevention training as well. At the neuronal level, an analogous switch is flipped, and electrical impulses travel down the long axons and dendrites (the wires of the brain) that connect neurons. This impulse releases neurotransmitters into the synapse (the space between neurons). The neurotransmitters, chemicals that are released between neurons, cause the adjacent neuron to fire (or not fire, in the case of inhibitory neurotransmitters) communicating that something important is happening; that is, the central nervous system knows about the stimulus (the trigger of the doorbell) and needs to respond. Using our crude house analogy, if we repeatedly flip the switch or ring the doorbell to allow the electricity to flow, then the synaptic connections are strengthened. These connections wire the brain (and change its structure over time) in order to function adaptively when similar stimuli are detected.

Neurons That Fire Together Wire Together

The whimsical line "neurons that fire together wire together" (commonly attributed to the neuropsychologist Donald Hebb) speaks to the physiological reality of how the structures of the brain change as clusters of neurons fire together, triggering gene activation and protein production, which in turn creates new synaptic connections and/or strengthens those that already exist (Siegel, 2010). Specifically, Cozolino writes that "(1) communication across the synapse (2) changes the internal biochemistry of the cell, which, in turn, (3) activates mRNA (messenger ribonucleic acid, the material that translates protein into new brain structure) and protein synthesis to change cellular structure" (Cozolino, 2006, p 5). Additionally, this process can alter the "packets of neurotransmitters that are released or the receptors that receive the messages, and even stimulate the growth of new neurons" (Siegel, 2010, p. 148). In educating clients about how we are wired to think, feel, and behave, this level of detail is most likely beyond what most individuals may want to know. However, what this information means on a practical level is that, by repeating positive experiences (such as having secure nurturing relationships, doing aerobic exercise, enjoying novel experiences, or simply focusing our attention and/or being emotionally aroused), the neural structure and function of our brain can change in positive ways. Describing this process, called neuroplasticity (Siegel 2007), to clients of all ages can provide a sense of hope for change. Simply put, if you change your mind and your life experiences (e.g., change your behaviors, thoughts, and/or relationships), then you can change your brain. And although it takes time and repeated experiences, these neuroplastic changes can happen throughout our lives. Therefore, the take-home message about neuroplasticity is this: The more that you stimulate healthy neural pathways in the brain and body (through learning intrapersonal skills and experiencing interpersonal healing in recovery), the more likely you will feel an increased general sense of health and wholeness.

Alternatively, the adaptive process of neuroplasticity can work to change the brain structure and function in negative ways when there is repeated exposure to chemicals that are foreign to the brain. For example, drugs of abuse, like cocaine and amphetamine, affect specific sections of the brain that are related to reward and motivation, such as the mesolimbic dopamine system (MDS; discussed below). These stimulants alter neural firing patterns by affecting the release and reuptake of the neurotransmitter dopamine. Stated simplistically, when there is excess dopamine in the MDS, it "communicates" pleasure subjectively and is involved in an emotional response system that motivates us to move and seek out whatever stimulus has triggered this effect. Because they affect dopamine in this way, cocaine and amphetamine trick the natural reward system (the MDS) that is hardwired to seek out new experiences and/or emotionally nurturing relationships.

Repeated chemical abuse and drug-seeking behavior can biochemically "stamp in" memories of drug experiences (Wise, 2002; as cited in Koob & Le Moal, 2006) that can alter the neural firing patterns, which, in turn, can drastically change a person's attitudes and behaviors over time. An analogy of this process would be walking through a grassy field using the same pathway over and over again until there is a distinct path through the grass that others can clearly see (Siegel, 2001). Likewise, if repeated drug and alcohol abuse stamp in neural pathways, then one's ability to regulate one's emotional states and behavior patterns related to drug seeking is compromised. Because of this effect, we often see addicted individuals make bizarre, illogical, and even inhumane decisions that can severely affect themselves and others.

AT THE HEART OF THE BRAIN: THE LIMBIC REGION

Using The Brain in the Palm of Your Hand model, we can see more concretely how the limbic region is at the center of the "action" and functions in relation to the neurobiology of addiction. We need to zoom in and see what specific brain structures, neural circuits, and neurotransmitters are in the limbic region that are connected to the process of substance abuse and addiction. For better or for worse, the limbic system is one of the "more plastic, or modifiable, areas of the brain" (Eliot, 2009, p. 253).

We have been referring to the thumb in our model as representing the limbic region, which includes several key structures whose functions relate to motivation, feelings of attachment to caregivers, the encoding of memories, and the appraisal of salient events in our lives. For example, the *amygdala* is involved in our initial *meaning-making* processes, helping us to feel whether something or someone is potentially good or bad for us (assessing threat), and in storing *implicit memories* (Siegel, 2007), especially those related to fear responses and the anticipation of panic and anxiety (Fogel, 2009). Implicit memories come into awareness as contextual perceptions, tacit feelings, sensations in the body, and impulses to do some type of behavior that involves moving toward someone or some place that feels safe or away from people and places that feel unsafe and threatening. There is a timeless quality to implicit memories, and, even though they may barely register, if at all, in one's consciousness (and "make no sense" in relation to a present-day experience), they can be intensely meaningful and compelling and can saturate the body with emotionally laden sensations. In this case, the amygdalae is involved in making meaning out of a stimulus that is "bringing to mind" something from the past that has not been encoded in the explicit memory system through the hippocampus.

In close proximity to the amygdalae is the *hippocampus*, which is seen as the "cognitive mapper" that assembles bits of information into *explicit memories* (Badenoch, 2008, p. 16). Stated simply, explicit memories are what we think of when we say "I remember that." Importantly, the hippocampus helps to bring together the events of our lives into "a coherent time-and-space story structure" (Fogel, 2009, p. 252). And while implicit memories have a more tacit quality that inform our embodied self-awareness, autobiographical memories are more concrete and help to inform our conceptual self-awareness (Fogel, 2009). We know that the hippocampus continues to "grow" throughout our lives as it is involved in storing memories that become the narratives of our life.

Close in proximity to the amygdalae and hippocampus is the *anterior cingulate cortex* (ACC), which is involved in *attentional processes and motivation*. Through its connections with the prefrontal cortex, the ACC helps us to regulate cognitive and affective information in order to make decisions about the future (Badenoch, 2008). In terms of the development of addictive processes, it is "responsible for the feeling of craving and the related actions of seeking, obtaining, and consuming" (Fogel, 2009, p. 139).

Another relevant structure to our discussion of the limbic region is the *hypothalamus*, which is the "master hormone regulator" (Siegel, 2007, p. 34). Through its connections in the hypothalamus-pituitary-adrenal (HPA) neuroendocrine system, it helps to regulate immune functioning and maintain homeostasis in our bodily states "by way of the autonomic nervous system with its brakes/accelerator divisions (the parasympathetic and sympathetic branches)" (Siegel, 2007, p. 35).

Before we add in the element of how substances of abuse affect the brain chemistry in the limbic region, let us take a look at an example of how this built-in stress-response system might work for a man in early recovery. We will call him "Bob" and say that it has been approximately 30 days since he last used his drugs of choice—cocaine and alcohol. Using our familiar scenario, Bob hears the doorbell ring. His heart starts racing. This seems odd to him since it is a Sunday afternoon and he is simply sitting at home watching television by himself, not expecting anyone in particular to be coming for a visit. As he approaches the door, memories of past experiences with a drug dealer start to come into awareness, and a fear response begins. When he opens the door, he sees an old friend standing there with a 12-pack of beer, a bag of chips, and a smile on his face. His old friend has decided to stop by unexpectedly (as he has done many times in the past) to "watch the game," or simply to "hang out and drink beer."

Several contextual elements are important to this story. First, it has been a while since Bob has seen his old friend, and, even though it was suggested to him in counseling that he let potential "high-risk" friends and family know that he has chosen to seek help for his substance abuse issues, he did not want to contact this old friend in particular, because in Bob's mind, if his old friend showed up, he would have no problem letting him know that he was "not partying anymore right now." Second, he has not been able to attend his last few aftercare support group meetings because of work, and he has not reached out to develop a social support system that he can depend on when he "feels shaky" in his new-found recovery.

Layers of *reactivity* are happening in Bob's embodied brain as he stands at the door greeting his old friend. Most of the reactivity is occurring in the structures of the limbic region that we have discussed, and although the following is a highly simplified version of a complex response system, in a nutshell, here is what is happening. The brainstem and the lower limbic regions have the heart racing because past doorbell ringing has brought a drug dealer with cocaine and all of the anticipatory fear and excitement attached to that experience in the limbic region. The amygdala, with its involvement in implicit memories and hedonic tone (positive or negative attributions), is feeling its way through the situation, asking: "Is this a friend or a foe?" This is clearly an old friend, and the limbic region remembers this, even though in counseling the neocortex processed him as a "high-risk" person related to potential relapse. The anterior cingulate cortex has brought its sub-cortical attentional and motivational processes to the sight of the 12-pack of beer in his old friend's hand, and a craving state has started to be activated in the limbic region as well. The ACC is located near the brain's cortical motor areas (associated with movement) and connected to the autonomic nervous system, and so "what the body wants to do (intentions and urges)" and "what the body does (emotion related behavior, including expressions and vocalizations)" (Fogel, 2009, p. 56) are quickly coordinated through this close structural and functional proximity.

The instinctive nature of Bob's almost mechanical and well-conditioned movement to welcome his old friend into his home is also aided by the fact that emotional memories are similar to procedural memories (Fogel, 2009), which function below awareness to facilitate routine movements like driving a car or riding a bike. For example, if we have ridden a bicycle for any amount time, we do not need to pay close attention when we peddle and balance to ride the bike. Memories of how to ride are ingrained in the implicit memory systems of our bodies and brains.

Additionally, because of Bob's implicit memories of answering the door to let in a drug dealer, which carries mixed feelings of excitement and stress, his heart is racing. As the heart races, an approach/avoidance system that includes the structures above as well as the hypothalamus-pituitary-adrenal system starts to be activated. Stress hormones are released, such as adrenaline and noradrenaline, and the hippocampus, involved in encoding and retrieving autobiographical memories, such as Bob's relatively new sense of self in recovery, begins to shutdown. In the extreme, this approach/avoidance system becomes a fight, flight, or freeze response that is engaged as we "approach what is life-sustaining and avoid that which is dangerous" (Cozolino, 2006, p. 28). And although this scenario, in theory, does not present a life-threatening situation to Bob, his "most primitive subcortical fight-flight circuitry—shared with our reptilian ancestors" is beginning to affect his experience. In that moment, the subcortical brainstem and lower limbic structures are in strong competition with the "later evolving emotional and cognitive processes" (p. 28). Unfortunately, without repeated experiences that successfully engage the higher cortical functions that support his recovery efforts in these types of high-risk situations, the "ancient, rapid-acting neural networks that are fundamental to survival" (Cozolino, 2006, p. 28) will very likely win out. Subsequently, Bob will be more *reactive* (sub-cortical and autonomic reactions) than *responsive* (higher-cortical response) in this situation.

All of these neural reactions are happening in a split second (sub-cortically in the limbic and brain stem regions, right at the threshold of his self-awareness) as Bob is standing there at the door greeting his old friend. In this scenario, the impact of the sub-cortical regions and the autonomic arousal system (Porges, 2009) narrows Bob's field of consciousness and behavioral options, as sensory and emotional networks triggered by internal and/or environmental cues are dissociated from those networks "that organize cognition, knowledge, and perspective" (Cozolino, 2006, p. 32). Through this process, the limbic region (at the center of our emotional neural circuitry) can be seen as truly at the heart of the relapse potential of this scenario, even before the substance of abuse has been re-introduced into this neural system. In short, at that moment, if Bob is to continue his progress in recovery, he will need to have every layer of his brain—and specifically the middle prefrontal cortex (Siegel, 2007; described in detail below)—processing this emotionally charged event so that he can act authentically and congruently in recovery as these types of high-risk situations arise.

The Mesolimbic Dopamine System

Within the limbic region lies the *mesolimbic dopamine system* (MDS), often associated with addiction, that moves "from the center of the brain forward" (Erickson, 2007, p. 52) through the ventral tegmental area (VTA), which has neural projections to (i.e., synaptic connections with) the nucleus accumbens (NAcc) (associated with reward and pleasure), the amygdalae (affective meaning-making), the anterior cingulate cortex (attentional processes and motivation), and the sections of the middle prefrontal cortex that are essential for social communication and self-observation. Importantly, the flow of the energy and information of the mind (Siegel, 2001) between and through these structures serves as a regional link from the sub-cortical to the higher cortical functions (Siegel, 2007). These limbic structures, along with the brainstem, "combine to influence our *motivational drives* and the activation of our *basic needs for survival* and for *affiliation* and *meaning*" (emphasis added; Siegel, 2007, p. 35). Because "essential portions are below the area of the neocortex and consciousness" (Erickson, 2007, p. 53), much of this affective appraisal and response system functions below our conscious awareness. Neurotransmitters in the mesolimbic dopamine system (described in Box 2.1) affect a vast array of psychological and emotional processes, including: emotional responses to stress and pain, feelings of pleasure and well-being, motivation and learning, muscle control and movement, and appetite, mood, and memory. A dysregulation in the neurotransmitter systems of the mesolimbic dopamine system, whether through genetic predisposition, environmental influences, and/or repeated drug use, is said to lead a person to connect "to certain drugs to 'balance' or 'correct' the brain dysregulations" (Erickson, 2007, p. 55).

BOX 2.1.

Neurotransmitters in the mesolimbic dopamine system include: *dopamine* (DA), associated with feelings of pleasure, motivation, emotional responses, and muscle control; *serotonin* (SER), associated with feelings of well-being; *gamma aminobutyric acid* (commonly known as GABA), an inhibitory neurotransmitter associated with anxiety and sleep; *glutamate* (GLU), an excitatory neurotransmitter involved in learning and memory, as well as in alcohol and other drug intoxication; *endorphins*, which are opioid peptides that function as neurotransmitters, soothing pain and creating a sense of well-being; *acetylcholine*, an excitatory neurotransmitter involved in memory and muscle movement; and *endocannabinoids*, associated with appetite, mood, and memory (Doweiko, 2009; Erickson, 2007).

The mesolimbic dopamine system serves essentially as a natural "appetitive motivational system" that "energizes the many engagements with the world as individuals seek goods from the environment as well as meaning from the everyday occurrences of life" (Panksepp, 2009, p. 9). Panksepp (2009) refers to this as our "seeking/desire system." Think of the implications of repeatedly saturating this delicate neurochemical system with chemicals of abuse, especially at an adolescent developmental level when these neural systems are going through intense and rapid changes. This is the time when the adaptive process of neuroplasticity can be a double-edged sword, as cellular adaptations to repeated drug use can cause "long-lasting changes in brain function" (Erickson, 2007, p. 60). For example, drugs of abuse sensitize the dopamine and glutamate pathways that run through the mesolimbic dopamine system, particularly in relation to the nucleus accumbens-related (NAcc) circuitry that "provides salience (meaning) to environmental stimuli associated with reward" (p. 62). Specifically, even though dopamine functioning is involved in the early stages, "repeated use of a drug causes a gradual involvement of the prefrontal cortex and its GLU projections to the NAcc" (p. 61). Significantly, what this means is that an area of the brain that is normally focused on social communication and self-observation (the middle prefrontal cortex), through its glutamate projections (an excitatory neurotransmitter involved in learning and memory), is repeatedly stimulating a structure (the amygdalae) that is associated with reward and pleasure. When these pathways are consistently activated by repeated drug use, there are plastic changes at the cellular level that are "remarkably persistent" (Erickson, 2007, p. 62).

In summary, the mesolimbic dopamine system is part of a larger neural circuitry in the center of the brain that connects the brainstem to the limbic region and the limbic region to the prefrontal cortex. It is through these circuits that "our feelings and interpersonal lives are governed ... bridging the connection between the rational and the instinctive parts of the nervous system" (Eliot, 2009, p. 253). If drugs of abuse are used repetitively, then the metabolic and electrochemical energy in the brain are frequently concentrated in the mesolimbic dopamine system. We can see this action (increased oxygen and blood flow) in brain imaging studies that suggest that that there is a disruption in the neural circuitry related to reward (nucleus accumbens), motivation (orbitofrontal cortex), memory and learning (amygdalae and hippocampus), and control (prefrontal cortex and the anterior cingulated cortex) (Koob & Le Moal, 2006). Although there are many questions to be answered about the neurobiology of addiction,

> evidence at the molecular, cellular, systems, behavioral, and computational levels of analysis is converging to suggest the view that addiction represents a pathological usurpation of the neural mechanisms of learning and memory that under normal circumstances serve to shape survival behaviors related to the pursuits of rewards and the cues that predict them. (Hyman, 2005, p. 1414; as cited in Erickson, 2007, p. 64)

When one is actively and repeatedly using drugs of abuse, the spotlight of the mind—one's attention and motivation to act—is centered in the "seeking/desire" processes of the mesolimbic dopamine system and not in the middle prefrontal cortex, the area of the brain that is essential for self-observation and social, empathic communication. Importantly, if the energy and information flow is happening primarily in the mesolimbic dopamine system, then it is creating a state of mind that is concentrating (through the anterior cingulated cortex's attentional processes) on reward and pleasure (through the nucleus accumbens). In a limbic-dominated state of mind, it feels subjectively like one "cannot live without the drug of choice." This feeling stems from the amygdalae's affective meaning-making and implicit memory system, along with the brainstem, which are connected to basic survival instincts. And as much of this activity is below conscious awareness and often involves the timeless qualities of our implicit memory systems, how one feels, behaves, thinks, plans, and communicates with others comes from a relatively unconscious and mindless place that is primarily seeking reward and pleasure "like there's no tomorrow."

Therefore, when we describe how substance abuse affects brain development, we can talk about how the structures and functions of the brain related to rational decision-making processes were compromised by repeatedly saturating the limbic region with substances of abuse. That is, we can include in this dialogue (in an attempt to help clients moderate feelings of guilt and shame) a discussion about the stigma of addiction and specifically how people who are suffering from addiction are often characterized as "crazy," "criminal," or "immoral." Without removing the culpability that clients may have related to their behaviors while intoxicated and/or drug seeking, we can have a dialogue about how their thinking processes involved in making rational, mature, and moral decisions were compromised and about how recovery from substance abuse and addiction involves strengthening the neural processing of information both from "top to bottom" and from "bottom to top" (i.e., bi-directionally) through the systems of the brain and body, especially with the aid of the executive functioning of the middle prefrontal cortex and a supportive therapeutic relationship.

Additionally, if we think about the desires and beliefs that are wrapped up in our client's struggles with ambivalence in the early stages of treatment—wanting to change and yet not wanting to change—we can see how these dissonant thoughts and feelings may emanate from the neuronal firing patterns of the brain. Specifically, this ambivalence may be indicative of the lack of integration between the major structural and functional areas of the brain. For example, the middle prefrontal cortex (discussed below) may hold the energy and information that wants to change based on one's desired self-concept and value systems, while the mesolimbic dopamine system may hold the energy and information related to not wanting to change based on an underlying feeling of "not being able to live without it" (the drug of choice), which has accrued over time with repeated chemical abuse. Although this is an overly simplistic view of the interplay of these complex neurobiological processes of the brain, this example can provide a way to normalize the ambivalence that clients are feeling as they attempt to live without their drug of choice.

Lastly, while the stamped-in neural pathways related to addiction represent the downside of the plastic nature of our brain chemistry, structure, and function, this same ability of the brain to change with experience, its neuroplasticity, can be harnessed in recovery from substance abuse and addiction. This process has been described as the "bidirectional causality between neural structure and experience" (Cozolino, 2006, p. 7). Given the right conditions, one's experiences in recovery can become the catalyst for creating the integrated neural circuits that are the vital systems of our mind (Siegel, 2001). And although current and/or future pharmacological interventions may help to change brain function to support the treatment process, the emphasis in this book is on the impact of changing our minds and our relationships in recovery.

Therefore, the hopeful message for boys and men that can be conveyed through this demonstration is this: Changing your mind and your behavior will change your brain and your relationships. Over time, by practicing the intrapersonal and interpersonal skills of recovery, new neural pathways will be strengthened that connect the emotional center of the brain with the higher cortical functions to create mature and lasting changes in long-term health and well-being. The brain region that is central to "changing our minds" through reflective self-awareness and enhanced personal relationships is the middle prefrontal cortex. It is instrumental in facilitating neural integration related to self-regulation (Siegel, 2007) in the midst of the storms of life.

MIDDLE PREFRONTAL BRAIN FUNCTIONS AND SELF-REGULATION

The middle prefrontal neural structures and their functional connections that are vitally important to building both mindful awareness and healthy relationships in recovery can be explained by continuing to use the Brain in the Palm of Your Hand model. In this model, the middle two fingers that are folded over the top of the thumb (from the fingernails to the second knuckles) represent roughly the structural region of the middle of the prefrontal cortex (Siegel, 2007). In the very center of these two fingers are the: *dorsomedial prefrontal cortex* (DMPFC) and *ventromedial prefrontal cortex* (VMPFC). These structures are related to *conceptual self-awareness* (how you think about yourself) and *embodied self-awareness* (how you feel about yourself) respectively (Fogel, 2009). Understanding these two types of self-awareness can be a key to helping boys and men to have a full sense of who they are and how they can fully experience themselves and others in recovery. Located on the side of the dorsomedial prefrontal cortex (point to the two outer fingers) is the *dorsolateral prefrontal cortex* (DLPFC). This structure has been called "the chalkboard of the mind" (Siegel, 2007) because it is involved in "holding" sensory information temporarily in awareness (Fogel, 2009). For our purposes here, we will think of these structures (DMPFC, VMPFC, and DLPFC) as being central to our "executive attention" processes and refer to them collectively as being essential structures in the middle prefrontal cortex (MPC; Siegel, 2007).

In our doorbell ringing scenario, Bob was ill-prepared for his old friend standing at the door with a 12-pack of beer and a smile on his face. As was mentioned, Bob's subcortical brain areas (the brainstem and limbic region) and his autonomic nervous system won out over his higher cortical functions, as Bob was unable to think, feel, and act from a solid, stable, and flexible state of mind in recovery at that moment in time. If you will remember, the anterior cingulate cortex (ACC) involved in attentional and motivational processes would focus on the 12-pack of beer in his friend's hand. The ACC functions as both a part of the upper limbic system and a lower part of the middle prefrontal cortex. Because Bob's neural pathways related to the mesolimbic dopamine system were strengthened over years of repeated drug and alcohol abuse (think about the pathways through the grass that have continually been stamped down), it felt instinctive for Bob to invite his friend into his home. What Bob lacked in this high-risk situation were the skills and the time-intensive training and experience that would strengthen the neural pathways that would engage his middle prefrontal cortex (MPC) to successfully navigate the situation. Using the grassy field metaphor, these latter pathways of the MPC were relatively less trodden, because Bob was new in recovery and only slightly engaged in the process of building new neural pathways through practicing being mindfully aware of his bodily and mental reactions and through modifying his behaviors in relationships to support his best efforts at recovery.

Mindful awareness is a state of being where our attention is focused intentionally on our experiences inside and outside of our mind and body. According to Siegel, these experiences can be

> divided into at least four sectors including the first five senses (data from the outside world), sixth sense (information from the body), seventh sense (elements of the mind itself thoughts, feelings, images, beliefs, intentions), and the eighth sense (relationships of oneself with others, something larger than the day-to-day self, or the feeling of attunement with oneself). (Siegel, 2007, p. 336)

Awareness of these internal and external stimuli requires the involvement of the pathways leading into the middle prefrontal cortex from "lower" (relatively speaking) structures in the brain, including the *orbitofrontal cortex* (OFC) (located just behind the eyes and below the ventromedial prefrontal cortex; involved in embodied self-awareness), which is adjacent to the *insula cortex* (IC) (implicated in the ability to feel the internal states of your body), and the *anterior cingulate cortex* (ACC) (related to emotion and motivation). These structures sit at the proverbial crossroads of the cortical ("higher") and sub-cortical ("lower") functions. The OFC and IC work with the ACC to affectively appraise bodily states and "to regulate whether to take approach (good) or withdrawal (not so good) action" (Fogel, 2009, p. 57). When there is impairment in communication between the OFC and the ACC, then "an unrestrained urge to use or obtain an addictive substance" is created (Fogel, 2009, p. 139). Similarly, if the insula cortex, which is the structure "through which information is transferred to and from the outer cortex and the inner limbic (amygdalae, hippocampus, hypothalamus) and bodily areas (by way of the brainstem and spinal cord)" (Siegel, 2007, p. 38), is left unchecked, then it is implicated in activating neural networks that "create constant cravings or fears that cannot be fully satisfied" (Fogel, 2009, p. 139).

Importantly, as the hippocampus helps to bind together our autobiographical memories (i.e., the stories of our lives), the insula cortex is involved in binding emotional memories, which as has been mentioned are more automatic, similar to procedural memories (which aid in functions like brushing one's teeth or riding a bike; Fogel, 2009). Siegel emphasizes that:

Becoming open to our body's states—the feelings in our heart, the sensations in our belly, the rhythm of our breathing is a powerful source of
knowledge. The insula flow that brings up this information and energy
colors our cortical awareness, shaping how we reason and make decisions. We cannot successfully ignore or suppress these subcortical springs.
Becoming open to them is a gateway to clear mindsight. (Siegel, 2010, p. 63)

Together, the orbitofrontal cortex, the insula cortex, and the anterior cingulate cortex are involved in bringing information (e.g., bodily
sensations, mental images, thoughts and feelings) into conscious awareness to be processed in the middle prefrontal cortex. The dorsolateral
prefrontal cortex temporarily holds the information (the chalkboard
of our mind), as it moves into awareness in the dorsomedial prefrontal cortex (conceptual self-awareness) and the ventromedial prefrontal
cortex (embodied self-awareness). This process allows us to pause and
reflect on the internal and external stimuli of our experiences. In this
way, our mind becomes filled with awareness (hence the use of the term
"mindful awareness" for this process).

Mindful Awareness in Recovery

Mindful awareness is essential for the integration of our consciousness
(Siegel, 2010). The neural net connections in the upper limbic and middle prefrontal region allow us to have conscious awareness of feelings
of pleasure and desire, to focus our motivation and learning processes,
to relate empathically with others, and to consciously evaluate situations (i.e., pause and reflect) and make conscious decisions. These neural
pathways, which are nurtured and strengthened through the counseling
relationship, also help us to deal with emotional or psychic pain, such
as states of stress, anxiety, shame, fear, or panic that reside in the lower
limbic structures such as the amygdalae. Therefore, engaging the upper
limbic and middle prefrontal regions in the therapeutic context is at
the heart of learning to self-regulate the mental and emotional storms
of life (which often involve the lower limbic region and implicit memories). This has enormous implications for substance abuse counseling.

We can harness the power of the counseling relationship to enhance
mental training (e.g., building mindful awareness) that will promote
the nine prefrontal functions outlined by Siegel (2007) to support
recovery. When the inevitable storms of life strike, we want to have
the clarity of mind and the sense of self not only to ride the storms out,
but also to remain flexible, adaptable, and fully engaged as authentic
human beings in the process. Siegel describes this ability as "response
flexibility" (2010, p. 27), and it is a skill that can be learned given the
right conditions. For example, when attention and reflective self-awareness are harnessed in the middle prefrontal region of the brain, there
are nine key functions (response flexibility is one of them) related to
mental health and well-being that are enhanced (Siegel, 2007). They are

(a) bodily regulation, (b) attuned communication, (c) emotional balance, (d) response flexibility, (e) fear modulation, (f) empathy, (g) insight, (h) moral awareness, and (i) intuition. These functions, which are related to the neural circuitry of the middle prefrontal region, are compromised by chronic substance abuse and addiction. Fortunately, strengthening connections between the middle prefrontal and the limbic regions of the brain is at the heart of learning how to navigate the storms of life in recovery.

Many of the intrapersonal skills that are taught in substance abuse treatment begin with consciousness raising and awareness; that is, bringing attention to one's intentions and being mindfully aware of our states of mind and body, as well as our relationships. For example, identifying relapse triggers begins with awareness about one's reactions to internal and external cues that may be a catalyst for craving states or urges to use substances. Similarly, in order to manage one's thoughts in general (such as negative thinking patterns), or more specifically thoughts about using substances that may be triggered in various contexts, one must build conscious awareness that these thoughts are actually happening in our brains and that they are leading to desires to use substances. Other activities, such as learning how to solve problems in recovery, manage stress, and choose enjoyable activities that are non-drug related, each require that one first be aware that there is a problem to be solved, that one is feeling stress, or that there are pleasant activities that one can do without using alcohol or other drugs. Likewise, having the ability to examine "apparently irrelevant decisions" (Marlatt & Donovan, 2005), plan for situations that may arise in recovery that could constitute an "emergency," or recommit after one has had a slip or relapse, will necessitate the involvement of awareness of one's emotional states through engagement of "executive attention" in the middle prefrontal region.

There are several excellent resources available that explain the process of teaching these intrapersonal skills in more detail than can be provided in this chapter (Daley & Marlatt, 2006; Monti et al., 2002; Velasquez et al., 2001). Additionally, an aftercare program, called Mindfulness-Based Relapse Prevention (Bowen, Chawla, & Marlatt, 2011), integrates a full spectrum of relapse prevention strategies with mindfulness-based activities using experiential, somatic awareness exercises (e.g., body scans) that "build the muscles of the mind" in the middle prefrontal areas. In fact, there are a number of mental health counseling resources that integrate mindful awareness as a key component of the therapeutic process for a variety of challenges, such as: acceptance and commitment therapy (ACT; Hayes, Luoma, Bond, Masuda & Lillis, 2006; Hayes, Strosahl, & Wilson, 2003), dialectical behavior therapy (DBT; Dimeff & Koerner, 2007; Linehan, 1993), and mindfulness-based stress reduction (MBSR; Grossman, Niemann, Schmidt, & Walach, 2006; Kabat-Zinn, 2003). Lastly, a more self-guided approach (designed for the lay reader) to foster the process of developing "mindsight" is described by Daniel Siegel as a way to use mindful awareness to facilitate integration across several domains related to the brain, mind, and relationships (Siegel, 2007, 2010).

The common denominator of these approaches (mindfulness, mindful awareness, or mindsight) is that they use a process of becoming aware of awareness and beginning to pay attention to one's own intentions through self-observation. These processes allow us to begin to find words that will describe what is happening in our mind and bodies. Interestingly, as we begin to tune in to ourselves in an intimate way, we can come to know ourselves as a good friend would know us. As Siegel states, "just as our attachment to our children promotes a healthy, secure attachment, tuning in to the self also promotes a foundation for resilience and flexibility" (Siegel, 2010, p. 86).

Over time, this behavior will stimulate neural growth, making healthy and functional connections in the brain in recovery. As clients begin to discuss with us (and other clients and supportive individuals in their network) how they are learning to navigate the storms of early recovery, self-efficacy will be enhanced. Situations that may have engendered anxiousness or caused emotionally avoidant behavior in the past can be noticed in the present moment, and, with reflection (with self and others), an approach state in one's mind can be cultivated.

In *The Psychophysiology of Self-Awareness*, Fogel (2009) describes how having a sense of "embodied self-awareness" is vital to our overall health and well-being. Embodied self-awareness allows us to be able to pay attention to our bodily sensations, as they affect the thoughts and feelings that arise into our moment-to-moment awareness. The interpersonal process of teaching clients to pay attention to their bodies and minds increases their reflective self-awareness. This is an important goal of many substance abuse and addiction treatment approaches because it is essential to the process of relapse prevention (Bowen, Chawla, & Marlatt, 2011; Marlatt & Donovan, 2005; Monti et al., 2002; Velasquez et al., 2001). Additionally, this same process of developing an embodied, reflective sense of self-awareness that aids in the stabilization and relapse prevention phase of treatment can be a foundation for deepening the healing process as counseling shifts into developing a consistent pattern of self-reflection in relationships with others that supports the maintenance of long-term recovery.

Therefore, while fostering emotional development can provide the true-north reference point for where we are heading in the counseling process, self-awareness that is nurtured through a well-attuned and resonant counseling relationship can provide the vehicle to get us there. In chapter 3, we will explore how we can help boys and men to strengthen their recovery by fostering self-awareness in relationships and by building the capacity for emotional intimacy with others. Having a deep connection with oneself opens the doorway for a deeper level of closeness with others in recovery.

CHAPTER

3

Strengthening Recovery by Fostering Emotional Intimacy in Males

Intimacy begins at home, with oneself. It does no good to try to find intimacy with friends, lovers and family if you are starting out from alienation and division within yourself.

–Thomas Moore, 1994, p. 24

EDUCATING BOYS AND MEN ABOUT EMOTIONS

Albert Einstein is credited with having coined the phrase "Insanity: Doing the same thing over and over again and expecting different results." How often has an individual's behavior while under the influence of alcohol or other drugs been described as "insane," "crazy," "criminal" or "immoral"? This question will resonate with men in substance abuse treatment, because it is very likely that they will have been seen by others (and themselves) in this mentally or morally deficient light. There is no doubt that people who are in the throes of addiction can and have acted in ways that merit these descriptions. Their behaviors often leave friends and loved ones asking: "What were they thinking?"

The nature of this question points to an interesting theoretical distinction, namely that the problem is fundamentally about a deficit in cognitive processes, i.e., that something within their mind has gone awry. There is a connotation that one's thoughts and decisional processes are somehow defective, damaged, or dysfunctional. To some extent, irrational thinking comes with the territory of substance abuse and addiction, and in fact, evidence-based treatment approaches have traditionally focused largely on using cognitive-behavioral strategies to alter irrational thinking patterns related to substance abusing behaviors (Miller, 2009).

However, research on affective neuroscience has highlighted the central role that emotions play in our experience and development as human beings. Emotions have been crucial to our survival as a species (e.g., alerting us to danger or drawing us towards potential mates) and they provide a vital link in our neural connections related to mental health and well-being (Fosha, Siegel, & Solomon, 2009). Specifically, emotions are at the heart of how we integrate (make whole) the systems of what Siegel (2010) calls the "triangle of well-being," which is composed of our *brain*, the states of our *mind* and sense of self in our bodies, and the saliency of our *relationships* with family and friends, and with our larger communities. As Fogel (2009) writes, "emotional salience activates awareness," which "leads eventually to the formation of learned patterns of response, experience dependent neural connections, and thus memories for the salient events and the actions that were involved" (p. 66).

In short, emotions play a key role in learning, memory, and motivation, all of which are processes that are relevant to human development across the lifespan, and to the development of, and the recovery from, substance abuse and addiction. Being open to, and aware of, our emotional states allows us to have a more flexible and personally meaningful response to challenging life decisions and relationships (Siegel, 2001). This leads us to "one of the most frequently discussed issues in men's studies," namely, the notion of "restrictive emotionality" in males and its potential consequences (e.g., physical illness, violence, and mental health problems, including substance abuse) (Kilmartin, 2007, p. 145).

Big Boys Don't Cry: Emotions and Their Expression in Males

Studies related to sex and gender differences and emotional expression look at gender stereotypes (what people believe about men and women) and self-descriptions of emotionality in terms of one's emotional experience and expression (which can be biased by one's gender stereotypes). Not surprisingly, gender stereotypes describe men as less emotionally expressive than women (Kilmartin, 2007). But the story is much more complicated than that. And in order to provide gender-responsive counseling services for men that address social and emotional development, we have to look more closely at how we as substance abuse professionals can better understand emotional expression in males.

First, although there is great cultural and within-group variability related to what, when, and how emotions can, and/or should be expressed by males and females, developmental research tells us that infant boys, in general, are in fact more emotionally expressive than girls. Eliot describes newborn males as being "more irritable, cry sooner when distressed, and are less easy to console than newborn females" (2009, p. 252). This difference starts to equalize during the pre-school years, and by age 6, consistent differences that are more in line with gender stereotypes ("girls are more emotionally expressive than boys") start to emerge, which continues into adolescence (Kilmartin, 2007). From a neuroscience perspective, the "social and emotional differences between boys and girls begin as tiny seeds planted by evolution and are nourished by hormones but blossom only under the hot sun of our highly gendered society" (Eliot, 2009, p. 252). This male socialization process related to emotional expressiveness or inexpressiveness is highlighted throughout the case studies in chapters 4 through 8. For now, the key point is that the male socialization process affects how boys and men think about expressing their emotions. For example, if they have internalized prohibitions about emotional expression in certain contexts but not in others (e.g., "I think it's OK to cry at funerals, but not when you lose a ballgame"), then this says more about their socio-cultural development than it does about their willingness and/or their innate ability to have and express emotions as boys and men (Wong & Rochlen, 2005). Likewise, if they have developed an "alexithymic style" of dealing with emotions (where alexithymia means "no words for feeling"), then they may have "such an impoverished emotional life that they cannot even identify feelings, much less express them" (Kilmartin, 2007, p. 156). The bottom line is that emotional behavior is more dynamic than the stereotypes suggest.

Second, if emotion is at the heart of developing an integrated sense of self in recovery, then understanding to what extent a boy or man lives by the prescriptions of traditional male gender roles will help us to better predict how they might react to a counseling strategy that targets their emotional awareness and expression. For example, if males see emotional expression as being feminine (e.g., as the behaviors of a "wimp" or a "sissy," or when homophobia intermingles with this dynamic, we may hear derogatory words like "fag" or "homo"), then they may not only be less likely to want to explore their emotional life with you, but they may decide that counseling is inherently a female realm, which may add to their ambivalence and apprehension about counseling. This has obvious implications for treatment retention.

Even though there is evidence that many men have "a desire to improve their abilities to express and disclose" emotions (Kilmartin, 2007, p. 161), it is rare that one finds boys or men entering substance abuse treatment with increasing emotional expression as a goal for themselves. However, there are several experiential change processes that can facilitate the start of this process. For example, as has been mentioned, *consciousness-raising*, i.e., increasing self-awareness, is recommended as a therapeutic change process to be used in the precontemplation and contemplation stages of change in the initial phases of treatment (Substance Abuse and Mental Health Services Administration, SAMHSA, 2002). As boys and men begin to look at themselves and the nature of their behavior, they become aware of the negative effects of their substance abuse on themselves and others.

Several other experiential change processes identified by Prochaska and DiClemente (1984) can help males increase motivation for change and move them from one stage to the next early on in treatment. For example, as one becomes more aware of the consequences of their substance abuse, they may experience *dramatic relief,* which can be a powerful emotional experience that is intensified by the fact that their bodies and minds are no longer numb from substances of abuse. Depending on how the boy or man has been socialized to express (or not express) these significant emotions, he may use this affective thrust as motivation to make changes in his life. A word of caution, however, is in order related to how males may or may not be able to handle a high level of intensity of emotional arousal in early recovery. Siegel (2001) writes:

> It is often at the moments in which emotion becomes most intense that we seem to have the greatest need to be understood and the most intense feelings of vulnerability. This sense of exposure may make many individuals, especially those with unsatisfying past experiences with communication, reluctant to reveal openly what they are feeling. At a moment of intensity, a failure to be understood, to be connected with emotionally, can result in a profound feeling of shame. The shame generated by missed opportunities for the alignment of states—for the feeling of emotional resonance, of "feeling felt"—can lead to withdrawal. (p. 247)

As we work with males in early recovery, we can recognize the potential that "dramatic relief" may have to trigger intrinsic motivation for change; while at the same time, we can be cognizant that their intensity of emotion, which may be masked in some men, can lead to feelings of vulnerability. Importantly, it is the interpersonal therapeutic relationship that can have a powerful regulating effect during these intense emotional encounters with feelings of shame.

Other experiential processes include *self-reevaluation* (recognizing how his behavior is in conflict with his personal values and life goals as a man) and *environmental reevaluation* (recognizing the effect that his behavior has had on others and his environment) can help to motivate change. Through a mindful and emotional appraisal of their behaviors, they can see who they have been while abusing substances and begin to visualize the type of man that they can be if they make positive changes in their lives. This process can begin through using psychoeducational discussions in individual and group counseling.

Emotions are Information

We need emotional information to identify triggers, to feel urges and cravings, to solve problems, to manage stress, and to feel good in recovery.

As was mentioned, many of these intrapersonal skills that are taught in substance abuse counseling settings begin with consciousness-raising and awareness. If we need to build awareness about the importance of emotional development in males, how do we help a man to find intrinsic motivation to pay close attention to his emotions and his overall affective state, especially when he may have been mandated—extrinsically motivated—to participate in the substance abuse counseling process? Why would a boy want to be aware of his emotional states? Other than anger, pride and excitement, aren't emotions painful. Isn't being emotional a "sissified" thing (big boys don't cry)? These may seem like odd questions if one is raised to value emotional awareness and expression; however, if male socialization processes affect how boys and men think about expressing their emotions, then they may have internalized prohibitions about seeing the value of discussing emotions (consciousness raising) and building emotional awareness (taking action) in treatment.

Indeed, although the context of a treatment setting may seem conducive to discuss the value of emotional awareness, the socio-cultural development of the boys or men in treatment may affect their willingness to have this discussion, and to express their emotions, particularly around other boys and men. Because emotional behavior is dynamic and affected by the context, we need to create the environment where discussions about emotions are not only possible, but are seen as important. Therefore, we need to shift perceptions about the value of emotions. There is no easy way to facilitate this shift.

This section began with the question: "What were they thinking?" Our look at the brain science and the neural pathways associated with substance abuse and addiction in chapter 2 pointed to the center of our basic drives and emotion, the limbic region, as being at the core of these seemingly out of control addictive behaviors. And although thinking processes are crucial to understanding and building recovery strategies related to relapse prevention, facilitating emotional awareness is essential to teaching boys and men the basic intrapersonal skills that will strengthen their treatment and recovery efforts.

Therefore, this simple phrase bears repeating: *Emotions are information.* Let us assume that we have the worst case scenario where feelings are seen by men as being feminine, and to go there even in counseling is seen as making him less of a man. This is where a shift in language from "talking about your feelings" to "understanding the basic mechanics of our survival instincts" can help to change perspectives about the role that feelings have in our lives. Understanding the mechanics of the brain (and having a balanced evolutionary perspective on the importance of emotions) can help us to underscore the value of paying attention to what one is feeling.

It is helpful to repeat the statement "emotions are information" in a matter-of-fact nonjudgmental way when working with boys and men. Additionally, we can change how the word "emotion" is perceived by discussing its origin. It is derived from the Latin words meaning "out" (e- which is a variation of ex-) and "move" (movere, which is related to the word "motivation"; *Webster's*, 2008). Emotions move us to act out, which has a negative connotation when associated with acting out behaviors. However, from an evolutionary standpoint, acting out was a positive behavior because it meant that we were motivated to move "out" towards things that kept us alive and away from things that might kill us. As Panksepp (2009) states: "To the best of our knowledge, emotional feelings arise from wide-scale neurodynamics that establish characteristic mentally experienced 'forces' that regulate and reflect certain types of action readiness within the nervous system" (p. 20).

Remember that as human beings we have depended upon our senses (our central nervous system of which our brain is a part) for our basic survival. As a species, we needed to be able to assess threat and to act quickly in order to survive the harsh environments of the jungles, forests or the plains of our ancestors. In fact, clients may have personal experiences where their instinctual awareness (senses in the body) may have helped them to survive in the dysfunctional environment of their family (e.g., if there was abuse) or their neighborhood (e.g., if there was bullying and/or gang-like activities). These instinctive senses are the basic bits of information that our bodies, brains, and minds use (through appraisal and recursive reappraisal processes) to make decisions that will affect our well-being.

In the basest sense, our senses are the data points for our affective appraisal system. For example, gut feelings are emotional information. They represent the "lower" end of the neural circuitry of emotional awareness and processing. So to put it briefly, emotional awareness (one piece of which is to "trust your gut") can be reframed as a survival skill. If we were working with females, we may use the language of "intuition" to describe this process. However, for males, becoming more aware of emotional states can be framed as opening up to our instincts for survival. Alternatively, by automatically shutting down our feelings (if that is possible) as being a nuisance to our manhood, we are losing valuable information about what is happening inside and outside of our bodies that affect our ability not only to survive, but to thrive and fully experience life.

Therefore, rather than seeing feelings as something that we need to get out (or get out of expressing), Siegel (2001) proposed an alternative way to view emotions; namely, that "emotions represent dynamic processes created within the socially influenced, value-appraising processes of the brain" (p. 123). We pay attention to things that we value. What we value has emotional salience. And the process for how we make decisions about what we value is deeply connected to our emotional needs.

By emphasizing that emotions are information, we can change the value that boys and men place on talking about feelings of fear, sadness, anger, or joy. All of these emotions can trigger behavioral impulses and thoughts of using substances for someone whose neural pathways are ingrained with this type of reactive (versus responsive) coping system.

An Affective, Value-Based Appraisal System

In order to teach boys and men how to access this information, we need to break down the mechanics of emotions to see them as being "a value system for the appraisal of meaning" (Siegel, 2001, p. 136). As we have seen, we are genetically and environmentally hard-wired with a system that seeks out what is of value to us and avoids what is not. The limbic system (e.g., amygdala, anterior cingulate cortex, etc.) and the neurotransmitters of the mesolimbic dopamine system affect our psychological and emotional drives and sense of well-being, and they move us (often unconsciously) towards what we value (and away from what we don't).

Long before we get to the point where we can manage emotions by acknowledging them and talking with someone about our feelings (e.g., saying "I feel angry" before engaging in acting out behaviors), we can begin to become aware of (i.e., broaden our consciousness of) the sub-cortical processes that underlie and precede the basic emotions that we identify with words. This increased awareness will deepen our relationship to our emotional states, and increase our response flexibility (Siegel, 2001) to whatever our affective appraisal system is sensing internally or externally in the environment. In short, broadening and deepening our awareness of our emotional states sets the stage for (and focuses the spotlight of the mind on) being able to respond flexibly to "internal and interpersonal processes" that have "a direct effect on self-regulation, relationships, and development across the lifespan" (p. 141).

Using Siegel's (1999) seminal writings from interpersonal neurobiology on emotion and self-regulation, we can break down emotional awareness into three phases: (a) initial orientation, appraisal, and arousal, (b) sensing primary emotions, and (c) having categorical (or basic) emotions, including the ability to put words to them (like fear, anger, sadness, surprise, or joy). By teaching about these phases of emotion (think emotions are information), we can approach them from the standpoint that they are the end product of an ancient neural circuitry system for appraisal and meaning-making related to what is happening inside and outside of our bodies and minds. Importantly, men's literature identifies places at various points in these phases where emotional awareness and emotional expression may be disrupted or blocked by a "cognitive-evaluative process" that relates to "internalized traditional masculine gender roles" (Wong & Rochlen, 2005, p. 63). As the phases are described below, examples will be given of potential barriers to facilitating emotional awareness in boys and men.

The *initial orientation, appraisal and arousal* phase involves two processes, an "initial orienting response," and an "elaborative appraisal and arousal," that activates certain neural circuits and deactivates others (Siegel, 2001, p. 124). There are two types of orienting responses that can occur. One is an overt orienting, whereby one's body and gaze literally shifts towards an external stimulus; while the other is a covert orienting that involves a slight internal shift of attention towards a stimulus that does not necessarily involve movement of the muscles or awareness in the prefrontal cortex (Ogden, Minton, & Pain, 2006). These two types of orienting responses are reflexive in nature and happen sub-cortically (without the involvement of the cortex). Discussion about "elaborative appraisal and arousal" began in our ringing doorbell analogy that provided some context for understanding how the limbic system might respond to a stimulus. This affective appraisal and arousal response attributes value to stimuli and together with the initial orienting response represents the beginning of emotional processing (Siegel, 2001) that says "Pay attention to this ... This is good (or bad) ... Now move!"

As the initial phase orients the body and mind towards a stimulus, there is a shift in one's state of mind that includes nonverbal, affective sensations, called primary emotions, which are feeling-states of mind rather than categorical feelings that one could label with words. Siegel describes this process of *sensing primary emotions* (that follows the initial orientation, appraisal and arousal phase) as shifts in one's state of mind that may be "subtle or intense" and "fleeting or persistent," and that "may continue as gentle sensations, like waves lapping on a shore, or they may evolve into larger, global changes, like a storm pounding on the beach" (pp. 125–126).

Using animal models, Panksepp (2009) describes seven basic "ancient emotional forces" that exist as instinctual emotional responses across species of mammals, including human beings. These seven core affective neural networks can be used as examples to describe the subtle shift from an orienting response (cross-species affective response) to a change in states of mind (a human primary emotional response): (a) the "seeking" system (a neural network) that is at the base of "the urge to find, to consume, and at times to hoard the fruits of the world" shifts in human beings into a state of mind that is focused on urgent interest and desire (Panksepp, 2009, p. 9). The remaining basic emotional systems identified by Panksepp (2009), and their related affective shifts in states of mind, include (b) the "fear" system (anxious state of mind), (c) the "rage" system (angry state of mind), (d) the "lust" system (erotic state of mind), (e) the "care" system (nurturing state of mind), (f) the "panic" system (sad state of mind), and (g) the "play" system (joyful state of mind). These emotional neural networks are the ancient instinctual systems that give us information about what is happening in our environments. Importantly, all of these emotional networks are related to our sense of connection with others—with lust, care, play, and seeking functionally opening during connected states, and rage, fear, and abandonment panic opening when we feel disconnected from others (Badenoch, 2008).

As we educate boys and men about these ancient emotional primes within the counseling relationship, we are building awareness (engaging their middle prefrontal region to connect to the limbic system) and helping them "to recognize how they can become masters over their primes rather than being mastered by them" (Panksepp, 2009, p. 18). By engaging their executive attentional circuits, we are changing how they think about emotions, and at the same time, increasing their awareness that there is a process of (a) *orienting to,* and (b) paying attention to *subtle shifts in states of mind* that precedes what we would call "feelings," where (c) *words can be used to describe our basic emotions.* Basic emotions, also known as "categorical emotions," such as sadness, anger, fear, surprise and joy are found to be expressed in different ways in cultures around the world, and "can be thought of as differentiated states of mind that have evolved into specific ingrained patterns of activation" (Siegel, 2001, p. 127).

As substance abuse professionals, we can attune to, observe, and begin to read the subtle orienting responses and shifts in our client's states of mind that may show up in body language and facial expressions long before there is an acknowledgement and potential verbal expression of their basic emotions. For example, as the therapeutic relationship develops, we can bring these observations into the process of counseling by having a dialogue about the subtle shifts in states of mind and body that we see happening in the moment. This requires that the counselor has the knowledge (e.g., awareness of one's own and other's affective orienting and appraisal processes) and the counseling skills (e.g., the use of immediacy in the moment) to bring this process to light in the session. Interestingly, there is evidence that attunement with the client's emotional state of being is healing with or without words (Siegel, 2006).

As we begin to educate boys and men about these subtle affective shifts in their body and mind, we may encounter some interesting dilemmas. For example, what happens when emotions begin to arise into awareness for boys and men? Will social prescriptions from traditional male gender roles be barriers to their ability to be with their emotional experiences? How might they react to their increasing emotional awareness? Will they be able to stay with their emotions and/or be willing or able to express them?

A Five-Step Process Model of Emotional Expression

A five-step process model of emotional expression and nonexpression from the psychology of boys and men (originally proposed by Kennedy-Moore & Watson, 1999; cited in Wong and Rochlen, 2005) provides a way that can help counselors to be more cognoscente about the possible causes of a male's inexpressiveness and adjust their counseling approach to fit the nature of the client's challenges. Consider phases one (orienting) and two (sensing primary emotions) that were outlined above. In this process model, these two initial phases would be considered a prereflective reaction step (Step 1), where a man may have a higher threshold for emotional arousal and therefore have a more limited emotional reaction to a stimulus than others may have. This could be due to this particular man having a less reactive set autonomic nervous system, or he may be less trained to sense when this subcortical system is activated.

For example, he may have no awareness that his heart is beating faster (brain stem level reaction) when he is told by his spouse or significant other that he is in danger of losing the relationship. Increased awareness about his heart beating faster is emotional information that enhances his response flexibility to this threatening situation. Being unaware increases the chances that he will suddenly realize (perhaps after the fact) that his emotional reactivity has exacerbated the challenges that he is facing (in this case in relationship to his significant other). Furthermore, in this scenario, if the reactions of the brainstem and lower limbic region (perhaps fear, rage and/or panic) go unnoticed, then he may find himself acting in a fight, flight, or freeze response (autonomic nervous system). At this point, the ingrained behavioral patterns of the past will likely be engaged. If heading to the bar to drink with the guys has been a past response to blow off steam, then this suddenly may seem like the best idea given the circumstances. Later on, he may find himself returning home to re-engage his spouse in a highly reactive (and intoxicated) way. This is a recipe for domestic violence, which is a significant concern for women, children, and other men, as is highlighted in the men's literature (Brooks & Good, 2001a,b).

This level of emotional reactivity can be processed in a substance abuse counseling setting when clients are retelling stories from their life, for example if they are telling a story about what happened in an alcohol-related domestic violence situation. There is the potential for a multitude of emotional states of mind to be created in the retelling of an incident like this. Anger, sadness, and anxiety could be expected. And states of shame would only exacerbate and complicate the expression of these emotions. This is an opportunity to say: "Can we take a minute to pause and reflect and see what is happening in your body as you are telling this story? Is your heart beating faster right now? Are you beginning to breathe differently? Are you feeling warmer or colder in your body? Were you feeling any of these sensations before, during or after the incident?" You are engaging an internal processing system that can be trained to check-in and pick up on subtle pieces of emotional information that are the canary in the mineshaft that warns boys and men that something important is happening in their environment, and in their bodies and minds. Learning the skill of mindful awareness of the bodily states can shift the trajectory of their emotional and behavioral responses.

Imagine if this man who is feeling threatened by someone or something could notice that his heart rate and breathing had changed, engender some curiosity about what that might mean, and then choose to step away for a few moments to check-in and breathe into the situation. Through this process, he can return to the situation with his middle prefrontal region fully engaged in responding (in this case to his significant other). His heart may still be beating faster; however, with the middle prefrontal region engaged, he will have enhanced (a) bodily regulation, (b) attuned communication, (c) emotional balance, (d) response flexibility, (e) fear modulation, (f) empathy, (g) insight, (h) moral awareness, and (i) intuition (Siegel, 2007). How different would his response be with these qualities of mind engaged?

Emotional reactivity is a common occurrence in early recovery as drugs of abuse leave the systems of the body and mind and clients seek to find equilibrium and a sense of stability. There will be ample opportunities to ask them to pause and reflect in the midst of this emotional chaos. Each repeated effort at engaging the middle prefrontal region to respond to these affective mind states will strengthen a client's neural pathways related to self-regulation. In other words, working out these muscles of the mind in treatment will increase response flexibility after treatment and into recovery. Each successful effort at moving through this process can increase a male's sense of self-efficacy for change and for dealing with these types of situations in the future. Therefore, in phases one (orienting) and two (sensing primary emotions), increased self-awareness can shorten the prereflective reaction step (Step 1; Wong & Rochlen, 2005) through training boys and men to sense when their subcortical nervous system is being activated and respond accordingly.

Let us take this a step further and suppose that we have had some success in substance abuse treatment, and our male client is becoming more aware of his affective responses (Step 2; Wong & Rochlen, 2005) through learning to recognize the subtle shifts in his body and his states of mind. One potential barrier that may surface related to male socialization processes is that because of gender role conflict (O'Neil, Good, & Holmes, 1995) boys and men may have internal prohibitions against having feelings, such as sadness (Lynch & Kilmartin, 1999) or grief (Rabinowitz & Cochran, 2002), shame or fear (Park, 2006) and "convince themselves that they are not experiencing feelings and therefore do not express them" (Wong & Rochlen, 2005, p. 63). As a gender-responsive professional, we can recognize when males may essentially be "putting the cap on" their emotional experiences, and explore what it may mean for them as males to begin to be aware of their emotional responses to internal and external stimuli.

Revisiting the new way of looking at emotion as information, while comparing this to the messages that they may have received from their peers, family members, and/or role models in their culture about feelings, can help to continue the process of consciousness-raising; which in turn, aids in moving males into the preparation and action stages of change in terms of using their emotions as information to navigate the storms of recovery.

This leads us to another potential barrier for this process, namely that "some men have difficulty identifying and describing what they feel and are thus unable to express their emotions" (Step 3; Wong & Rochlen, 2005, p. 64). In this scenario, we may have a male who is able to begin to feel the subtle affective shifts in his state of body and mind (Step 1), and may have moved through some of the limiting socialization processes that are related to expressing emotions (Step 2), and yet may not be able to put words to what he is feeling because he has not been socialized to interpret and label his emotions, i.e., "I am feeling sad" (or angry, afraid, surprised, or happy). Intimately related to these first three steps is the process of being able to read other people's emotional states and respond to feelings (one's own and others) in relationships (which will be discussed in the developmental case studies in chapter 4 through 8 related to building interpersonal skills). Using writing activities, role-plays, and other experiential exercises in individual and group counseling can be helpful to build the skills of interpreting and labeling emotional states.

During these processes, it will be necessary to be acutely aware of the ambivalence that may arise from time to time related to male socialization processes and emotional awareness and expression. For example, even if a male is able to label and interpret his feelings (Step 3), he may find himself in conflict with his values and personal beliefs about emotional expression that have been deeply rooted in his development as a boy and man. He may "evaluate certain emotions as negative" (Step 4; Wong & Rochlen, 2005, p. 64) and believe that it is both unacceptable to feel and express certain basic emotions, such as fear and vulnerability. The same decisional balance processes that are involved in exploring whether or not to change any behavior that is problematic can be used to explore the ambivalence related to expressing certain basic emotions with others. Specifically, exploring the developmentally influenced values and belief systems related to emotions and emotional expression in various contexts will be crucial to moving through this potential barrier.

Lastly, we must consider the influence of the social context for emotional expression (Step 5; Wong & Rochlan, 2005). In most social contexts, men tend to display most feelings less frequently and less intensely than females (Kilmartin, 2007). The exception is the expression of anger by men, which may not only be seen as an appropriate male affective response, but may be forgiven in extreme, out of control responses, particularly in certain contexts. For example, consider the social context of a funeral. When a boy or man knows that he is feeling sad or afraid, for example, his emotional expression may be inhibited by his perception of the appropriateness of males expressing fear or sadness in a given social context. At a funeral, a male may perceive that it is okay to express extreme anger at the death of a loved one, but he may feel that intense grief and sadness would be perceived as him falling apart and being less of a man, or not being strong for his family during this time of grief. Conversely, add the consumption of alcohol in this context, and it may be culturally accepted, and even appropriate, for him to show intense grief, because he (and others) can say after the fact that it was the alcohol talking. The end result in this scenario may be unresolved grief and a socially learned response to drink alcohol when feelings of sadness begin to come into awareness.

If anger, pride, and loneliness are generally the most frequently expressed emotions in males (Kilmartin, 2007), then we are very likely to see them surface in the substance abuse treatment context. We can explore these feelings as gateways to a more expansive and healthy array of emotional awareness and expression. As Wong and Rochlen (2005) state: "Men's emotional behavior is not a stable property but a multidimensional construct with many causes, modes, and consequences" (p. 62).

In summary, to explore these multidimensional factors related to emotional expression, we can consider several key questions in our assessment about our male clients related to the potential barriers that have been outlined above: Are they able to sense affective arousal in their body (Step 1)? Are they automatically repressing their feelings because of gender-based expectations (Step 2)? Are they able to identify and label their feelings (Step 3)? Are they uncomfortable and avoidant of negative emotions (Step 4)? Or are they feeling that they have very limited social contexts for the expression of their emotions (Step 5)? We can incorporate these important assessment questions into the dialogue that we have with males in counseling as they begin to pause and reflect, for example, on what is happening when a subtle sense of uneasiness or distressing feeling begins to enter their awareness.

When the Storm Hits: Check-In (Not Out)

Emotions are information. Whether we are aware of it or not, they are the energy that flows through our body and mind in an affective, value-based appraisal system that helps us to make meaningful decisions about whether to act out or not (remember "e-" and "-motion" combine to mean moving out towards or away from something in the environment). As boys and men learn to tune in to this ancient, instinctual system in their bodies, they are strengthening the neural pathways that flow through the body and between the layers of their triune brain, i.e., the brain stem (associated with maintaining homeostasis related to our basic bodily functions), the limbic region (associated with basic drives and emotions), and the cortex (that allows us to be conscious, to have ideas, and to reflect upon, and communicate about, abstract concepts).

Let us take a moment to review (remember that repetition stimulates neural growth and memory) the connections related to the brain structures that were presented in chapter 2 that are involved with the effective functional flow of energy and information bi-directionally from top to bottom in our brain and bodies. Whereas, the dorsomedial, ventromedial, and dorsolateral prefrontal cortices (DMPFC, VMPFC, and the DLPFC) are central to our executive attention processes, the orbitofrontal, insula, and anterior cingulate cortices (OFC, IC, and the

ACC) sit at the proverbial crossroad between the "higher" executive structures and the "lower" limbic and brain stem areas associated with emotions, basic drives, and survival. The fact that the words "higher" and "lower" are in quotation marks denotes structural proximity. It does not suggest that one area is more important than the other relative to the overall functioning of our mental and emotional capacities. This latter distinction gets to the point that we are hoping to make in our discussion with boys and men about the importance of emotional development to their overall well-being. That is, if males can make the shift from dismissing emotions as irrelevant or a sign of weakness or femininity into emotions are information, then they can begin to focus more intentionally through their executive attentional circuits on (a) monitoring their emotional state of being, (b) modulating their emotional states in a flexible and adaptable way, and (c) modifying their behaviors in relation to self and others. As has been described, this begins by increasing awareness of the processes of *orienting to,* and paying attention to *subtle shifts in states of mind* that precedes the process of *finding words to describe one's basic emotions* and *expressing one's basic needs and values with others.*

Boys and men can be taught processes in counseling that include *monitoring, modulating, and modifying* one's thoughts, feelings, and behaviors (using a type of check-in system like the one described below). When practiced in day-to-day life, these processes can strengthen the neural pathways of mindful awareness, and perhaps lower the threshold for males to be more quickly aware of their affective shifts in emotional states or moods in various situational and relational contexts, and act in a more responsively flexible and adaptable (versus reactive) way.

This last point about emotional states or moods brings up an interesting and important distinction related to the terminology that we can use to discuss the often vague and mysterious word: feelings. As we expand the discussion with males about how emotions are information, we can begin to have a dialogue regarding how this information is primarily related to our needs and values, i.e., emotions are part of an affective, value-based appraisal system. Therefore, as we are educating boys and men about emotion, we may need to step back for a moment and define our terms more explicitly.

First, *emotion* represents a state of being in a particular moment, e.g., calm, excited, proud, happy, lonely, etc. It carries information about what is needed or valued in that moment in time. The more attuned that we are to our emotional states of being, the more likely it will be that we can see the value of the moment, or understand what we need in that instant.

Second, if we begin to notice that there is a pattern of emotion that develops over an attenuated period of time (e.g., throughout the progression of the day), then we can describe that emotional pattern as a *mood.* A "mood" is often described as less intense and not attributable to anything in particular (Kassel & Veilleux, 2010). For several reasons, mood states are particularly troublesome for boys and men in recovery. First, if the mood states are less intense and not associated with anything or anyone in particular, then it is very likely that they will remain below conscious awareness and motivate them in ways in which they are not even aware. Oftentimes, it is only after a relapse, for example, that someone will reflect (consciously) on the fact that: "Oh yeah, I *was* in a bad mood that day." Second, moodiness is stereotypically associated with females. For a male to recognize a mood state, he would need to move beyond the notion that moods are representative of femininity. Again, emotions (and mood states) are information about what we need and value, and whether we are able to get what we need, or live out the values that we profess.

Lastly, there is the notion of *affect* that "is generally perceived to be a superordinate category defined by valence (positive or negative) feelings" that "encompasses the phenomena of mood and emotion" (Kassel, & Veilleux, 2010, p. 4). As we discuss emotional processes (awareness, regulation, expression, etc.) with boys and men, we start to see patterns of affect that occurred during specific developmental periods in their lives, or were triggered by events that changed their emotional valence (positive or negative) related to longer-standing emotional patterns in their life.

To summarize, as we teach boys and men how to focus more intentionally on *monitoring, modulating, and modifying* their thoughts, feelings, and behaviors, it will be important for us to include a discussion about the differences between *emotion, mood, and affect.* To use a weather analogy, as they develop a day-to-day practice of mindful awareness, they will be better able to reflect upon, and delineate between, the types of affective "storms" in their life. Is this emotion a temporary squall (e.g., and emotional reaction to an altercation with a co-worker) or is this current state of mind indicative of a weather event that has set-in for the day or the week (e.g., a mood that cannot be attributed to an activating event, but nonetheless is causing mild distress and is in need of some exploration)? In order for males to get to this level of affective discernment, they will need guidance about how to develop a process for attending to their subtle or severe shifts in emotional states or moods in various situational and relational contexts.

Checking In: Developing Embodied Self-Awareness

While the name of this process of checking the weather should fit with the client's personal frame of reference, for explanation purposes here we will call it a Check-In System. And although each part of this process is described in detail in separate sections below, Appendix A provides a sample handout that can be used in individual or group counseling settings, e.g., in an aftercare group that is focused on self-awareness and/or relapse prevention.

The first point in this process would be to simply ask the client to check-in:

Hold _____ in your awareness and breathe down into your body. (You fill in the blank. It can be a difficult situation, a crisis event, an actual person's name, etc.)

Use your mind to scan yourself from head to toe for any sensations in your body.

Where are these sensations located physically in your body?

As you hold your attention on these bodily sensations, what images are coming to your mind (past memories, recent events, or future expectations)?

How do you feel about these images? What do you think about them?

Checking In facilitates a process of mindful awareness that allows us to broaden our consciousness and to notice what is happening in our experience; to pause and reflect on the *sensations, images, feelings* and *thoughts* (Siegel, 2010) in our body and mind. Siegel uses the acronym SIFT to help us remember this process. When we notice that something isn't quite right within our awareness, we can use this process of holding our awareness and SIFTing through our experience to see what is influencing us to act in certain ways in different relational contexts. From the perspective of neuroscience, this process effectively begins to connect the energy and information flow between the upper and lower parts of the brain and central nervous system through using mindful awareness, i.e., intentionally focusing on the sensations and feelings in the body (embodied self-awareness) and the thoughts and images that are coming into the mind (conceptual self-awareness). The following information about the importance of connecting embodied and conceptual self-awareness in this way represents an annotated version of the well-researched ideas that are detailed in Alan Fogel's highly informative book, *The Psychophysiology of Self-Awareness: Rediscovering the Lost Art of Body Sense* (2009).

As we ask clients to breathe down into their bodies, we are energizing what Fogel (2009) calls our "interoceptive" awareness (our ability to feel our internal bodily states). We are engaging the crossroad areas of our brain (the orbitofrontal, insula, and anterior cingulate cortices) to bring up awareness from our bodily states and sensations into our executive attentional areas (dorsomedial, ventramedial, and dorsolateral prefrontal cortices). Essentially, this process opens up communication of energy and information between these larger structural areas that are involved in: (a) conceptually reflecting on, and making interpretations, judgments, and decisions about what is happening (through the conceptual self-awareness of the dorsomedial prefrontal cortex); and (b) making embodied choices about how to experience what is happening to the self in that moment (through the ventromedial prefrontal cortex). Interestingly, Fogel explains that activation of these two main structures of the brain in the middle prefrontal cortex happens much like a switch flipping back and forth between ventral (embodied self-awareness) and dorsal (conceptual self-awareness) processes. Fogel writes: "Any way you want to look at it, the fact is that we cannot be in conceptual and embodied states of self-awareness at the same time," however, "you can under certain circumstances, self-regulate the switch" (p. 99).

This latter process is essentially what we are training males to do with this Check-In System. Their thoughts, judgments, and decisions can be checked for accuracy by switching from their conceptual self-awareness to their embodied self-awareness. In other words, what they may think is accurate about the activating event in their conceptually-guided self-awareness may shift when they feel it through their embodied-guided self-awareness that occurs when they take the time to breathe down into their experience of the event. In this way, the thought patterns that do not fit with their felt embodied experience can help to create a more grounded, embodied decision-making process in relation to the event.

Additionally, the neural pathways related to embodied self-awareness are literally slower than the pathways related to conceptual self-awareness, because interoceptive pathways involve unmyelinated nerve fibers (myelinated nerve fibers speed up transmission of energy and information through neural circuits). Therefore, since "expanding embodied self-awareness is slow and deliberate in comparison to the rapid and instantaneous generation of ideas and thoughts in conceptual self-awareness" (Fogel, 2009, p. 47), the first point of our Check-In System asks the client to slow down, take a deep breath into their body, and trust the information that their physiology (i.e., their gut, as well as their heart) may have to guide their responses to the activating event.

Doing a Gut Check: Getting a Felt Sense of One's Needs and Values

Continuing with initiating the systematic check-in, we can ask the client to do the second part of this process, which is to do a Gut Check:

Continue to hold these bodily sensations and images in your awareness.

If they are from the past, what does your gut tell you that you needed and valued the most at that time in your life?

If they are from the present, what does your gut tell you that you need and value the most right now?

If they are about the future, what does your gut tell you that you will need and value at that point in your life?

As you hold your needs and values in your awareness, what value-based
actions can you take right now that will be your best efforts at *both* (a)
getting your needs met and (b) "doing the next right thing" in recovery?

In facilitating this Gut-Check process with a client, they may ask:
"Why look back at the past?" It's because, as we have explored in chapter 1, "states of mind become traits of mine," and as such, the chances
are good that the current situation that is the activating event of the
moment is being fueled by (i.e., intensified by) the implicit, embodied
memories of the past. Implicit memories may be reactivated into our
present awareness; giving us the opportunity to build on the autobiographical narratives of our life. That is, through this process, we can
explicitly fill in and deepen our understanding of ourselves, and create a narrative that is coherent and unifying, particularly around making sense of what has happened in our life and relationships related to
the consequences of our substance abuse and addiction. This narrative
process, especially related to attachment system, emotional communication, and the developing sense of self as a boy or man, directly influences emotional regulation and the organizing of a coherent sense of
self in recovery.

This process may be inhibited by the "experience dependent brain
development" (Fogel, 2009, p. 100) that may have occurred through
socialization processes that valued thinking over feeling. If we have
spent most of our lives with the switch of conceptual self-awareness
turned on, then it may be difficult to switch on the embodied self-awareness that may be less valued by the traditional male gender role norms
of stoicism and restrictive emotionality. In the heat of a fierce battle, it
may be helpful to be able to switch off embodied self-awareness to fight
through the pain of a wound in order survive. However, in the day-to-
day practice of living, the paradigm of winning or losing can be shifted
to a more fluid process of finding yourself again and again by intentionally bringing both embodied and conceptual awareness to yourself and
your relationships.

In a trusting therapeutic relationship, we can help clients to build a
coherent self-narrative that is influenced by both the internal, embodied, gut-level experiences of met or unmet developmental needs, as well
as the internal, conceptual value-based thoughts and judgments about
what was happening "then" in the past. At the heart of each male's
development are beliefs about what it means to be a man. Packaged in
this phrase are notions about masculinity and male gender roles that
shape the developing selves of boys and men. What we are looking
for in this dialogue with these boys and men are developmental and
gender-specific themes that may emerge and help us to make sense of
both the current activating event and the continuity (or discontinuity)
of their sense of self and their current life direction.

Appendices B through E contain query-based exercises that can be
helpful with initiating this Gut-Check process related to unmet devel-

opmental and gender-based needs and values in their life. The questions in these exercises can be used to guide discussions in the assessment and/or treatment phases of the counseling process. These appendices are essentially the same exercise that is adapted for the developmental level of your client (e.g., Appendix B is "An Exercise for Early Adolescent Males, Ages 12 to 18," while Appendix C is "An Exercise for Later Adolescent and Young Adult Males, Ages 18 to 34," etc.). The appendices are also designed to be used as self-reflective homework assignments called "Looking Back to Plan Ahead: Setting Personal Goals." However, it is highly recommended that the writings that come from these homework assignments be processed in the context of the person-to-person therapeutic relationship. This is the optimal situation because, through the dynamic of being seen and feeling felt in the counseling relationship, the client can experience a level of intimacy from sharing these often shame-based, emotionally painful memories that can deepen the healing process far beyond what might occur if clients simply write down responses and never share them in a nurturing therapeutic environment with another person(s).

These exercises in Appendices B through E were created as an adaptation of processes for gathering information from participants that were used in a qualitative research study of psychosocial stages and the accessibility of autobiographical memories across the life cycle (Conway & Holmes, 2004). Designed to be used as a process to supplement the assessment and rapport-building phase of treatment, the questions (and/or the written answers that can be reviewed in session) will illicit autobiographical memories from client's earlier socialization experiences, which tend to be emotionally laden (and may be quite painful). As we process the memories, we can look for events and themes that reflect psychosocial developmental tasks, and gender-based challenges, needs, and values. For example, we can look for the ways in which they talk about notions of masculinity and femininity in their stories. We can ask such questions as: What would happen if they deviated from traditional gender role norms? How did they experience the women and men in their lives? Were they nurturing or emotionally aloof (i.e., examining stereotypical and other behaviors without judgments)? Were their caregivers able to experience, label, and express their emotions, and were they able to receive their children's emotional expressions? Were there events or patterns of gender role devaluations, restrictions, or violations (O'Neil, 2006)? How might these gender role issues contribute to their current emotional and interpersonal problems? What are the major gender role themes and how do they manifest in the present life challenges? How will these themes affect their ability to change? Were there events, patterns, or themes that emerged across their lifespan, specifically in relationship to their family of origin, peer relations, and their perceptions of societal and ethno-cultural expectations? Where were the transition points in terms of specific pivotal experiences? How did alcohol and other drugs (and the expectations and actual effects of the drugs and alcohol) play a role in shaping their subjective experiences (states of mind that became traits of mine) around these issues?

As we are processing these questions, we can also ask ourselves where the opportunities lie to reframe the problems or issues that we are hearing as developmental challenges and transitions, and help them to shift perspectives on these gender role issues (using metaphors and analogies) whenever possible. These transformed narratives can be unifying to "otherwise disparate aspects of memory within the individual" (Siegel, 2001, p. 63). Through this process, we are encouraging men to recreate themselves and not be defined by their past. As they process their bodily sensations and images, and their thoughts and emotions, we can help them to mediate their fears related to trust, intimacy, power, and giving up control (O'Neil, 2006).

Additionally, in this second part of the systematic check-in, we are asking clients to do a Gut Check now. That is, if the bodily sensations and images that are in their awareness are from their present life circumstances, then we ask them to consider what their gut may be telling them about what they need and value the most *right now* in their life? This question moves them from the realm of contemplation about what they needed and valued but did not get in the past (most likely as children and adolescents) into identifying what it is that they presently need and value (in their current developmental life stage as adolescents or adults in this moment). As they are switching back and forth from embodied self-awareness and conceptual self-awareness, and from past experiences to the present moment (with its needs and values), they are reorganizing memories and seeing and experiencing the themes in their lives that provide detailed information for their hippocampus to store explicit autobiographical memories. Importantly, they are also identifying, and preparing to move toward what they need and value (in their mind and in their gut) right now in the present moment.

Doing a Reality Check with Trusted Others

As the Rolling Stones song says, "You can't always get what you want, but if you try sometimes you just might find you get what you need." The processes that have been initiated in this systematic Gut Check thus far have laid the foundation for males to have access to the emotional energy and information from their past and their present, which serve as personal data for contemplating with others (e.g., a counselor or another trusted confidante in recovery) what *value-based actions* can be taken in the present moment that will be their best efforts at *both* (a) getting their needs met and (b) doing the next right thing in recovery? This question moves into the realm of action and takes us to the third (and final) part of the Check-In System, which asks the clients to do a Reality Check:

What people and places do you trust as being safe to talk about what you need? Who can you speak openly with about what you value the most right now in your life?

Seek out those people and places that will respect your best efforts to act according to your emotional integrity. Talking with people that you trust and respect can help to give you some perspective and an objective viewpoint. It gives you a reality check on your needs and values.

If you are unable to identify or get in touch with specific people that you trust, then find a safe place where you can come home to yourself and gain a sense of stability and peace in the present moment. Journaling can be an excellent way to process through these sensations, images, feelings, and thoughts as they arise into your awareness.

One of the most challenging aspects in recovery can be putting together a social support network that you can turn to when you need to do anything from ventilating to celebrating, i.e., when you need to act out from the basic emotional systems that were identified by Panksepp (2009): (a) seeking/urgent interest, (b) fear/anxiety, (c) rage/anger, (d) lust/eroticism, (e) care/nurturing, (f) panic/sadness, and (g) play/joyfulness, without turning to the ingrained and conditioned patterns that are associated with drug-seeking and substance abusing behaviors.

It is also a reality check of sorts for a boy or man to realize that in recovery he must identify who in his social environment he *can* trust when he needs to talk about these basic affective needs. Additionally, and perhaps more importantly, he must understand that these emotional systems are basic, fundamental needs of all human beings. Therefore, as he can create a map (or mental representations) in his mind of his own needs and values through this process, i.e., his "Me-Maps," he can also build "You-Maps" to understand another person's needs and values. Furthermore, when he enters into a conscious relationship with another human being, he is also creating a "We-Map," which is a mental representation of the relationship of which he is a part (Siegel, 2010).

This process of bringing attention to, and reflecting upon, another person's states of being engages and strengthens the neural circuitry involved in having empathy for others. As was discussed in chapter 2, when attention and reflective self-awareness are harnessed in the middle prefrontal region of the brain, there are several key functions that are enhanced which are crucial to having mature, intimate relationships with others, e.g., attuned communication, empathy, insight, and intuition (Siegel, 2007). And even though these functions are compromised by chronic substance abuse and addiction, it is fortunate that they are at the heart of learning how to do a systemic check-in with oneself and others in recovery.

These notions of having *conceptual and embodied awareness* of me, you, and we states of mind are essential to developing an integrated sense of self that is capable of having mature relationships with others. Consequently, there are multiples examples in the developmental case studies (in the chapters that follow) that show how crucial the process of understanding the me-, you-, and we-states of mind can be to having healthy, mature, and intimate relationships in recovery. With this increased awareness of self and others, males can find in their relationships in recovery that they can get a reality check from their trusted friends or loved ones about their thoughts and feelings related to the value-based actions that they may want to take in the moment that represent their best efforts at getting their needs met and doing the next right thing in recovery.

In summary, with an attuned and resonant therapeutic relationship with our clients, we can create the space to explore difficult gender- and developmentally-specific questions, especially related to the influences of the male socialization processes and how boys and men have learned to deal with and express their emotions in various relational contexts. Additionally, by asking our clients to repeatedly pause and reflect with us on their emotional experiences (current and past), we are helping them to work out the muscles of their mind interpersonally in treatment to increase their ability to respond flexibility to high-risk situations after treatment and into recovery. Through this process, we are engaging their middle prefrontal region to hold their attention so that that they can respond to their emotional arousal, their conditioned impulsive reactions, and their negative and positive affective mind states in a flexible and adaptable way. Over time, they will be strengthening new neural pathways related to self-regulation and emotional development. We will see in the developmental case studies in the chapters that follow that emotional awareness (within oneself and in relationships with others) is at the heart of developing an integrated sense of self that can weather the storms of life in recovery.

CHAPTER

4

Substance Abuse Counseling with Early Adolescent Males (Ages 12 to 18)

If you think about the basic biological and psychosocial developmental challenges that 12- to 18-year-old boys face as they mature, it is almost overwhelming to grasp the multi-layered aspects of their development, i.e., how their rapidly changing bodies intersect with their self-concept as boys, and how these elements are influenced by their peer's comments, which in turn are affected by familial and societal expectations about what it means to be a man. These intertwined biopsychosocial elements have a powerful influence on how boys will make choices around drinking alcohol, smoking cigarettes or marijuana, or choosing to use any other substances of abuse.

Early adolescence is defined by the beginning of a major biological developmental leap, namely, the entrance into puberty, which occurs for most boys around the age of 12. This stage represents a period of rapid physical changes that are initiated by the production of hormones that cause increases in physical size, as well as a number of cognitive and emotional changes, that combine to affect appearance, coordination, changes in sexual interests, and swings in mood and energy levels (Newman & Newman, 2012). Although there is variability in terms of how and when these changes manifest in boys, there are some generalizations in the biopsychosocial development for this age group that are important to understand, particularly in relation to the initiation and potential continuation of substance use.

Adolescent development includes an inherent tension between developing a sense of independence (from one's family of origin) and a sense of group belonging or mutuality (with one's peers and larger social groups). Interestingly, the same characteristic behaviors that are associated with moving through this normal adolescent transition, i.e., high levels of exploration, risk-taking, and novelty and sensation seeking, as well as increased social interaction and play behaviors, place adolescents in a "critical period of addiction vulnerability" as evidenced by three major observations: (a) that "adolescents and young adults generally exhibit higher rates of experimental use and substance use disorders than older adults," (b) that "addictive disorders identified in adults most commonly have onset in adolescence or young adulthood," and (c) that "earlier onset of substance use predicts greater addiction severity and morbidity, including use of—and substance use disorders associated with—multiple substances" (Chambers, Taylor, & Potenza, 2003, p. 1041). In short, the neurobiological and socio-cultural aspects of this developmental period are both a blessing and a curse, because they are needed to initiate the development of a mature adult who has both a sense of self and a sense of connection to others, and yet they heighten the vulnerability to substance use disorders.

During early adolescence, there is a neurobiological feedback system that is developing between the brain, the glands (hypothalamus, pituitary, and adrenal), and hormones that is crucial to the stability of mood, energy level, sleep patterns, digestion and the functioning of the immune system (Newman & Newman, 2012). These linkages help to control how boys (and girls) react to stress, and in tandem with socio-cultural factors, affect how they will learn to self-regulate their emotional and mental states of being. One can imagine how saturating these biological systems with substances of abuse could play havoc on the delicate balance of the developing boy's mind, body, and spirit. Additionally, there are important neurological changes that are interconnected with the endocrine system that are related to mood and energy levels.

In terms of brain development, adolescence has been described as a "period of remodeling" where early puberty marks an "overproduction of axons and synapses," while later adolescence shifts to "rapid pruning" of these same synaptic connections (Crews, He, & Hodge, 2007, p. 190). Importantly, many of the structural areas of the brain that were highlighted in chapter 2 of this book in terms of being important to the "stamping-in" of addictive behaviors (primarily in the limbic region) and "working out the muscles of mind" in recovery (strengthening connections between the middle prefrontal and limbic regions) undergo massive reorganization in adolescence (e.g., the amygdalae, nucleus accumbens, hippocampus, and structures of the middle prefrontal cortex). Examples of this remodeling process include a decline in the absolute volume of the prefrontal cortex, with peaks in levels of dopamine and serotonin inputs to this same structure (Crews et al., 2007). Details about how this re-modeling occurs during adolescence is beyond the scope of this chapter, however, there are excellent sources in the literature that describe specific changes in brain structures and the neurotransmitter systems that are related to both normal adolescent development and the neurocircuitry associated with substance abuse and addictive behaviors (Casey & Jones, 2010; Chambers, Taylor, & Potenza, 2003; Crews et al., 2007; Tapert & Schweinsburg, 2005; Thatcher & Clarke, 2010). Importantly, these sources point to a "tension between early emerging 'bottom-up' systems that express exaggerated reactivity to motivational stimuli and later maturing 'top-down' cognitive control regions" (Casey & Jones, 2010, p. 1197). Adolescence is also characterized by intense emotional states where the appearance of striking changes in mood are often difficult to distinguish between the normal developmental processes of learning to modulate affective states and the development of clinical syndromes, such as depression (Crews et al., 2007).

The challenge of modulating this tension between bottom-up and top-down systems in adolescence is essentially the same challenge that all individuals face when they move from active addictive behaviors into active recovery behaviors. That is, the bottom-up neurobiological system that is related to sensation-seeking and risk-taking (i.e., emotion and motivation) will, over time and with repeated mindful experiences, gradually lose "its competitive edge with the progressive emergence of 'top-down' regulation" (i.e., executive functioning will strengthen in the prefrontal cortices as individuals learn to monitor, modulate, and modify their thoughts, feelings, and behaviors), which is the case when adolescents move successfully into adulthood (Casey & Jones, 2010, p. 1197).

This self-regulatory process in adolescence has also been described as a "period of developmental imbalance in the brain's 'Go!' and 'Stop!' circuitry" (Childress, 2006, p. 49). One can explain this process to clients using the analogy of a car with its accelerator (or gas pedal) as the "Go!" circuitry, and its braking system (or brake pedal) as the "Stop!" circuitry in the brain. The "Go!" brain circuitry is embedded in the limbic region and is involved in every individual's desires and motivation for the natural rewards in our environment that have kept us alive, and surviving and thriving, as a species for ages. That is, the natural drives for food and sex (that are the gas pedals of the brain moving us to eat and to reproduce) are part of the "Go!" circuitry and are involved in stimulating basic survival behaviors. In contrast, the "Stop!" circuitry, located primarily in the prefrontal region, is involved in inhibiting or putting on the brakes in order for the individual to pause and reflect before making decisions about when to pursue a reward (Childress, 2006).

Adolescents with less of the top-down regulatory abilities (or "Stop!" circuitry) may be more susceptible to develop substance abusing and addictive behaviors. For example, studies in samples of high-risk populations show "impairments in frontal functioning before alcohol and drug exposure," which is also apparent in "clinical findings in attention-deficit/hyperactivity disorder populations who show decreased prefrontal activity and are four times as likely to develop a substance use disorder compared with healthy controls" (Casey & Jones, 2010, p. 1197). Add to this systemic susceptibility repeated heavy doses of alcohol, and cortical development in adolescence is further disrupted as higher executive functions are altered "in a manner that promotes continued impulsive behavior, alcohol abuse and risk of alcohol dependence" (Crews et al., p. 196).

Alternatively, during adolescence cortical changes can be induced through environmental experiences and training, such as educational tasks to improve selective attention, working memory, and problem solving (each of which are correlated with increased myelination and synaptic pruning in the frontal cortical areas) (Crews et al., 2007). Experiences such as these can be included in substance abuse treatment processes, e.g., cognitive behavioral strategies to improve cognitive control or refusal skills to decrease harmful risk-taking behaviors (Casey & Jones, 2010), in order to alter executive functioning in a way that increases top-down regulation over bottom-up functioning. Additionally, even though risk-taking behaviors are often seen as troubling, in the right environments (e.g., therapeutic recreational activities like rock-climbing or high-ropes courses), risk-taking can be adaptive. As Casey and Jones conclude: "Because the adolescent brain is a reflection of experiences, with these safe risk-taking opportunities, the teenager can shape long-term behavior by fine-tuning the connections between top-down control regions and bottom-up drives for maturity of this circuitry" (p. 1198).

In summary, in the developmental period of early adolescence, there are pronounced changes in physical maturation that involve endocrinological and neurological systemic transformations within boys and girls that affect their internal states of being. From a purely biological standpoint, drugs of abuse shape these internal states in dramatic ways because they affect the neurobiological processes that are involved in the development of formal operational thinking and emotional development, as well as interactions between the two that are related to self-regulation.

Additionally, research indicates that substance abuse problems are a result of a mixture of genes and environment, with approximately 50% being genetically determined (e.g., family history of alcohol dependence, genetically influenced temperaments, etc.) and 50% being psychosocially determined (e.g., peer relations, cognitive factors, etc.) (Hesselbrock & Hesselbrock, 2006). Importantly, it appears that "environmental factors may play a larger role in *initiation* and *continuation of use past an experimental level*, while genetic factors take precedence among individuals who move from use to dependence" (italics added for emphasis) (Hasin, Hatzenbuehler, & Waxman, 2006, p. 70). This is particularly troublesome for boys who are influenced by a male socialization process (an environmental factor) that is mediated through peer groups affiliations, relationships with family members, and the notions of masculinity that are found in popular culture. Images of virile males drinking alcohol (partying hard) are often associated with sports or enhancing sexual experiences. These two areas of interest loom large in the psyche of developing boys and are an accepted phenomenon in the media (TV shows and commercials, movies, music videos, etc.). Messages about masculinity (implicit or explicit) are often reinforced through peer and family interactions, encouraging adolescent males to drink like a man and be a tank, i.e., be impervious to the risks associated with heavy drinking. Interestingly, having tolerance to alcohol, which is one criteria used to establish a diagnosis of dependence, could be seen as manly, because the male who is drinking more heavily than his cohort (i.e., in increasing amounts to achieve the desired effect) may be viewed as a man who can hold is liquor. Isenhart (2001) states that "traditional masculine role expectations promote alcohol use as a way for a man to better fit in to the masculine role and also as a way to manage stress associated with not fitting into the role" (p. 249).

The two case studies that follow show the challenges that are involved in dealing with the aftermath of substance abusing behaviors while trying to navigate not only the normal physical, mental, and emotional transitions of early adolescence, but also the male gender role transitions that occur when (a) changes in gender role identity are sparked by the maturation of the reproductive system and the appearance of secondary sex characteristics, (b) boys internalize male role norms for masculinity and manhood, (c) tentative career interests and aspirations related to masculine gender role norms begin to manifest, (d) male role norms and standards related to romantic and sexual relationships are expressed, and (e) the initiation of heterosexual or homosexual relations plays a role in the understanding and validation of one's masculinity and value as a man (O'Neil & Egan, 1992). Additionally, as boys' feelings, thoughts, and behaviors are deeply influenced by their memberships in peer groups, their families of origin, and other larger systemic and contextual factors (e.g., popular music, movies, or the media), it is important to remember that it is the confluence of these sociocultural and developmental aspects that help to shape and to manifest the behaviors that we see as either troubling or inspiring.

Having an understanding about these influences will help us to have greater empathy for boys as developing human beings who are trying to navigate the rough waters of their adolescent lives as males. If we are talking about substance abuse, then we often see these behaviors as troubling. On the other hand, when we see a boy recovering from these difficulties by learning to be flexible and adaptable when the storms of life hit, then we are inspired.

JACK (AGE 14): A DEVELOPMENTAL CASE STUDY

Imagine that you are working as a substance abuse professional with adolescents in an organization that has both residential group homes for boys and an in-home family counseling program that is designed to prevent out-of-home placement whenever possible. Jack, who is a 14-year-old Caucasian male (5'3" and 130 lbs.), has been referred to your organization for substance abuse and family counseling by his probation officer after he violated the rules of probation agreement by testing positive for marijuana use during a random urine screen in the first month of his 1-year probationary period. His probation officer is concerned that if Jack continues to test positive for marijuana, he will be in violation of his probation and will be placed in juvenile detention where he will be mixed in even further with the wrong crowd. Jack says that he "just wants to get off probation." He apparently is in the pre-contemplation stage of change in regards to altering his substance abusing behaviors.

The in-home counseling team of which you are a part operates under the general philosophy that it is better in the long-term to work with adolescents and their families within the systemic context of their home and neighborhood to preserve the family unit rather than to remove the adolescent from the home and place them into residential facilities, even though the latter may be necessary for a period of time if home-based family services are initially unable to affect change. The idea is that by working with the parents or the primary guardian to deal effectively with the adolescent's behaviors in their home environment we can affect the larger systemic challenges that are crucial to long-term stability in recovery. How often have we worked diligently to stabilize clients in residential or inpatient treatment settings only to have them return home to an environment that is not conducive to their recovery? In this latter instance, if aftercare services are inadequate, then clients often go back to the behaviors that led to their need for professional help in the first place.

Alternatively, by working with the adolescent in their systemic context, an in-home family counselor can affect long-term change by facilitating a transformation not only in the individual adolescent's behaviors, but also in the behaviors of the parents or primary guardians. In this particular treatment setting, the option also exists for the boy to be removed temporarily from the home, and be placed into a group home that has both an educational and counseling component. During this out of home placement, the in-home family counselor can continue to work with the family while the home environment is stabilized; at which time the boy can be transitioned back into the family home where further individual and family counseling continues in order to maintain treatment gains. In this treatment model, the same substance abuse professional can work with the adolescent and their family throughout the continuum of care.

Jack's case is presented using the domain areas that are outlined as being critical to a comprehensive adolescent assessment, mirroring the domain areas that are found in the Comprehensive Adolescent

Severity Inventory (CASI), e.g., the clinically pertinent life areas of *health, stressful life events, education, drug/alcohol use, use of free time, peer relationships, sexual behavior, family/household members, legal issues,* and *mental health* (Meyers et al., 1999). However, the information that is normally gathered in the initial psychosocial assessment (which in this case was done through preliminary interviews with Jack and his mother, grandmother, probation officer, and school counselor) was assessed further with Jack by using the "Looking Back to Plan Ahead: Setting Personal Goals" exercise found in Appendix B, designed as "An Exercise for Early Adolescent Males (Ages 12 to 18)." Jack was asked to complete the exercise after the second individual session per the instructions on the exercise sheet. However, as can be the case with adolescent (and adult) clients, he did not fully complete the homework assignment. Instead, he did a minimal amount of writing, which became the starting point for further discussion using the questions from the exercise in individual counseling sessions over an approximately three-week period to deepen both the assessment and the rapport-building processes of the initial phase of treatment. Jack was relatively open during this assessment process, perhaps because few people had shown a high level of interest in his life prior to the start of counseling.

Psychosocial Case Presentation of Jack

Jack often dresses in baggy pants and a hooded sweatshirt and wears a cap sporting the logo of the local professional sports team. He openly engages in conversations about sports and is articulate about how the team, coaches, and players are doing this season. He has good hygiene and appears to take pride in his appearance. Jack has never been in a controlled environment, such as a youth detention center, shelter, or inpatient treatment facility for substance abuse and/or mental health issues, and he says that his "only jail time" (spoken with bravado) happened directly at the time of his recent arrest.

Jack lives with his mother in a poverty-stricken neighborhood. They receive food stamps and are renting their home, which has one bedroom (with two single beds), a bathroom, and an open kitchen and living room area. Jack often finds his mother sleeping on the couch when he returns home in the afternoon. His mother is a registered nurse; however, she is currently not practicing in the medical field and instead works evenings in a local bar and restaurant waiting tables. Jack's paternal grandmother lives in the neighborhood several blocks from their home and is a support in terms of occasionally providing food and conversation for Jack at the dinner table. Importantly, there is a strained relationship between Jack's mother and his paternal grandmother.

Health

Jack reports no health concerns and a physical examination reveals no medical conditions. There is no evidence that Jack has had regular physical or dental check-ups, and he is not currently taking medications. Additionally, he appears to squint when he reads paperwork at intake and may require an eye-exam as part of his treatment.

Stressful Life Events

When asked about any stressful life events that come to his mind, Jack begins by talking about "being busted for being at the wrong place at the wrong time." He was referring to his relatively recent arrest and subsequent probationary status. Jack also tells stories about his father who left home when Jack was age 6. His father had moved to another state and left Jack and his mother and older brother without a family income. He reported this as a major loss in his childhood and said that this time period was significantly stressful for Jack and his mother and brother. Prior to his father leaving, Jack has a vague memory of intense arguments between his father and mother, including one significant incident where his father physically shoved his mother, and his brother, who came to his mother's defense. Jack is uncertain about whether alcohol or other drug intoxication was involved during these altercations; however, he stated that his father "drank beer when he worked on cars ... and he worked on cars a lot." In addition to the significance of the early loss of his relationship with his father, Jack has dealt with serious challenges in terms of lack of family finances and unstable relationships with his mother (due to her substance abuse issues and relationships with abusive men) and his brother, who is 5 years older and "getting into some serious shit" (quote from Jack) (e.g., drug abuse and legal issues).

Education

Jack is entering the eighth grade. He was held back a year in elementary school, i.e., moving from first to second grade, which was the year that his father left the family. Due to his physical size, he is not seen by his peers as older for his grade level, and yet he is street smart and uses this savvy to gain acceptance from his peers. His grades have remained average (i.e., at the B and C level) throughout his time in elementary and middle school.

When asked about what he likes in terms of subjects in school, Jack says that he has an interest in music and art; however, he shows no interest in completing homework assignments, has multiple absences from school, and has had in-school suspension for cutting class. Jack says that neither his brother nor his father finished high school, and that he could "always just get a GED at some point." He does not have a plan in terms of getting a college education, learning a trade, or joining the military. In terms of involvement in athletics, Jack says that he is "lightning fast" and would like to run track; however, he states that "the coach doesn't like me." When discussing school and future plans, Jack appears to be resigned to "tracking down" his father and seeing if he can work with him repairing and restoring old cars.

Drug/Alcohol Use

Jack reported that the first substance of abuse that he ever tried was alcohol at age 5 when: "I took a sip of my Dad's beer." He began using primarily alcohol and tobacco with his friends in the neighborhood at age 12. However, at age 13, marijuana use was initiated and quickly increased to a pattern of daily use. He often uses alone "wandering around the neighborhood." During these times of substance use, he has engaged in high risk behaviors, such as stealing cigarettes and other merchandise (which he sells to get money) and being chased by the store owner, climbing on the local water tower "to hang out," and riding his bike dangerously with his friends weaving erratically in and out of traffic. He has had no physical injuries from these incidents with the exception of falling out of a tree and straining his wrist. He often wears an ace bandage around his wrist and tells people that he was injured in a fight. At age 14, he began smoking marijuana before school on a regular basis and has had altercations with school personnel as a result (with the consequence of getting in-school suspension). Jack has also obtained money by stealing from his mother's purse. There is no evidence of tolerance or withdrawal and Jack reports no loss of memory during his use of either marijuana or alcohol. He has never received any form of counseling or treatment for substance abuse issues.

Use of Free Time

What Jack does during free time is a mystery to his mother and his grandmother. He mentions spending time with other boys (usually older) in the neighborhood, but on several occasions his mother has found him wandering alone around the neighborhood and the local park. Jack enjoys riding his bike and hiking through wooded areas in the local park, as well as doing drawings of sports logos, cars, and mythical creatures (e.g., dragons). Jack also does odd jobs for his grandmother and neighbors to make money, such as shovel snow or wash cars; however, he has never been officially employed. His major source of support is his mother, although he does not receive regular allowance from her. On occasion, Jack will stop by the bar and restaurant where his mother works and she will supply him with an evening meal.

When discussing possible options for after school and weekend activities, no one has talked with Jack about getting a work permit, playing on a sports team (such as track), participating in any clubs or other activities at school (such as the art club), exploring his interest in music, or volunteering or doing civic work in the community. Importantly, Jack has received little guidance from his mother about completing his homework assignments. Instead, watching TV, playing video games with friends, and riding his bike are his primary leisure activities, all of which seem to happen while he is under the influence of alcohol and/or marijuana.

Peer Relationships

Most of Jack's friends use alcohol or other drugs. It is unclear how close his friendships are with these peers. He is not satisfied with the quality of his friendships, and he alludes to the fact that he has been "pushed around" quite a bit (i.e., bullied) by them, and that he does not fully trust them "to have my back" if he needed them. This may partially explain why he feels more comfortable alone and in nature. Jack reports that he often carries a knife "for protection" but that he usually does not take it to school with him. When he has taken a knife to school, he stated that he "was wicked paranoid" all day. When asked if there was anyone that he felt that he could really trust, he stated that he didn't think so. His grandmother appears to be the most solid adult attachment figure in his life.

Sexual Behavior

Jack has no "romantic" relationships and indicates that he is heterosexual, scoffing at the possibility of homosexuality. Jack reports that he has witnessed sexual behavior in videos and on the Internet, and that he has stolen pornographic magazines from his brother and friends, which he hides in the park. He says that he had a girlfriend briefly in the past year who had performed oral sex on him while they were both under the influence of alcohol and marijuana, but that they did not have intercourse. He reported no history of sexual abuse.

Family/Household Members

Jack lives with his mother who is divorced and who appears to be addicted to pain killers and alcohol, which may explain why she lost her job as a nurse. It is uncertain whether her nursing license has been suspended or permanently revoked. Jack's relationship with his mother vacillates between affectionate and volatile. Much depends on the time of day and his mother's level of intoxication. For example, Jack's mother often works the dinner shift at a local bar and restaurant and will come home late at night, occasionally with a man that she has met at the bar.

Jack has awakened to noises in the living room of his mother having sex with these men. Once when he confronted her about this behavior, she was intoxicated and called him derogatory names (e.g.., "little shit") and later only partially remembered her interaction with her son. Although Jack reports that she seemed genuine in her apology to him when she spoke to him about the altercation, he has not confronted her about this behavior since. Rather, when his mother brings home a man after work (which is often as late as midnight), he chooses to leave the household and "go out and get high" either alone or with friends.

Apparently, Jack's mother provides little to no structure for him in the home. When she has tried to establish rules for Jack, she finds that she has no credibility, or earned sense of respect, from him because of her erratic and often untrustworthy behaviors. For example, because of her late night schedule, Jack is responsible for getting himself up and ready for school in the mornings. In the afternoons, his will often find his mother asleep on the couch and will wake her up in time to get ready for her evening shift. Because they have only one bedroom, Jack finds that he has little personal space of his own in their home. When affectionate, Jack's mother refers to him as her "little man" and says that she would be lost without him. When angry or depressed, her behaviors turn to criticism of Jack (and his father) and she will insult Jack by saying "you're just like him" (referring to Jack's father). There is no evidence that there has been physical abuse involved in their relationship.

Jack's relationship with his father has been sporadic, in that his father "will just show up out of nowhere" (quote from Jack's mother) and want to take Jack for a ride in his car or go fishing for the day, which Jack reports enjoying immensely. Jack's father does not provide child support on a regular basis. He provides money only when Jack's mother threatens to file charges against him. It is Jack's fantasy to go to live with his father in another state and work with him repairing cars. Jack identified his father as the man that he thought best represented what he would like to be like when he grows up, "without the divorce and not being around his son part."

Jack's older brother Tim (age 19) dropped out of school and left home when he was 17 years old. Tim tried living with his father, but the relationship was strained and a violent incident between Tim and his father resulted in Tim moving out within two weeks. Tim told his father that he was moving back home with his mother, and he told his mother that he was "doing great" and still living with his father. In the meantime, he moved back to the area where Jack and his mother lived and was residing in an apartment with several males in their early 20s who were apparently dealing drugs and frequently engaging in substance abusing behaviors. Because Jack's parents did not communicate with one another, Tim remained in this living situation in close proximity to Jack and his mother without her knowledge. At one point, Jack saw

Tim in public with the older males, and they warned Jack that if he told his mother where Tim was living that he would be seriously hurt. Jack feared that this was true, and he kept this secret from his mother for over a year, at which point Jack's father stopped by unannounced for a visit and the truth came out. Subsequently, Jack received the brunt of his mother's anger and frustration and Jack has not since spoken with his brother, who has continued to live with his friends in the local vicinity of Jack's home.

Jack does not see himself as religious; however, his grandmother attends church (Protestant faith) regularly and often invites him to join her. She has done so particularly since the time that he was arrested and placed on probation. Jack's relationship with his paternal grandmother is warm and cordial; however, she does not approve of his behaviors of "running the neighborhood" unsupervised "at all hours of the night," and she has confronted both Jack and his mother about their behaviors on many occasions. This has left strained relations for days at a time between Jack's mother and his paternal grandmother, and subsequently, Jack will miss out on warm meals with his grandmother, as well as her supportive caring style of attachment to him.

Legal Issues

Jack is on probation because he was caught "breaking and entering" in a local business. He was "the look-out guy" for a group of boys who were breaking into a pawn shop to steal items that they had identified during the day. He was intoxicated at the time of the break-in and felt that he was talked into something that he otherwise would not have done on his own. The probation officer feels that Jack "is one of those kids with basically a good heart who just needs some help before he gets into more serious trouble," and has therefore provided funding for in-home family counseling services to prevent out-of-home placement. Jack will need to pay restitution in the amount of $500 for property damages in the break-in.

Mental Health

Jack reports that he has never been treated for psychological, emotional, or behavioral problems. He meets the criteria for Cannabis Abuse in the DSM-IV-TR (APA, 2000), and there are no apparent co-occurring mental health issues. Jack's mental status examination is unremarkable, and he reports that he has "more good days than bad." A successful intervention at Jack's developmental level can be seen as a form of indicated prevention (Hogan, Gabrielsen, Luna, & Grothaus, 2003), especially in terms of preventing further legal issues, as well as potential mental health issues associated with substance abuse.

A Developmentally-Informed, Gender-Responsive Approach with Jack

Understanding Brain-States and Self-Traits

As was mentioned above, the approach in working with Jack from a home-based family therapy model included a combination of motivational interviewing, cognitive-behavioral strategies, and family systems therapy, which incorporated primarily structural and strategic interventions (Haley, 1976; Minuchin, 1974). Services that are provided through home-based family therapy models are generally intensive with sessions two to three times per week (lasting anywhere from 1 to 2 hours), and include at least one family session per week and two individual counseling sessions with the identified client. The home-based family therapy services for Jack and his family were funded for 3 months initially with the possibility of extending to 6 months, which included 24-hour-a-day emergency visits or phone consultation if needed.

Two forms of assessment, i.e., a family genogram (McGoldrick, 1985) with Jack and his mother, and the completion of the "Looking Back to Plan Ahead" exercise in Appendix B with Jack, set the stage for discussing brain-states and self-traits with Jack and his mother. In addition to giving them factual information about the interaction of socialization processes and brain development (e.g., how our neurophysiology and social experiences interact to create a sense of self, our ideals and values, etc.), coherent self- and family-narratives were being created as they discussed their experiences in relationship with each other and other family members.

One striking example of having a brain-states and self-traits dialogue with clients is a series of interactions that took place between Jack and his mother over several family sessions while completing the family genogram. In conversations about Jack's grandparents on both sides of the family, Jack's mother began to share about her relationship with her parents (i.e., Jack's maternal grandparents whom he had only met once as a very young child around the age of 4). Jack's mother revealed that her father, who was an alcoholic, had beaten her mother repeatedly when she was a young girl. Despite this fact, her mother apparently continued to enable his drinking and abusive behavior. Jack's mother talked about her state of mind during that time in her life, e.g., the states of fear, anxiety, and shame that were created in her during these repeated domestic violence incidents. As she was relaying these states of being from her early socialization processes, she was able to feel emotions swelling in her body. Through this process, she was also able to see how these past memories changed her state of mind in the present moment, and see more clearly how these repeated states of mind had created traits in her that affected her ability to cope with fear and anxiety as an adult.

Up until that point, Jack did not know about these incidents because his mother had grown up with a sense of shame about her parents and a family legacy of not talking about these family issues with anyone. While Jack's mother realized that she was repeating this family pattern of not dealing directly with her thoughts and feelings of being neglected as a child and adolescent, Jack was able to see why his mother had reacted so harshly to his father's drinking behaviors and the shoving incident that precipitated the separation and divorce, which his father had always claimed was "a onetime thing." Jack's mother insisted that his father had shoved her on more than one occasion, and that his abusive behavior included verbal insults and attacks. Through these discussions, both Jack and his mother gained a sense of perspective on their family's over-arching legacy of substance abuse and domestic violence. Over time, these conversations deepened and Jack's mother began to see the importance of addressing her own substance abuse issues as an aspect of her own recovery from an abusive childhood. Importantly, she started to be honest with herself about why her nursing license had been suspended (e.g., she had been accused of stealing medications from work) and she began to make plans to address her substance abuse issues and to apply to get her nursing license re-instated.

For Jack, this dialogue also included a discussion about his fantasies of moving in with his father, i.e., he had repeatedly stated that "if I move in with my Dad, everything will be great." Two processes served to create a reality check on how Jack perceived his father as a man, and what that perception meant to him in terms of his own budding notions about masculinity and his ability to see himself as a man in the future. One process involved the discussions about the past related to how his Dad had behaved in the roles of husband and father. He began to see that his father was unable to give him or his brother the attention or guidance that they needed in order to learn how to become men who were capable of having relationships with others, and specifically how substance abuse had played a key role in his father's inability to "be there" for him. The second process involved a discussion about the future where Jack was able to imagine himself at later developmental ages as a male (see Appendix B for the questions that facilitated this discussion). For example, although Jack clearly had fantasies about fixing up old cars with his father as a way to make money, he had not considered the number of career options that were available in the automobile industry as a whole that might include using his strengths and natural talents that he could build upon in school. His father had often ostracized him for doing drawings, calling him a "girly-girl artist" even when Jack had switched to drawing cars thinking that his father would appreciate his drawings, which in turn would have meant that he appreciated and recognized Jack's talents. Through talking about the states of mind that were created during some of the early interactions that he had with his father involving gender-related insults and neglect, Jack was able to re-conceptualize his creativity and artistry as human traits and as skills that, if cultivated and nurtured, might lead him into an job (e.g., a career in automobile design) as an adult that he would love on many levels. Even though Jack was only 14 years of age with many years ahead of him to make career decisions, this realization shifted his perceptions about himself and his potential that could be enhanced by being more actively engaged in his schoolwork.

Therefore, in this case, the traditional strategies of cognitive-behavioral relapse prevention skills that were focused on preventing relapse so that Jack could stay within the boundaries of his probation were enhanced by discussions about his states of mind in various relational and situational contexts (which included "emotional states of being" as triggers for acting impulsively). Similarly, the family systems approach was augmented by focusing on states of mind that were created in the family interactions and communication patterns across generations within his family. In this way, discussions about how "states of mind become traits of mine" can allow for a straightforward conversation about the effects of substance abuse on the developing brain and relationships. Ultimately, this dialogue can shift to what "recovery" will mean for Jack beyond the initial stabilization phase of treatment, i.e., recovery is about building the capacity for emotional responsiveness instead of reactivity when the old individual and family patterns of behavior seem ingrained and insurmountable.

Educating Males about Emotions

From the assessment processes, it became clear that Jack carried with him a legacy of restrictive emotionality, not only from his mother's avoidance of emotions because of her family history of abuse, but also from his male socialization processes in his relationship with his brother and father, as well as his peers educating him that "feelings were for girls and sissies." For example, Jack recounted a story about how he had injured himself on the playground in elementary school. He said that he would never forget how a group of boys had laughed at him and mocked him for "crying like a girl" when he was hurt.

Jack also had a strong positive reaction to the idea that emotions are information that had helped him to survive difficult situations in his life. When talking about neighborhood encounters with people who were at best not concerned with his ultimate welfare, he was able to see how his brain, i.e., his affective, value-based appraisal system, had functioned as a quick reactive system that had moved him away from danger, e.g., in a fight with a group of boys in the neighborhood or away from a man whom he later found out had abused another boy in his neighborhood. Yet he could see how this same system could be slowed down to process tough decisions that were related to whether he should go in one direction or the other when friends invite him to participate in old behaviors. In a nutshell, he was developing an awareness of his emotional states of being that could serve as a Gut Check about what he needed and valued in circumstances that once left him puzzled and "twisted in knots" emotionally. He stated that he always thought that he was "going crazy" in his mind, but in hindsight he was able to reframe this "craziness" as his emotions trying to tell him something that he had been taught to ignore in his socialization processes as a male.

Importantly, Jack was able to process the night of the arrest that led to his probationary status by looking at it from an affective standpoint. That is, what he needed earlier that night on an emotional level was friendship and a sense of connection to other people. He was lonely and his reactive brain moved quickly into acting impulsively when his peers had invited him to smoke pot and drink alcohol, which later led to their urging him to serve as a look-out for a robbery. In hindsight, Jack sees that if he had paused and reflected on his needs and values that night, he may have been in a better state of mind to make decisions that would have led to a better outcome for himself (and potentially even his friends who are also on probation). As he begins to see the value of emotions, he is starting to conceptualize himself in a different way.

Conceptual and Embodied Self-Awareness: Monitoring Me-States of Mind

Learning how to manage thoughts, feelings, cravings, and urges to use substances are part and parcel of most (if not all) substance abuse treatment approaches that are used with adolescents and adults, and females and males alike (Brady, Back, & Greenfield, 2009; Daley & Marlatt, 2006; Miller, 2009; Monti, Barnett, O'Leary, & Colby, 2001). These processes are a key feature of relapse prevention and managing relapses when and if they occur. From a neurophysiological perspective, they require intentionally focusing on the sensations and feelings in the body (embodied self-awareness) and the thoughts and images that are coming into the mind (conceptual self-awareness) (Fogel, 2009). These forms of self-awareness are what can be referred to here as the "me-states of mind" (or states of being). As was discussed in chapter 2, when we engage the crossroad areas of our brain (the orbitofrontal, insula, and anterior cingulate cortices) to bring up awareness from our bodily states and sensations into our executive attentional areas (dorsomedial, ventramedial, and dorsolateral prefrontal cortices), we are essentially opening up the communication channels of energy and information between the structural areas that are involved in conceptual and embodied self-awareness (Fogel, 2009). Fogel explained that we can, under certain circumstances, move our awareness back and forth between these two distinct forms of self-awareness to have a more holistic perspective and *feeling for* what we are dealing with in our lives.

For Jack, this broadened awareness meant that during a crucial internal storm, he could test his thoughts (e.g., "I don't think I can deal with this"), his self-judgments ("I'm must be a wimp if I can't"), and his apparent impulsive decisions ("I have to do this right now") for accuracy. By switching from his conceptual self-awareness into his embodied self-awareness, he could make a more balanced and informed decision (e.g., "When I feel this out in my gut, and talk it over with you, I feel like I can deal with it better"). In other words, on impulse, what he may think is accurate about his "self" as seen through his conceptually-guided self-awareness may not fit with his embodied-guided self-awareness that is created when he takes the time to breathe down into his body and do a Gut Check of his experiences in the present. In this way, the old thought patterns that come from his socialization processes that do not fit with his felt embodied experience in the present moment can help to create a more grounded, embodied decision-making process in relation to whatever he is dealing with in his recovery.

For Jack, slowing down and taking a deep breath into his body was not something that he was often willing to do, especially when he was around his peers. And he reported that he did not enjoy learning about how to do body scans. Instead, for him, doing vigorous exercise, like intense bike riding or running through the woods, and then stopping to feel what was going on when he was breathless and "needed a break," allowed him to get in touch with the information that his physiology (i.e., which he chose to call his "gut") was providing for him, which in turn helped to guide his responses to whatever emotionally charged (positive or negative) event was happening in his life. It was as if he needed to burn off excess energy (i.e., emotional tension) before he could "take a break" (pause and reflect) and settle into his body and feel what was going on for him.

Finding the right process for each individual to build embodied self-awareness in a way that makes sense to them takes patience and a scientific approach, i.e., "let's try this and see how it works for you," which can be anything from doing body scans to playing basketball. Once the individual's unique processes have been identified, it takes repetitive practice to build the neural nets that will make switching from conceptual and embodied self-awareness swifter and more solidly felt in their bodies.

Educating Males about "Others": Modulating Me-, You-, and We-States of Mind

Dealing with family and interpersonal problems, especially within significant relationships with others (e.g., parents and other family members and friends), can be one of the most emotionally challenging skills that can be learned in treatment. Oftentimes, these skills include learning how to resist social pressures and refuse offers to use substances in various relational and situational contexts (Daley & Marlatt, 2006). The discussions about becoming more aware of me-states of being that are started in relapse prevention education can be extended to include an increased awareness of others' states of being (you-states), as well as an even larger awareness of our relationships, or our we-states of mind (Seigel, 2010), which are crucial in feeling our way through the development of lasting relationships and in building social networks in recovery.

For Jack, this awareness of his we-states of being was essential because he felt that he was alone in the world, especially when his mother was either actually physically absent or mentally absent under the influences of substances. The only exception to this reprieve from loneliness that he could identify early on in treatment was his relationship with his paternal grandmother, who seemed to him to be able to be aware of his state of being in a way that he "felt felt" by her. Likewise, he could see how he was able to tune in to her state of being when she would share her feelings and thoughts with him in an honest, integrity-filled way. For him, his relationship with his paternal grandmother was his prototypical example of a we-state of mind.

As family therapy proceeded, reconnections between Jack's mother and paternal grandmother increased the opportunity for him to have situational and relational contexts in his life that fostered a felt-sense of security. Visiting with his grandmother became one example of a place where he could go when he needed to talk with another person about his feelings, i.e., where he could participate in another person's experiences of living (which is an example of a we-state of mind). Additionally, through making connections with groups in his vicinity, e.g., youth groups at his grandmother's church and counseling groups and clubs at his school, he was able to begin to build a pro-social peer support network, as well as relationships with adults in his community who could support his recovery.

Learning to Check-In (Not Out)

Because early recovery is often a roller-coaster ride of emotions, there will be ample opportunities to teach clients how to develop a personalized working system to deal with the storms of life in recovery as they arise. Chapter 3 discussed both a Check-In system and five-step process model of emotional expression and non-expression from the psychology of boys and men. This Check-In system can be used "as is" (see Appendix A) or as a template for building a personalized model for a client to check-in with themselves and others. The essential elements of the system for a client like Jack would include helping him to (a) learn how to hold in awareness whatever situation, crisis event, or an actual person who may be triggering a strong emotional reaction in him, and paying attention to the sensation, images, feelings, and thoughts (Seigel, 2010) that are coming into his awareness; (b) learn how to check back into his past and see what memories might be triggered by the situation; (c) identify and label what needs and values were not being met in his life at that time; (d) identify and label what needs and values in the present are not being met; and (e) ask himself what he can do right now to *both* get his needs met in the present moment and do the next right thing in recovery within the limits of his social context. If he has the support network in place, he can discuss this process with people that he trusts (i.e., do a Reality Check).

As was mentioned earlier, Jack enjoyed vigorous exercise, and if you will remember from the psychosocial assessment information that was presented, he also enjoyed disappearing into the woods for extended periods of time to be by himself. Prior to starting counseling, this behavior often included smoking marijuana, looking at pornographic magazines, and engaging in high-risk behaviors like climbing the local water tower (and throwing objects at cars passing by). Even though this behavior is troubling, it can be reframed as adaptive, in that he was trying to find a place to cope with the challenges in his life. In recovery, Jack can harness his love of nature to check-in (not out). That is, where he used to unconsciously try to get away from the feelings that he was having about his life by escaping into the woods, in recovery he can intentionally bring himself to a place in nature where he can check-in and see what is going on for him from an emotional standpoint using his version of the Check-In system.

Although these five processes described in this developmentally-informed, gender-responsive approach have been discussed separately, they are inextricably intertwined. For example, as Jack's behavior in recovery of heading into the woods to check-in with himself is seen as an example of a strategy to find balance in his life (Daley & Marlatt, 2006), it represents a larger movement that he has made from a gender-based standpoint in making the shift from dismissing his emotions as irrelevant or a sign of weakness or femininity into emotions are information. In this example, he is exercising the muscles of his mind by beginning the lifelong process of focusing more intentionally through his executive attentional circuits on (a) monitoring his emotional states of being, (b) modulating his emotional states in a flexible and adaptable way, and (c) modifying his behaviors in relation to himself and the significant others in his life. Measuring progress from the standpoint of fostering emotional development will include finding examples where clients like Jack are making the choices to increase their awareness of the processes of orienting to, and paying attention to the subtle shifts in their states of mind that precedes the process of their finding the words to describe their basic emotions and expressing what it is that they need and value in order to deepen the relationships in their life, create a coherent narrative that makes sense of their lives in the aftermath of substance abuse and addiction, and engenders the capacity to enjoy their lives in recovery.

TJ (AGE 17): A DEVELOPMENTAL CASE STUDY

Imagine that you work as a mental health professional in an outpatient behavioral health setting with adolescents who are suffering from substance abuse and co-occurring disorders. The counseling format includes a combination of individual, group, and family counseling and incorporates motivational enhancement and cognitive-behavioral strategies, as well as structural and strategic family counseling models. You have been assigned a client named TJ, a 17-year-old African American male, who has been referred for outpatient counseling as part of an aftercare plan following inpatient treatment for diagnoses of Alcohol Abuse and Major Depression. His mood has been stabilized during the 3-week inpatient stay using a combination of medication and psychotherapy, and he is currently vacillating between the contemplation and preparation stages of change in terms of establishing a long-term plan for maintaining the treatment gains that he made in inpatient treatment.

As in the previous case with Jack, the initial psychosocial case information for TJ is presented using the domain areas outlined in the Comprehensive Adolescent Severity Inventory (CASI; Meyers et al., 1999). The information gathered in the initial psychosocial assessment was obtained from preliminary interviews with both TJ and his parents, and supplemented by a more in-depth interview with TJ using the questions from the "Looking Back to Plan Ahead" exercise found in Appendix B.

Psychosocial Case Presentation of TJ

Health

TJ is 6'1" and 190 lbs. and appears to be in excellent physical shape. Documentation from his inpatient stay revealed that TJ had a comprehensive health examination that confirmed that he is in good physical health. In fact, TJ is a three sport athlete (soccer, basketball, and track) and has the potential to receive an athletic scholarship in the coming year.

Stressful Life Events

TJ reports that the most stressful life event that he has ever experienced was the sequence of incidents that preceded his recent episode into treatment. A month prior to his admission into outpatient counseling, TJ had what he thought would be a routine wisdom teeth extraction. A day after the procedure, he attended a party where alcohol was being served. He was warned by his dentist not to drink alcohol in combination with the post-operative pain medication. However, TJ, feeling that his dentist was exaggerating the dangers involved in mixing pain medication with alcohol, drank in excess of 16 beers over a 3-hour period. The next day, TJ found that he was vacillating between extreme agitation and depression to the point that he felt suicidal. He then drank heavily the next night with his friends and was found by his mother the following morning in a catatonic state sitting in their living room. He was taken to the hospital where he was given a psychiatric evaluation and admitted into an inpatient psychiatric ward. After a week of observation and evaluation, he began to disclose in treatment the amount of alcohol that he had been drinking in combination with the pain medication. He was then moved to a dual-diagnosis treatment facility for 2 weeks and was discharged into outpatient treatment in order for him to be able return to school as soon as possible to "catch up with his studies and rejoin his team" (quote from his parents).

Education

TJ is in the fall semester of his senior year. He is considered to be a top student in his high school, and his grades are mostly As with an occasional B, which his parents (particularly his father) frown upon. Although TJ's father is pushing him towards subjects related to pre-med, he is an exceptional student in history. TJ's interest in history was kindled by the fact that his family moved every three to four years (mostly around Europe) as his father's military career dictated. Most of the moves when TJ was a young boy occurred in military-affiliated international schools until 2 years ago when he returned to the United States and began attending a public high school.

Drug/Alcohol Use

TJ first tried alcohol at age 10 in Italy at a party of mostly military families hosted by his father. Several factors helped to formulate TJ's relationship to the use of alcohol, not the least of which was his father's status as an officer in the military. TJ often witnessed his father's daily use of alcohol after work with his fellow officers. Additionally, in Europe, TJ reported that the children of American military families took advantage of the lower drinking age and would often drink to intoxication when their parents were having a party, or when they would go to the beach on the weekends. TJ's alcohol use intensified from ages 13 to 15 into a binge drinking pattern on the weekends. When he returned to the United States with his family at age 16, he continued this pattern of heavy drinking on the weekends; however, he found that his peers were also using prescription drugs and marijuana and he began experimenting with combinations of these drugs with alcohol.

Importantly, TJ had received the message his entire life that alcohol use was accepted as a rite of passage and part of becoming a man, while drug use was seen as being illegal and for "liberal degenerates" (quote from his father). This was acceptable for TJ because he preferred alcohol over marijuana and only occasionally used prescription drugs when his friends showed up at parties with their parents "leftover meds." Because TJ was in the process of applying to a military academy, he knew that he would need to get a physical at some point and was ever cognoscente of being drug tested. Subsequently, he was more likely to excuse himself when marijuana was being passed around at a party.

TJ had only minor consequences from his binge drinking episodes, e.g., falling and cutting his face and arm in a blackout, which required stitches. This incident had the opposite effect from being a negative consequence, in that, he received a tacit message from his friends, and even his father, that these were akin to "battle scars" as they were highly visible and discussed openly. Prior to his admission of binge drinking patterns in treatment, TJ had never considered counseling to try to stop or cut back on his drinking.

Use of Free Time

Over the last few years, TJ has developed an extreme dichotomy in terms of his public and private self. During the week, TJ is a highly focused student-athlete who is seen by his parents, teachers, and coaches as "a high potential, confident young man" (quote from his father). On the weekends when he has "free time," he is seen by his peers as a guy who "parties hard." His family attends church (Protestant) occasionally; however, TJ does not consider himself to be religious, and he has not developed a sense of connection to a church community because of the fact that his family moved around frequently.

Peer Relationships

Socially, as TJ moved to new schools and joined new sports teams, he felt that he needed to be extroverted in order to fit in with his peers. In actuality, he reports being more introverted and that the alcohol helped him to feel more comfortable with the social demands on the weekends with his peers. Even though TJ is an extremely popular student-athlete, he reported that he never has really felt that he fit in anywhere and that he "never had a best friend" growing up. With Caucasian student-athletes, he was respected and admired, but always felt different and was once challenged when he was interested in dating a popular Caucasian cheerleader. With African American students, he reported feeling that they saw him as "more White" because he had been raised mostly in the European and military culture. Even though he loved participating in sports, he felt that his social life would have been very difficult had he not been one of the star athletes at his school.

Sexual Behavior

TJ became sexually active at age 15 and had engaged in intercourse with a 16-year-old Italian girlfriend when his family was living in Europe. This was his "first love" experience that resulted in "breaking his heart" (quote from parents) when he moved to the United States. TJ reports having a feeling of guilt when he "fooled around" with girls after he moved to the United States, as he was continuing to keep in touch with his girlfriend in Europe through electronic means (e.g., emails and Skype).

Family/Household Members

Prior to entering treatment, TJ lived at home with his parents and his younger brother. His relationships with his family are complex. As the first born, his father has expectations that TJ will achieve "great things." His father was the first person in his family to attain a college education and he did so through ROTC scholarships. He heavily emphasizes the traditional male role expectations of success, power, and competition, and he has always wanted TJ to attend one of the military academies (specifically West Point). With TJ's good grades and athletic achievement, particularly in soccer, he has a good chance to achieve this goal. However, with the recent hospitalizations and missed time in school, he may have reduced his profile as a viable candidate for West Point, as his congressional district only allows for two appointed candidates each year. This has been extremely troubling for TJ's father and he is angry that TJ "may have already blown his chances at success." TJ does not appear to be as troubled as his father about his future.

TJ's mother is a quiet and unassuming woman who has dutifully followed her husband from place to place in the military. His father and mother met in college and, although she received a degree in elementary education, she has never been employed full-time as a teacher. Instead, she has worked outside the home as a substitute teacher and teacher's aide because of the frequent moves and her commitment to working at home as a homemaker. She was instrumental in TJ's academic success-ful and has kindled his interest in history, taking TJ and his younger brother on day trips to various historical and cultural sites while in Europe.

TJ has a younger brother, Rob, who is 12 years old. At present, Rob aspires to follow in TJ's footsteps both academically and athletically. TJ's parents reported that Rob is very puzzled by the events that have followed TJ's hospitalization.

Legal Issues

There were no prior legal concerns, nor has there been any current legal issues related to TJ's drinking incidents.

Mental Health

At the time of TJ's admission into outpatient aftercare services, he had received a diagnosis of Alcohol Abuse and Major Depression. His mood was stabilized as he is on antidepressant medication and was no longer having suicidal thoughts. Both he and his father strongly object to his continuing on these medications for several reasons. First, they believe that there is a social stigma associated with mental illness and taking medications for the same. Second, they feel that there are potential side effects of the medication that could have a detrimental effect on TJ's athletic performance, which is extremely troubling for both of them. TJ's mother has quietly expressed her concerns that she feels that TJ should stay on the medication until he is "out of the woods." She was shocked by the suicidal thoughts that accompanied TJ's first weeks in treatment and was worried that they might occur again. She had an uncle with whom she was close who took his life when she was an adolescent and she had been bewildered by this as a teenager. To think that her son had thoughts of killing himself was beyond her imagination and she felt that this was far more pressing of a concern than his athletic performance or his college admissions process.

A Developmentally-Informed, Gender-Responsive Approach with TJ

Understanding Brain-States and Self-Traits

Educating TJ about brain development and substance abuse occurred in a psycho-educational group counseling setting and was later processed further in individual counseling. TJ reported that the Brain in the Palm of Your Hand model "made sense" and was the first time that he understood from a biological standpoint why alcohol "helped" him to feel more comfortable in social settings and why he had such a difficult time falling asleep during the first few nights of each week after having drunk heavily on the weekends. Specifically, he could see how the neurotransmitters that were affected by alcohol, specifically gamma aminobutyric acid (GABA), as an inhibitory neurotransmitter, soothed the limbic region and helped him with anxiety before going to parties and getting to sleep on the weekends. Making connections between the abstract neuroscience and concrete life examples helped to reduce the stigma associated with the resultant mental health conditions in which he was currently struggling. TJ reported that the depressive episodes usually coincided with the binge drinking episodes and that he had always thought that he had inherited a mental illness from his mother's side of the family. He struggled with this for two reasons.

First, it bothered him that he might have something happening to him mentally that was beyond his control, i.e., "if it's genetic, then there's not a lot you can do about it ... you just take your meds and deal with it." This did not fit with his sense of self as a young male athlete who had been taught that if there is some physical limitation that you think may be a deficit to your overall performance, and it is beyond your control to change (e.g., like your physical height, which is genetic), then you just need to focus your energies to train harder in other areas to be faster or quicker, etc. Seeing medication as the only answer was not what TJ or his father wanted to hear. Because he saw depression as a "brain-state," and alcohol as being integral to the formation of this particular brain-state, he could see how exercising the "muscles of the mind" could have the potential to change his "self-trait" of "someone with depression" to someone who was able to train themselves to adapt to and cope with a genetic vulnerability to depressive states of mind.

Educating Males about Emotions

The second reason that he struggled with the idea that he had inherited a mental illness was the fact that it was a mood disorder. TJ (and his father) had always thought of his mother and her side of the family as being "emotional," and as a male, TJ did not want to see himself in this light. This was particularly troubling for him when he was compared to his mother's uncle who had struggled with depression. As TJ learned about mental health issues from a neuroscience perspective, he began to understand the interconnectedness of brain development, emotions, and socialization processes. He also learned from his mother that her brother who had taken his own life also struggled with alcohol abuse. This gave TJ further incentive to address his own alcohol abuse because he could see its connection to his depression, i.e., that drinking alcohol exacerbated his problems with depressive symptoms.

Additionally, the idea that "emotions are information for surviving and thriving" fit within his schema associated with athletic performance. TJ could see this concept more clearly as he discussed the relationship between emotions and sports. Specifically, on the athletic field, as in life, you have to modulate your emotions in order to thrive. Too much emotion and you are playing without control of your skills and abilities. Too little emotion and you lose your competitive edge. Framing emotions as being a part of a larger affective, value-based appraisal system helped him to see the value of tuning in to what one was feeling as a way to increase one's athletic performance. In short, if he could harness the emotional energy and information that was fueling his passion and motivation on the athletic field, then he would be able to use his emotional nature to be a better athlete. This helped him to reframe the idea and importance of "being emotional" as a young male athlete.

Conceptual and Embodied Self-Awareness: Monitoring Me-States of Mind

Understanding how one's state of being could change in relation to one's situational and relational context was a relatively easy concept for TJ to grasp, specifically because of his understanding and *feeling for* athletic and social performance anxiety. He had experiences to draw from in his life where he could describe the difference between conceptual and embodied self-awareness. For example, on the basketball court or soccer field, he had practiced feeling his way through difficult performance tasks where he could tell the difference between when he was seeing himself take a shot (conceptually) and feeling himself taking the shot (from an embodied state of mind). The latter had a more fluid quality to his state of being and had what he called "rhythm and flow." He did not experience a similar state of being socially with other adolescents and he had found that drinking created this type of "flow" at parties.

Educating Males about "Others": Modulating Me-, You-, and We-States of Mind

Prior to counseling, TJ had not considered that he could "practice" how to be more present and embodied in social situations with others. This started with building awareness of his states of being (or his me-states of mind) in social contexts in treatment and talking out loud to others about how he was managing his thoughts of using prior to social situations and managing his emotions in general at school or at home. This process helped him to define his recovery as building the capacity "to find rhythm and flow" in all areas of his life, not only to manage cravings and urges to use substances, but simply to enjoy his life more fully. Dealing with family issues and interpersonal problems became an exercise in paying attention to his "me-state of mind" and feel his way through relating to others.

This was particularly challenging in relation to two social situations. The first was in relationship to his father. He began to see that his father had a picture in his mind about what his son was to become. TJ could see this as a "concept of TJ" rather than the actual "embodied TJ." Specifically, he began to notice and to feel the pull of his father's expectations of him on his motivation and "passion for the game." He began to discern, particularly in relation to his athletic performance, what were his own feelings about playing sports and what were his feelings about trying to live up to his father's expectations about how he should play sports. In order for TJ to have a more honest, intimate relationship with his father, he had to modulate his sense of self (me-state of being) with how he perceived his father's expectations of him (you-state of being) and then begin to share more openly with his father about what he wanted to achieve even if it did not match with his father's expectations (we-states of being).

The second challenging social situation was dealing with his peers' (particularly his peer athletes') expectations about "partying hard" on the weekends. This is a common challenge for early adolescents whose identity is intimately wrapped up in their social peer groups. Not only do they have to learn how to resist social pressure to use, but they also have to find new social outlets that "fit" with their identity as an adolescent in the context of their school, neighborhood, and larger cultural communities.

TJ's identity was embedded in the athletic culture of his school. It was a challenge for him to feel his way through a process of developing more varied interests and friendships. One way that he was able to do this was to harness his interest in and passion for history that he had developed as a boy growing up in a military culture and in Europe. Although he was hesitant at first, he joined the History Club at school. He framed this choice to his father and any questioning peers as "building extra-curricular activities for his college admissions process." However, he knew in his heart (and expressed in outpatient treatment) that he was enjoying both the content of the discussions and the process of stepping outside of his restrictive role of "jock" to have relationships with other students who did not have the heavy emphasis on "partying hard." This helped him to build a social support network that included alcohol-free activities, e.g., weekend field trips to museums with his newfound friends. He found one particular male friend who not only loved history, but was also a sports fanatic. TJ connected with him to go to college and semi-pro sports events as well.

Learning to Check-In (Not Out)

TJ, who preferred "not to focus on the past," adapted the Check-In System in Appendix A by reducing it to a more simple process of (a) Checking-In, holding whatever emotional issue was important to him to process through in the moment, (b) Doing a Gut Check now to see what he needed and valued in the current situation, and (c) Doing a Reality Check with his counselor and peers in group, and occasionally with his new friend, as well as his father and mother. Interestingly, TJ found that he was able to teach his younger brother how to do this same process as they were "shooting hoops in the drive-way." His younger brother was dealing with a comment that their Dad had made to him about his grades, and TJ was able to share how he had done a check-in related to a similar situation, and subsequently, had been able to talk with his father about the issue that might have sent him into a depressive state of mind in the past.

Measuring progress in treatment and recovery for TJ involved his recognizing that he was building the ability to deal with a number of situations that at one point would have been a trigger for both substance abuse and depressive symptoms. Additionally, although the stigma of mental illness loomed large within his family and in the larger society,

TJ was able to build a coherent narrative that made sense of "his ordeal in the mental ward." Through talking about his life in counseling, he was beginning to frame his experiences as something that he was overcoming (and would need to continue to overcome) from a strength-based perspective, rather than from a pathological, deficit-based perspective. This strength-based perspective of overcoming hardship was congruent with the cultural narrative of his family history, and therefore engendered pride in him and from his father and mother.

5

Substance Abuse Counseling with Later Adolescent Males (Ages 18 to 24)

The age group defined as "later adolescence," which includes individuals who range in age from 18 to 24 years (Newman & Newman, 2012), is considered by most laypeople (and especially by those who find themselves in this particular age group) as *young adulthood* (and not "adolescence"), even though the neurobiological, developmental processes that started in the early adolescent brain (discussed in chapter 4) continue throughout this later adolescent developmental level. If you will remember, as individuals move from adolescence into mature adulthood, the "bottom-up" neurobiological systems related to sensation-seeking and risk-taking gradually lose their "competitive edge with the progressive emergence of 'top-down' regulation" (i.e., executive functioning in the prefrontal cortices of the brain) (Casey & Jones, 2010, p. 1197). This process continues until approximately age 25 (Crews, He, & Hodge, 2007). Therefore, in many ways, even though there are multiple socio-cultural factors involved in defining normative "adolescent" or "adult" behaviors, the underlying biological processes of building mature bridges of neural circuitry between higher and lower cortical structures in the brain runs parallel to the building of the bridge that spans over the developmental ravine between adolescence on one side and mature adulthood on the other.

The early adolescent developmental challenges of physical maturation, cognitive, and emotional development, and membership in peer groups, expands into the later adolescent challenges of (a) further autonomy from one's parents or guardians; (b) further exploration of romantic, sexual, and intimate relationships that may lead to long-term commitment, such as marriage and/or having children; and (c) further exploration of work, career, and lifestyle considerations; all of which are interwoven with one's developing sense of morality and identity as a "man" or "woman" (i.e., one's gender identity) (Newman & Newman, 2012). Although the economic and societal circumstances that change from generation to generation have an effect on when it will occur, later adolescence is often associated with pressures to achieve an actual physical separation from one's parents that can be related to going off to college, joining the military, obtaining gainful employment, etc., all of which are associated with increasing the chances for financial independence.

O'Neil and Egan (1992) describe several male-specific transition points of later adolescence that are related to leaving home, getting steady work, and developing intimate long-term relationships. First, there may be a sense of autonomy and independence that a male feels when he leaves his parent's home that fits with his traditional gender role expectations of self-reliance and success. However, if he has feelings of fear, sadness, or grief about this process, he may also be reluctant to express these feelings to his family or peers because of rigid gender role expectations. Second, as he moves into further exploring romantic, sexual, and intimate relationships, he may be faced with gender role conflict (e.g., devaluing different aspects of himself as a man) related to how and when he chooses to be vulnerable and to self-disclose about his personal feelings in intimate relationships. Third, as he begins to try to establish a career and work life, his first jobs may be experienced through the gender-based lens of a male having to achieve success and power, and be competitive in the workplace in order to be considered a real man. If his sense of self is deeply rooted in this expectation that is associated with traditional male roles, then he may sacrifice his mental and physical health, and/or his relationships as well, in order to try to live up to this standard as a man. Fourth, if he finds that he is moving into a monogamous relationship, then gender role norms and standards may begin to affect his personal (i.e., related to familial and ethno-cultural values) and legal (i.e., related to marriage) expectations about the continuation of this relationship. And fifth, if he moves into the adult roles of husband and father, then he will no doubt be faced with his own and other's expectations about what an acceptable protector and nurturer of one's family and children looks like (i.e., if those descriptors are even a part of his male socialization processes). It is important to remember that these adult male role expectations are interwoven within the context of his culture, ethnicity, race, religion, nationality, and sexual orientation. Therefore, there will be as many examples and descriptors of what it means to be a good dad or a loving husband as there are families in the world.

As we consider the importance of these developmental transitions for later adolescent males, it is even more troubling to remember that this age group has the highest rates of substance abuse among any other demographic group in the United States (Park, Mulye, Adams, Brindis, & Irwin, 2006). This trend appears to continue well into adulthood for males across the lifespan (Office of Applied Studies, 2004). And for this reason, we have the opportunity as substance abuse professionals to see our work as being a form of indicated prevention (Hogan, Gabrielson, Luna, & Grothaus, 2003). Specifically, we can intervene at a crisis point where changes in the course of our clients' lives can have an incredibly important preventative effect on the positive roles that our male client's will play in the lives of their children, families, friends, and co-workers.

Because addiction can progress to unpredictable depths, an intervention at the developmental age of later adolescence can have a huge impact on the negative trajectory of the behavioral, cognitive, social, and emotional problems that can arise from substance use disorders in boys and men. Said with a positive spin, if we can have an impact on these males' lives in terms of reducing the harm that comes from gender role strain and/or substance abuse during this period in their lives, then we can help them to make better choices (i.e., more self- and other-reflective choices) related to some of the most crucial decisions of their lives, e.g., where they will work or if they will attend college, and with whom they will partner (and possibly become husbands and fathers). Imagine the positive outcome of helping our male clients in this developmental period of 18 to 24 years of age to realize the importance of being emotionally mature adult men who are present and available for relationships with the women, children, and other men in their lives.

The following case studies offer insights into how to conceptualize work with this age group that harnesses the processes of intentional behavior change (DiClemente, 2003) as a foundation for this gender-responsive substance abuse counseling approach with boys and men. Whenever possible, the underlying neurobiological developmental processes will be discussed that may have been stunted by substance abuse and addiction, and yet may be enhanced by the social and emotional processes of recovery. Likewise, related concepts that come from the field of interpersonal neurobiology will be interwoven with the importance of understanding the developmental transitions points mentioned above, particularly the emotional development of these males who are struggling to find a sense of stability and emotional maturity in the aftermath of their substance abusing and addictive behaviors.

BEN (AGE 19): A DEVELOPMENTAL CASE STUDY

Imagine that you are a college counselor who has been instrumental in helping a 19-year-old Asian American college student named Ben to enter an outpatient substance abuse treatment program. He agreed to participate in treatment because his parents were pressuring him to get help or he would lose their financial support. Additionally, the campus administration was threatening to remove him from college housing due to an incident involving severe alcohol intoxication and possession of marijuana in his dorm room. Even though they have no evidence to substantiate their suspicions, the campus residential life staff believes that either he or his roommate is selling drugs on campus.

Ben has completed 4 weeks of an outpatient treatment program and is being referred back to you for individual counseling as part of his aftercare plan. To remain in college housing, he has been mandated to meet with you for the remainder of the spring semester (an 8-week time period). The psychosocial assessment information that follows is organized according to the domain areas of the Comprehensive Adolescent Severity Index (CASI) (e.g., *health, stressful life events, education, drug/alcohol use, use of free time, peer relationships, sexual behavior, family/household members, legal issues,* and *mental health*) (Meyers et al., 1999) and was gathered in meetings with Ben both prior to, and immediately following, his outpatient treatment program. All direct quotes are from Ben during the assessment process.

Psychosocial Case Presentation of Ben

Health Information

Prior to entering the outpatient treatment program, Ben was transported to the emergency room because of severe alcohol intoxication. Upon returning to campus, he was given a full physical examination by the college health center. Ben has no medical concerns requiring treatment at this time. He appears to be a healthy 19-year-old male who is 5'6" and 145 lbs.

Stressful Life Events

At intake, Ben stated that he had no major stressful life events or trauma in his background, "except for whatever trauma you get from moving every few years." During his childhood and adolescence, Ben reports that he was "always stressed out" because he never knew when his father was going to come home from work and say "OK, we are moving again." Ben's father worked as an executive in a corporation that required that he move to new locations every few years, primarily between locations in the United States and Europe. Because his family moved often, Ben reports that he had a difficult time fitting in at each new school that he entered: "I was always smaller physically than the other guys in the elementary schools. So I was always picked on for being the new kid and being the new guy."

Education

Ben was a precocious elementary school student and excelled academically throughout his middle and high school years. Two of his high school years were spent in Europe, and he said that he was able to take advantage of the "awesome school trips" that were an integral part of the educational experiences at the international schools that he attended.

In the summer prior to his senior year in high school, Ben's father decided to retire from his job and moved his family back to the United States from Germany. Ben had difficulty transitioning to the new high school situation in the United States. He reports that he felt more discriminated against in the United States because he was Asian American and that there were expectations about how he should behave "as the quiet Asian kid," which did not fit with his view of himself. Ben joined the cross-country track team and immediately made friends with one of the runners who happened to be a drug dealer who sold marijuana. Ben started buying drugs from him in small quantities, "probably an eighth of an ounce, or even less for the most part."

In the winter of his senior year in high school, Ben's father moved without his family back to Europe, because he had decided to come out of retirement. This had a destabilizing effect on the family: "I think that kind of threw our family off balance." At one point during this time that his father was away, Ben's mother found a bag of marijuana when she was cleaning his room. Ben stated that "she really freaked out a lot, and we had big conversations about it. And the next time my dad was home ... my dad and I had a big talk about it. And they basically told me this was wrong, and 'You can't do this,' and 'It's bad for you.'" Ben stated that at that time he felt like he could easily navigate these types of difficulties and that he had simply "screwed up by leaving that under a chair in my room ... I felt like I could definitely do a better job of hiding my drugs (laughs)."

During the spring of his senior year in high school, Ben applied for an army ROTC scholarship to go to college in the fall. His intention was to gain an officer training scholarship to pay for his pre-med undergraduate education and then use his college fund that his parents had created for him (and potentially further GI Bill funding) to attend medical school. He knew that through this process he would be given a battery of tests, including a drug screen. For the 3 months prior to the drug screen, Ben continued to drink alcohol, because he believed that it would not show up on a drug screen. He managed to stop smoking marijuana through the first 3 months of the spring of his senior year. After the drug screen, Ben "just picked up right where I left off." For Ben, this was a point of escalation because he was now smoking marijuana by himself on a daily basis.

At the end of his senior year in high school, Ben's parents once again found some more marijuana in his room. His father happened to be home during one of his breaks from work in Europe at the time. Ben says that he worked hard at lying and disowning the marijuana by not admitting to anything "and not being truthful." At the time, Ben felt threatened by his parents, but says that he managed "to escape without any consequences."

Ben received the ROTC scholarship that he had applied for as well as other academic scholarships to attend a private university near his parent's home. Prior to moving in at college, Ben met his roommate at spring orientation and found out that his new roommate smoked marijuana as well, and on "day one ... it was like all day, every day, and I just really failed to ever get in the swing of really going to school." The university was in a large city with a significant international student population, and Ben began to enjoy the environment with his new friends from around the United States and abroad. Alcohol and drug use was a large part of Ben's new social experiences at college.

During Thanksgiving break, Ben's parents once again found a bag of marijuana in his pockets. This time they were "extremely concerned," because, in addition to finding the marijuana, they had received a "concerned call and letter from my ROTC people saying that 'Ben never comes to ROTC ... he's pretty much dropped out of the program, and we have to withdraw him from the scholarship'." Ben's parent's immediately sent him for a substance abuse assessment and counseling on an outpatient basis in the city where his college was located.

Ben said that he was not cooperative during his first few weeks in substance abuse counseling and that he continued to use despite negative consequences. However, this changed when the head of residential dorm system threatened to remove him from college housing due to an incident involving severe alcohol intoxication and possession of marijuana in his dorm room. Because he had lost his ROTC scholarship, he could not fathom the idea of facing his parents with the additional burden of finding off-campus housing. Therefore, he decided, in consultation with his substance abuse counselor, to "step-up his treatment process" and attend an intensive outpatient program to show his parents that he "was serious" about making a change in his life. After Ben completed 4 weeks of an intensive outpatient treatment, he was referred to the college counseling center for individual counseling as part of his aftercare plan. In order to remain in college housing, he was mandated to receive weekly counseling session for the remainder of the school year.

Drug/Alcohol Use

In addition to the information provided above, Ben reports that he had his first drank of alcohol when he was 17 and his family was living in Europe. He does not remember this as an important event in his life. More significantly, his initiation into drug use occurred when he was on a student field trip to Holland, where he smoked marijuana for the first time. Ben stated that "my grades were suffering a little bit that semester, but only because I was really traveling a lot ... I really took advantage of living in Europe in high school." Ben reports that he had liked drinking alcohol earlier in the school year, but that with marijuana he "felt that now I had discovered some secret recipe for life that I had been lacking." Simply put, Ben feels that marijuana is his drug of choice and he believes that alcohol is "less of a problem" for him.

Use of Free Time

This is an area where Ben readily admits that he is having challenges. Currently, Ben says that he does not have any hobbies or interests that hold his attention for any amount of time. He has started to take up jogging again and he enjoys going to the movies and playing videogames in the student center. He is trying to avoid hanging out in his dorm room because his roommate "continues to smoke pot ... although he definitely gets it that I can't smoke right now, and so he doesn't invite me to join him anymore." Ben said that he is also trying to concentrate on his studies so that he can improve his grade point average and possibly appeal to the ROTC program to be re-instated in the fall under probationary status.

Peer Relationships

In remembering his early adolescence, Ben said that the feeling of not fitting in anywhere continued to grow as his family moved around, and he remembers feeling "so relieved" whenever he could make friendships in the schools where his family relocated. Ben says that this was easier in college because all of his college friends "are partiers." However, currently he would not consider any of them to be close friendships. He does feel that he would like to develop relationships that are not centered on alcohol and drug use. Ben said that his father told him that it was important to make friends in college, stating specifically that "I know that college friendships last a lifetime ... at least that's what my Dad says ... and I only have tokers for friends right now."

Sexual Behavior

Ben reports that he is heterosexual and that he went out on a few dates in high school. He says that he has not had "any serious relationships in college either"; however, he has had sexual intercourse with a girl that he met at a party. He says that "it was actually not a great experience, because she ended up puking right in the middle of the whole thing ... she was pretty drunk, I think."

Family/Household Member

Despite moving often, Ben reports that he feels like his family was "very supportive." He describes his father as a first generation Japanese American and his mother as being Caucasian from mixed European descent. Ben says that he was an only child until he was 7 years old, at which time his twin sisters were born. He remembers feeling like his parents, especially his mother, were too "overwhelmed and exhausted to do a lot with me after my sisters were born." Ben reports that he has a good relationship with his younger sisters and that they are "starting to realize that I am getting into some trouble," which bothers Ben.

In terms of alcohol and other drug use in his family, Ben said that his father "drinks a little," but not to intoxication, and that his mother does not drink alcohol "at all" (spoken emphatically). He believes that is mother does not drink because there is "quite a bit of alcoholism in my mother's side of the family." There are five children in his mother's family, "and there are several uncles that have been to jail, pretty much for alcoholism, and have health problems and stuff like that ... health problems from drinking too much."

Legal Issues

The incident that prompted Ben's needing to increase the level of care of his outpatient substance abuse treatment services involved his being severely intoxicated (from alcohol and marijuana use) in the hallways of his dorm. When he was confronted by residence life staff, he hurried back to his dorm room where he tried to act as if nothing had happened and that he was not intoxicated. When the residence life staff member confronted him again in his dorm room, a small amount of marijuana (one joint) was found on his nightstand. Subsequently, he was written up by residence life staff for being severely intoxicated and the marijuana was confiscated by campus police. Because this was Ben's first offense on this private school campus, there were no charges filed, but he was adjudicated through the residence life judicial processes.

Mental Health

Ben was given a mental health status exam and screened for mental disorders at the beginning of his outpatient treatment. Documentation from this process indicated that he has no co-occurring diagnoses other than alcohol and cannabis abuse.

A Developmentally-Informed, Gender-Responsive Approach with Ben

Understanding Brain-States and Self-Traits

As a pre-med student, Ben was interested in having discussions about the effects of drugs of abuse on the brain. He was particularly intrigued by the connections between the brain, body, and mind in relation to addiction. Although he was interested in understanding the Twelve-Step approach that was a mainstay of his treatment in the outpatient counseling setting, he was not able to reconcile the "spiritual aspects" of his recovery.

Therefore, providing the scientific underpinning for understanding how the body and mind are connected and develop through our relationships with others shifted his perspective on the challenges that he faced in having a substance use disorder (a diagnosis that he struggled to accept). The brain science provided a sense of the architecture for how substances and addictive processes develop neural pathways in the brain (chapter 2) and how you can "recover" through changing your mind and your relationships (chapter 3).

Following his interest in understanding the neurobiological processes in the brain, Ben began writing research papers for classes related to neuroscience and became a self-proclaimed "expert" on the right- and left-brain modes of functioning. He wanted to have discussions in counseling about the states of mind that were created when various activities caused shifts in the right- and left-brain processing of reality. For example, part of his studies included reading *My Stroke of Insight: A Brain Scientist's Personal Journey* (Taylor, 2006). In her book, Dr. Jill Bolte Taylor, a neuroanatomist, describes how she had a stroke that disabled most of the left-hemisphere of her brain for a significant period of time and the experience of being right-brain dominant for months until she was able to slowly recover her abilities in language, logic, and linear thinking, which are all aspects of the left-brain mode of functioning. For Ben, he saw the states of right-brain functioning that were described by Dr. Taylor, i.e., the holistic, abstract, artistic aspects of life, as being an essential part of how he wanted to exist as a human being in the world. Interestingly, he described marijuana use for him as creating a similar state of being as a right-brain mode of functioning. Therefore, he wanted to learn more about right-brain processes (like meditation, drawing, listening deeply to music, etc.) so that he could create a state of being in recovery that brought him peace, enjoyment, and serenity, all aspects of spirituality in which he was slowly beginning to grasp. This was his adaptation of the relapse prevention strategies that he had learned in his outpatient treatment setting.

Educating Males about Emotions

Even though Ben was highly engaged intellectually in his recovery efforts, one of the challenging aspects in working with him related to his motivation to be aware of and express his emotional states of being with others. For example, if you asked Ben a question about the structures in the brain related to emotions, he could name them (e.g., amygdalae, nucleus accumbens, etc.). However, if you asked him to talk about his emotional life in relationship to others (e.g., how he feels when he asks a female out on a date and she says that she is not interested), then he struggled to find the words to express the emotional impact of the existence or non-existence of his relational life.

Evidence of this communication pattern existed in the way that he responded to questions about his relationships. He would begin to respond by saying, "I think ..." to every question related to connecting with others. And although thinking is obviously an important process for functioning as a college student, expressing feelings are also vital to deepening relationships. Ben's tendency to begin discussions with his thoughts was balanced in counseling by actively listening and reflecting back the thoughts that he was conveying, and then asking him again how he felt about his interactions with others. Repeating this process set a pattern in place of attending to feeling without neglecting or negating the intellectual and conceptual side of his awareness that with Ben appeared to be his dominant way of communicating aspects of himself.

Additionally, as was mentioned in chapter 3, defining our terms more explicitly can help to shift awareness about the overall impact of emotions in our lives. Information about the differences between emotion, mood, and affect helped Ben to attend to his feeling states in a more intentional way. For example, differentiating between (a) his *emotions*, i.e., what represented his specific states of being in a particular moment (e.g., a calm, excited, or lonely emotion) versus (b) an emotional pattern (or *mood* that may last for a day or days) versus (c) patterns of *affect* that occur during specific developmental periods in a person's life (and could be triggered by emotionally-laden events, like his family moving frequently) helped him to focus more intentionally on monitoring, modulating, and modifying the full-spectrum (beyond his intellectual self) of his thoughts, feelings, and behaviors in recovery.

Conceptual and Embodied Self-Awareness: Monitoring Me-States of Mind

In regard to the latter point about Ben's "intellectual self," fostering his emotional development included asking him to pay attention to the potential for multiple other states of being, and the subsequent self-states in his life that may manifest in various relational and situational contexts. For example, he was asked to consider whether he could sense a private, inner self-state versus a public, outer self-state. In addition to his intellectual self, did he have an emotional self that could be expressed? Perhaps it was during his alcohol or marijuana use in the past? Or perhaps it could be in his right-brain activities in recovery? Through examining this process, Ben came to understand that he could have any number of other selves that may have been created to function in various relational contexts. The challenge was to increase his awareness of these aspects and get a sense of congruency or continuity of his self-states over time.

This was a particular challenge for Ben who could grasp the notion of having both conceptual and embodied self-awareness intellectually, but struggled to get a sense of continuity in terms of embodied self-awareness. The right metaphor for increasing this awareness came with his experiences as a cross-country runner. Oddly enough, the example that he shared of having a keen sense of embodied awareness involved a cross-country race in high school where he was suddenly struck by an urge to go to the bathroom "right in the middle of the race." He said that he would notice getting more anxious during the race when he pictured himself (conceptual self-awareness) in the race as not being able to finish and thinking obsessively about being embarrassed when he would have to explain to people why he had to drop out. Ben said that this thought process increased his anxiety. However, when he was able to focus on his bodily sensations in the race (which seemed counterintuitive to him at the time), he was able to literally feel his way to the finish line (and then go to the bathroom). In a nutshell, Ben said that the thought of having to go to the bathroom and dropping out of the race was worse than the feeling of needing to relieve himself quickly in the middle of the race.

The same process of tuning into embodied self-awareness was used to explain "urge surfing" as a way to manage cravings and urges, and thoughts of using, substances of abuse (Daley & Marlatt, 2006). Additionally, he noticed that when he did tune into his emotional states of being, even though it was uncomfortable (like having to go to the bathroom in the middle of a race) he was able to manage his emotions and consider the possibility of talking with others about what he was feeling.

Educating Males about "Others": Modulating Me-, You-, and We-States of Mind

This area of understanding himself in relation to others was by far the most difficult for Ben. As he completed the "Looking Back to Plan Ahead" exercise (see Appendix C for the "Later Adolescent Male and Young Adult" version of this exercise), he became increasingly aware that his socialization processes had engendered an emotionally avoidant affective state of being in him when it came to relating to others beyond intellectual discussions. Perhaps it was his male socialization processes from the corporate-minded traditional male aspects of his father's interactions with him, or his mother's preoccupation with his two younger twin sisters as they were born when he was age seven. Figuring out the reasons why was less important than gaining an understanding that what he felt was the impact of a socialization experience where he did not see that he had any role models for interacting on an emotional level with other human beings. Ben felt that he had "escaped through the intellectual pursuits" that were valued by both his father and his mother, as well as the cultural expectations that were placed on him as an Asian-American male early on in life (i.e., being a "precocious, studious boy" fit the cultural stereotype). Later on, he had escaped with marijuana and alcohol abuse when he was challenged by the normal developmental task of early adolescence, e.g., testing out a sense of self in belonging to peer groups, and in social interactions with females where gender role norms were being expressed. Therefore, in a sense, he felt like he was an early adolescent male at age nineteen, particularly from a social and emotional standpoint. Ben's "work" in substance abuse counseling was to recognize opportunities that he had in his life to test himself socially and emotionally and to process his feelings about these experiences with his counselor.

Learning to Check-In (Not Out)

He approached this task as he would a science experiment in one of his pre-med courses. He would notice that he wanted to pursue a relationship, and he would make a hypothesis in counseling about what he could do to get his needs met. Then he would "perform an experiment" and gather social and emotional information about himself and report back to the counselor with details, e.g., whether he felt like he wanted to "check out" emotionally and avoid his feelings by smoking pot, or "check-in" and have the chance for a positive social and emotional experience. Ben kept a journal with "records" of his experiments, which he would later describe in counseling.

After several weeks of individual counseling, it was mutually determined by Ben and his counselor that he should also attend a counseling group that was formed through the college counseling center for both males and females who were struggling with substance abuse issues in the college setting. Attendance in this group was not a stipulation of his judicial hearing to remain in college housing. Rather his choice to attend was a sign of his progress in counseling, i.e., that he was intentionally seeking out additional places where he could regularly "test out" and process his "social and emotional experiments." This combination of individual counseling with a college counselor, and group counseling with individuals in his peer age group, helped him to find strategies for balancing his social, emotional, and intellectual selves in recovery.

TONY (AGE 22): A DEVELOPMENTAL CASE STUDY

Imagine that you are a substance abuse professional working as part of a treatment team in a residential facility for homeless adult males who are suffering from addiction and co-occurring disorders. The facility is located in a densely populated urban environment in a neighborhood that is largely seen as being part of a lower socio-economic, somewhat poverty stricken area in relation to other sections of the city. The organization is financed through state and veterans administration funding. You have a caseload of 12 to 15 adult males and you provide individual and group counseling that is based on a combination of Twelve-Step facilitation, motivational enhancement, cognitive-behavioral and psychodynamic strategies, as well as pharmacological interventions.

The information that is provided in the psychosocial case presentation that follows was gathered at intake from Tony. No documentation related to biopsychosocial issues was provided by the referring detoxification center. Additionally, no collateral information from friends, family, probation officers, or prior social workers or counselors was available. Therefore, the information that follows originated from the self-report of the client while participating in a structured clinical intake interview using the Addiction Severity Index (ASI) (McLellan, Luborsky, O'Brien, & Woody, 1980), which includes the assessment domains of *medical status, employment/support status, alcohol/drugs, legal status, family/social relationships,* and *psychiatric status.* All quotes below come directly from the interview with Tony.

Psychosocial Case Presentation of Tony

Tony is a 22-year-old, Caucasian male of Irish descent who is 5'8" and 225 lbs. He grew up in public housing projects and has been homeless for the past month due to a loss of employment as a carpet layer's apprentice. He was caught using crack cocaine on the job and was immediately fired. After "a month of wandering the streets" drinking alcohol and begging for money from friends and strangers, Tony admitted himself for detoxification and was presently referred for continued care into a 6-month government funded residential facility.

With the exception of a 2-month vocational training program for youth when he was on probation as an adolescent, Tony has received no form of professional help for mental health and/or substance abuse issues. He reported that he attended Twelve-Step meetings as an adolescent to comply with the terms of his juvenile probation, however, at the time, "it felt like a joke" to him because he felt that "a 16-year-old didn't belong there" as most of the individuals in attendance were older than him.

Medical Status

In terms of his physical health, Tony tested positive for Hepatitis C, and he has a gunshot wound on his leg. Both of these conditions require continued medical attention through case management in the residential program. Despite the injured leg, Tony is ambulatory and walks with a slight limp. He is currently not taking any medications for pain and expressed no other health concerns at the time of intake. A physical examination confirmed his health status.

Employment/Support Status

Tony did not complete high school, having dropped out in the 10th grade. He states that he would like to complete his GED in the future. Vocational training led to his being hired as an apprentice to a carpet layer, which he referred to as "just a job that kept me off the streets ... it helped me support my son."

Alcohol/Drugs

Tony reported that he started using alcohol and marijuana when he was 11 years old, which expanded to crack cocaine, heroin, and benzo-diazepines (e.g., valium) in later adolescence. Most recently, however, he reported severe alcohol and crack cocaine abuse and showed signs of withdrawal and tolerance upon entering the detoxification process. Tony reported having four to five blackouts per week after drinking a fifth of vodka (or a 12-pack of beer) and "as much crack as I could afford." He explains that his first use of mood-altering substances coincided with the murder of his older sister when he was age eleven.

Legal Status

Tony has a significant history of violence, including an extensive juvenile record that is comprised of mostly assault and battery charges going back to the age of 14. He said that his mother encouraged him "to take martial arts for protection" by paying for his lessons. At one point, around the age of 15, he earned a scholarship to attend a summer training program in another state with a "world champion kick boxer." However, most recently, this physical skill in combination with his aggression has translated into "an ability to break bones" and "to collect debts that people owed." He said that working with the criminal element in the city was "a desperate way to support my habit." There is an air of bravado as Tony discusses his ability to "take care of himself" physically in fights "with guys twice my size." One incident that Tony described included a high-speed car chase with police. There is the possibility of head trauma due to reports of being hit with "sledgehammers, baseball bats, and police flashlights." Without collateral data from friends and family members, it is difficult to determine the level of reliability of this information. There is both a verbal and non-verbal quality of exaggeration that exists in the re-telling of these violent incidents in his life. Additionally, although there are no charges that have been pressed against Tony, there is an ongoing investigation by the police into the shooting that occurred during the altercation that he had with his ex-girlfriend's current boyfriend.

Family/Social Relationships

Tony reported that his parents divorced when he was 8 years old and that he lived with his mother and five older siblings (two brothers and three sisters) in housing projects in a small town located approximately 30 miles from the large urban center in which the treatment facility was located. As he was growing up, his father provided some financial support but little apparent nurturance. Tony describes his father as "an alcoholic" who was "influential" in the town where his family lived, having owned a popular restaurant and bar. Tony bragged that his father had "friends in high places," e.g., that he was "good friends with the judge."

Tony has a 5-month-old son by an ex-girlfriend, which was the major motivating factor for him entering detoxification, as his ex-girlfriend threatened to get a restraining order against him and "never let him spend time with his son again." Tony stated: "I couldn't see my son ... so I wanted to get my act together so that I could be a father to my son." Unfortunately, Tony's relationship with his mother's son is extremely strained. She has a current boyfriend who is, according to Tony, "an ex-convicted rapist," with whom Tony has had numerous violent fights, including an incident in which the boyfriend was "thrown through a glass door" and retaliated by shooting Tony in the leg. Tony's ex-girlfriend is pregnant with a second child, and there is a possibility that Tony could be the father of this child.

As an early adolescent, Tony reported that "there were times when I would be gone for weeks at a time wandering (a large city nearby) and my mother was worried sick about me." Today, he says that "she's still worried sick," and even though she will send him money for transportation and food, she refuses to let him live at home with her because of his history of violence and alcohol and drug abuse. Tony said that his mother was instrumental in helping him to get visitation with his 5-month-old son; however, with the past months decline in his stability after losing his job and apartment, his mother is no longer responding to his requests for financial help and other forms of assistance. Attempts to contact his mother while he was in the detoxification facility and since entering residential treatment have been unsuccessful.

Tony has an older brother (age 31) who lives in a nearby town and has 2 years of sobriety from alcohol and other drug dependence. His brother helped him to get into detox and is asking him to "get active in AA and NA" and to attend Twelve-Step meetings with him on a regular basis. Apparently, Tony's older brother is the only family member who is stepping forward to help Tony find a sense of stability in his life.

Tony stated that he has "no friends ... only business associates." He reported that in his adolescence he had a few close friends, but that they "went their own way" after altercations with Tony while he was intoxicated. He also reported that he would "hit them up for money" later on and after repeatedly not paying them back, they began to refuse his offers to get together.

At age 11, Tony said that his 15-year-old sister was murdered in his family's home. As he states: "My cousin and I were playing at a playground nearby, and I came home to see my sister who was babysitting us and found a trail of blood leading to the closet. I opened the door and saw her lying in a pile of clothes ... she was cut up and covered in blood. The police said she was stabbed 17 times by a crack addict looking for money." Tony reports running to a neighbor's house to tell them what he saw and the neighbor's did not believe him. "I just lost it after that ... and grabbed a bottle of Jack ... and I haven't really stopped since."

Psychiatric Status

As Tony has gone through detoxification, he has begun to have dreams and intrusive thoughts about his sister who was murdered. He is showing signs that he is beginning a grieving process related to this loss. He also is showing signs of Post-Traumatic Stress Disorder (PTSD), e.g., a process of cold sweats, crying, nightmares, and "flashbacks of her staring at me when I go to sleep or wake up." Tony denies any current suicidal ideation; however, he had thoughts of wanting to kill himself while under the influence on several occasions as an adolescent.

Despite having struggled with all of the ramifications that go along with diagnoses of Alcohol and Cocaine Dependence, Tony has visible strengths, e.g., he is very personable and engaging, and appears to be able to recognize, and accept responsibility for, the challenges that he faces. He states that he wants to "start a new life" and that he plans on working on the following clinical issues in residential treatment: "... get a hold of my anger and stop beating the crap out of people," and "get a job and be able to keep it." Additionally, he noticed that he was one of the youngest males in the treatment facility at the time of his admission, and he stated that: "I'm 22 years old ... I want to do this right the first time." He was immediately encouraged upon arrival by the older members of the residential facility to "try to find some long-term sober living housing in the area" after the residential program completion in order to establish some stability and structure in his life. Although he is in the pre-contemplation stage in regards to his PSTD, his treatment will need to include dealing with the numerous traumatic incidents from his adolescence, and in particular, the dramatic events surrounding his sister's murder.

A Developmentally-Informed, Gender-Responsive Approach with Tony

Understanding Brain-States and Self-Traits

One of the major motivating factors for Tony to enter treatment was the fact that he had lost the privilege of being able to spend time with his young son. When Tony spoke about his son, one could see in his face that he was determined to do what he needed to do in order to have visitation on a regular basis with his son. An emotionally charged, intrinsic motivational factor, such as having love for one's child, can be an excellent place to start in order to get a client engaged in conversation about how and when to begin the change process.

However, Tony's life up until the age of 22 had been filled with anger, violence, and trauma. These experiences were repeated states of mind that had created in him traits that were not unlike someone who had been living in a war zone. Tony was hyper-vigilant and suspicious around other men (particularly "the crack addicts" in the rehab). He was having nightmares about his sister who was murdered. He said that he would wake up in cold sweats and remember only that his sister was "standing there staring at him and not saying anything ... like she was waiting for me to do something to help her."

Incredibly, Tony was excellent at hiding these internals storms that were challenging his emotional stability early on in recovery. Rather than directly processing with others these thoughts, feelings, and images that were coming into his awareness, his way of talking about his memories with others (counselors and fellow clients alike) was to speak with a sense of bravado and convey stories about his life that were almost unbelievable (e.g., police car chases, being attacked "by 10 guys," etc.). As a substance abuse professional, one can recognize that these war stories can have the potential to both hold others at bay (in amazement and/or fear) and keep Tony from sitting with the reality of the full range of his emotional experiences that may have been associated with the actual events of his life. That is, as the major focus in his stories from an emotional standpoint were his tremendous anger at the injustices that he suffered, and the sense of pride at being able to conquer the adversaries that he faced, he was avoiding sitting with (pausing and reflecting upon) the fear, shame, guilt, and often self-loathing that have been emotional undercurrents that were shielded or masked by the bravado of his self-presentation as a male.

With these traits of hyper-vigilance and mistrust of others, engaging Tony in treatment was a challenge. Meeting him "where he was" included listening to the war stories and actively reflecting his pride and his anger at the events of his formative life, i.e., essentially being there with him and honoring his efforts to adapt and cope to a harsh and non-nurturing, social environment, while at the same time, helping him to understand the impact of these experiences on his ability to respond (versus react) to his emotional needs (and the needs of others, including his ex-girlfriend and his son) in recovery.

For example, there was an emotional impact of the psychological trauma of experiencing the aftermath of his sister's murder that was never processed with others in a healing way. This very likely had an effect on the development of his middle prefrontal cortex (whose functions are described in detail in chapter 2). Importantly, trauma affects how the middle prefrontal cortex is able to exert its inhibitory influences (i.e., the Stop! circuitry) over the limbic system, specifically in terms of regulating "the generalization of fear and overall increase in fearful behavior mediated by the amydgala" resulting in the potential for "attentional and frontal deficits," as well as a suppression of the "stress response mediated by the hypothalamic-pituitary-adrenal axis" (Ogden, Minton, & Pain, 2006, pp. 148–149). In short, the ability to self-regulate through the functioning of the middle prefrontal cortex is compromised by trauma. Tony was compensating for these fears by increasing his bravado, which manifested as stories of masculine heroics (e.g., extreme examples of success, power, and competition over other men). Therefore, strengthening Tony's recovery included helping him to recognize the "brain-states" that were created by his early life experiences, which were quite traumatic and still affecting his current emotional states and sense of well-being as a young man.

Educating Males about Emotions

Like the case of Jack in chapter 4, Tony had multiple experiences to draw from where his emotions could be framed as information from an affective appraisal system that was central to his survival "on the streets." Additionally, like TJ (also in chapter 4), Tony had the experiences from his martial arts training of understanding how modulating emotions was key to his athletic performance.

In a sense, even though Tony entered martial arts originally to learn how to physically protect himself, the skills of centering and focusing his mind on the exercises had the fortunate effect of also initiating top-down regulation processes over his intense emotional states of being as an adolescent male with a history of trauma and very little family support to process his emotions. This explanation made sense to Tony, in that he could see how there were periods of time where his substance abusing behaviors were lessened as his practices with martial arts increased. For example, as an adolescent, there was an inverse relationship between his intense training leading up to a martial arts match and his substance abusing behaviors, i.e., when he was in "training mode," his desire to drink alcohol lessened significantly.

Conceptual and Embodied Self-Awareness: Monitoring Me-States of Mind

Tony could also see that in the 5 years leading up to his entrance into treatment, his substance abuse had increased as his martial arts training had decreased. He had previously downplayed this process more as his "just getting sloppy" in fights with other men, rather than his losing focus on the centering aspects of the martial arts. This process of learning how to focus and center one's self through martial arts practice is an example of monitoring me-states, a key experience upon which Tony could draw to enhance his recovery efforts. In treatment, Tony could see that approaching martial arts in recovery could be a significant resource for him to find emotional stability in his life. This process was actively re-engaging the top-down neural circuitry that would enhance his ability to be aware of and process his emotions in recovery.

Additionally, in the same way that TJ (in chapter 4) could contrast conceptual (seeing himself taking a shot) and embodied (feeling his way through the shot) self-awareness on the soccer field, Tony could translate his ability to be in the moment on the martial arts mat in competition as really being in an embodied state of mind. In this way, for Tony, doing martial arts was building his body awareness in a way that strengthened his ability to not only "stay with" and move through his cravings and urges to use substances, but also be present with his embodied self enough to monitor how his traumatic experiences from the past might affect his orienting towards, and arousal states from, internal and external triggers related to the psychological trauma that was embedded in his physiology.

Educating Males about "Others": Modulating Me-, You-, and We-States of Mind

Because of his childhood history that included a lack of any secure attachment figure in his life, Tony had developed an adult attachment style that could be characterized as avoidant, which is described as having "discomfort with closeness and depending on relationship partners, preference for emotional distance and self-reliance, and use of deactivating strategies to deal with insecurity and distress" (Mikulincer & Shaver, 2007, p. 27). Mikulincer and Shaver describe two goals for these "deactivating strategies" in relationships with others: "(1) gaining whatever they need while maintaining distance, control, and self-reliance, and (2) ignoring or denying needs and avoiding negative emotional states that might trigger attachment-system activation" (p. 41). Couple this relational style with the effects of psychological trauma, and you have the "perfect storm" where a client may not have developed the "interactive regulatory and social engagement abilities necessary for resolving interpersonal conflicts" (Ogden et al., 2006, p. 56).

In a substance abuse counseling setting, these qualities may be inaccurately read as resistant to the counseling process. They can also be seen as an example of the resultant behaviors from traditional male socialization processes (e.g., restrictive emotionality, taking an anti-dependent self-reliant stance in relationships, etc.). Teasing out whether this type of behavior is more the result of attachment wounds or gender socialization processes is beyond the scope of this book. However, the important take-away assessment and treatment piece related to these dynamics is that in order for Tony to learn how to deal with family and interpersonal challenges, he will need to grapple with the states of mind (and resultant self-traits) that were engendered in him by his socialization processes related to both his attachment needs and his male socialization process.

Using a family genogram (McGoldrick, 1985) or an exercise like the one in Appendix C ("Looking Back to Plan Ahead: Setting Personal Goals," and exercise for later adolescent and young adult males) can facilitate self-awareness about the developmental and gender-based patterns of relational styles that may be ingrained in clients from their family and peer interactions. These patterns represent we-states of mind that will affect Tony's ability to develop lasting relationships and build a supportive recovery network. The awareness that can be cultivated in this process is that an emotionally avoidant style of relationship, i.e., avoiding "interactions that require emotional involvement, intimacy, self-disclosure, or interdependence" (Mikulincer & Shaver, 2007, p. 41), is not conducive to developing the interpersonal experiences and resources in treatment that can strengthen long-term recovery.

Learning to Check-In (Not Out)

For Tony, learning to check in with himself through mindfulness-based relapse prevention practices (Bowen, Chawla, & Marlatt, 2011) and embodied self-awareness on the martial arts mat was relatively simple compared to the difficulties that he had with doing the Reality Check portion of the Check-In system found in Appendix A. Specifically, when he was asked to think about whether there are people and places that you trust as being safe to put out what you need, initially he could not commit to any one person that he thought would respect your best efforts to act according to your emotional integrity.

This changed gradually over time as Tony began to develop trust in the therapeutic relationship as being a safe place. He also found that he had begun to trust and respect his older brother who was in long-term recovery from substance abuse and addiction. Through bringing his brother into the counseling process in treatment, he was able to see that he was not alone in his anger and grieving related to the losses in his family (specifically his older sister's death), and he was able to say that he honestly trusted his brother as a resource to check-in about his thoughts, feelings, and values related to dealing with difficult emotional situations in recovery. Although Tony was extremely cautious about disclosing his feelings with others, he was beginning to find people and places where he could come home and find stability and peace in the present moment.

6

Substance Abuse Counseling with Males in Early Adulthood (Ages 24 to 34)

Whereas 18- to 24-year-olds are described as being in a later adolescent transitional period where major life decisions are being made about work and long-term relationships, the developmental life stage of "early adulthood" is characterized by accepting these choices and fulfilling and beginning to actualize the roles that come as a result of these decisions (Newman & Newman, 2012). In essence, in early adulthood, we begin to reap what was sown in later adolescence, and we settle in to deepening our experiences in these life roles.

If what was sown was the beginning of intimacy in relationships, then males in early adulthood are faced with deepening these relationships into longer-term commitments and/or marriage. This deepening of intimacy brings with it the challenge of greater social and emotional awareness and the ability to communicate with others in a personal way. This capacity to deepen intimacy may be limited by what has been described in the psychology of men as a confining gender role pattern of "restrictive emotionally" (O'Neil, 1981). Additionally, the priorities of traditional male socialization processes that favor success, power, and competition in the workplace, may in turn cause conflicts between work and family relations (O'Neil, Helm, Gable, David, & Wrightsman, 1986; as cited in Englar-Carlson, 2006), and complicate this deepening of intimate relationships for males in young adulthood.

Furthermore, when one is engaged in using substances in a detrimental way that has reached the point where one's substance use has become the central organizing feature of their life (e.g., daily plans cannot be made without considering when and where substance use will take place), then one's ability to have intimate relationships with others becomes inversely related to one's level of substance abuse and addiction. Specifically, when men who engage in addictive behaviors have a primary relationship with their addiction, then their desire (and often their developing ability at this developmental level) to have intimate relationships with others is severely comprised. As intimate relationships become secondary to the addictive behavior, the neural circuitry of active addiction (which has been described earlier in the book as creating a limbic-dominated state of mind) trumps the neural circuitry related to intimacy-seeking (which requires integrative—limbic and cortical—states of mind). The result is that addiction and intimacy become behavioral processes that oppose one another in terms of having a relationship with one's self and others.

Interestingly, even though the rates of substance abuse among later adolescent males (ages 18 to 24) are disturbingly high (i.e., as had been stated, they have the highest rates of substance abuse among all age groups in the United States; Park. Mulye, Adams, Brindis, & Irwin, 2006), there is a normal aging out process that occurs for a majority of later adolescent males as they move into young adulthood (ages 24 to 34) and take on increasingly greater responsibilities in their career and work life, as well as greater involvement in their family life (Bachman et al., 2002). Evidence for this normative transition away from substance abuse in young adulthood exists from the national Monitoring the Future (MTF) surveys that have been conducted with high school students across the United States for decades (Johnston, O'Malley, Bachman, & Schulenberg, 2010).

Since this research commenced in the 1970s, nearly 40,000 young people have been surveyed about their patterns of alcohol and other drug use, as well as their attitudes and experiences related to such factors as social activities, religion, freedom, and responsibilities. Bachman et al. (2002) published a monograph, *The Decline of Substance Use in Young Adulthood: Changes in Social Activities, Roles, and Beliefs,* that provides a detailed examination of how attitudes toward substance use have been observed to change in young adulthood in relation to transitions into family life, childrearing, and increased work responsibilities. Importantly, as young men take on (and have a more vested interest in) greater work, family, and relationship responsibilities, their substance use declines. And as the MTF surveys have tracked these adolescents into their 30s, they have found that there are consistent patterns in relation to these aging out transitions across demographic groups. These changes in behavioral patterns fit with the description above of the competing neural structures in the brain related to the inverse relationship between addiction and intimacy.

Therefore, to put it briefly, when utilizing evidence-based substance abuse counseling approaches with males in early adulthood, it is helpful to conceptualize your work from the perspective that you are facilitating the normative process of maturity that occurs during this developmental life stage. For example, in addition to the importance of career development, one could argue that the key area for this maturing out process lies specifically in the realm of social and emotional development, which very likely may have been stunted by earlier substance abusing behaviors, especially if there has been a long-standing pattern of abuse that extends back into early adolescence when important neurobiological changes in the brain and body (described in chapter 4) were occurring.

From a developmentally informed, gender-responsive counseling approach, as we discuss these normative developmental challenges of one's late teens and early to mid-20s with a male client (e.g., exploring intimate relationships, leaving home to initiate work and lifestyle changes, and the possibility of having children, etc.) (O'Neil & Egan, 1992), we can educate him (at least on a very basic level) about the neurobiological, social, and emotional impact that substance abuse and addiction have had on his states of mind and relationships across time. This psycho-educational process has been described in detail in chapter 2.

Additionally, as we will see in the two case studies that follow, for these young men to find a sense of stability and meaning in their lives and in their intimate relationships, as substance abuse professionals, we can foster their emotional development by teaching them how to (a) pay attention to their states of mind and their patterns of emotional arousal in various situational and relational contexts, (b) recognize their own (and others) affective communication styles, (c) monitor their goals and expected outcomes in communicating with others, and (d) modify their behaviors in relation to how they seek to repair not only the relational harm that may have come as a consequence of years of substance abuse, but also in the day-to-day reparations that are often needed in intimate relationships between all human beings.

DAVID (AGE 25): A DEVELOPMENTAL CASE STUDY

Imagine that you are a substance abuse counselor in an outpatient counseling program that is affiliated with a local medical hospital in a small rural town. Because of limited resources, which includes the absence of any local inpatient treatment facility, following a brief inpatient detoxification process, clients are referred for either a day treatment program that provides individual and group counseling Monday through Friday from 8:30 am to 4:30 pm, or an outpatient program in the early evenings that provides individual counseling once a week and group counseling three times a week. Clients in need of inpatient treatment may be referred to facilities in a large urban center nearby, but unfortunately, are often not able to follow through with this referral because they do not have the resources to attend treatment away from their small town. As a consequence, they choose to enter the treatment program that works with their hours of employment and family budget closer to home. Although this is by no means the ideal patient placement process, it is the reality of this particular location in terms of treatment options. The outpatient programs use a combination of motivational enhancement, cognitive-behavioral strategies, and Twelve-Step facilitation. Clients are also referred for attendance at local Twelve-Step meetings.

You have been assigned a client named David, who is a 25-year-old Caucasian American male of mostly British descent. He is 6 feet tall and weighs 235 lbs. David has been referred by the employee assistance program at the local paper mill where he is currently employed. He was referred for substance abuse counseling because he was repeatedly returning to work intoxicated after lunch. His chief complaint is that he "is stuck in a dead-end job." The information provided in the psychosocial case presentation that follows was gathered in a structured clinical interview with David using the Addiction Severity Index (ASI; McLellan, Luborsky, O'Brien, & Woody, 1980). David appeared to be a reliable informant. All quotes below come directly from David during this intake interview.

Psychosocial Case Presentation of David

Medical Status

A physical examination reveals that David has high blood pressure (150 over 100) and elevated liver enzymes. He reports that he feels overweight and has "gained 65 pounds since freshman year in college." He has no other medical complications at intake.

Employment/Support Status

David dropped out of college at age 21 after two-and-a-half years of alcohol and other drug abuse. His work history prior to college and during the summer months included working for his family's retail business. In his second year of college, he worked as a resident assistant in a freshman dorm, during which time he was nearly fired for being found "lying drunk in the grass outside my dorm." He also worked as a waiter at a local restaurant during his third year in college. David reported that he was taking out loans to pay for college and working part-time to pay for books and living expenses because his parents were only able to provide him with minimal financial support.

In high school, David was an A student, president of his high school's honor society, a two sport athlete (basketball and track), and played saxophone in the marching band. David reports that: "Coming out of high school, I had high hopes for doing something really cool with my life, even though I really had no idea what it would be."

When he dropped out of college, he worked a variety of jobs that each lasted for approximately three to six months. For example, he worked in retail at a hardware store, a plant nursery, and a bookstore. He tried starting a lawn service company with his friends one summer that did not survive the winter months. It was during this time that he began to work in the local paper mill. He started as a general employee working twelve hour night shifts, alternating three nights on, two nights off. During this time, he would go to breakfast with his co-workers each morning at 7:00 am and then go to the local billiard hall and drink alcohol and take amphetamines so that he could "stay awake, drink beer, and play pool" for the morning. David would then take a nap for 3 hours before waking up and beginning this process all over again. He would drink large amounts of coffee and caffeinated soft drinks to stay awake at work each night. This pattern would repeat itself for 3 days in a row, and then David would be off work for several days, during which time he would binge drink with his friends or alone around his home, and then sleep for 10 or 11 hours at a time.

After several months of working the night shift, his supervisor found out that he had been in college and suggested that David "go for a desk job" that was open in the supply office. He applied for this job and was promptly moved into this new position where he worked during daylight hours and had an hour each day for lunch. Even though David often went out after work in the evenings with his new boss to drink alcohol and occasionally smoke marijuana, he would also buy a six-pack of beer and drink it in his car during his lunch hour. It was after these lunch breaks that his boss began to smell alcohol on his breath. Even though his job performance at the paper mill was never in question, David's boss referred him to human resources for counseling.

Alcohol/Drugs

David took his first sip of beer with friends when he was 17 years old. His first impression was that "it tasted awful and I didn't see what the big deal was." Because David was an athlete in high school and enjoyed his school work and being in the band, he says that he was not interested in "joining in on the teenage party scene" at his school. It was not until the last day of classes his senior year that he decided to attend a local party near his home. At the party, he drank wine for the first time, and as he reports: "I drank enough alcohol to begin to feel the effects ... and I was amazed at how good I felt." During this initial episode, David drank to intoxication, rode his bicycle home under the influence, and had a confrontation with his mother. The next day, he had his first hangover and realized that there were large periods of time when he had forgotten what had happened during the party.

During the summer months preceding college, David had several episodes of drinking alcohol to intoxication. It was during this time that he began a pattern of thinking that he was avoiding any negative consequences through careful planning before each drinking episode (sleeping over at friend's house, etc.). However, in reality, there were several "close calls" with car accidents that he sees now were warning signs that high risk drinking behaviors would follow during his first few years of college.

Once at college, David began to binge brink on the weekends and on an occasional week night. Although David reports that alcohol was his drug of choice, he also began experimenting with other drugs such as marijuana, LSD, ecstasy, and psilocybin mushrooms. By the second semester of his junior year, David was struggling academically because of his daily drinking patterns. After a spring break spent drinking alcohol and taking psilocybin mushrooms for three days straight, David decided to drop out of college and return home "to try to figure out where I had gone wrong."

Family/Social Relationships

David lives alone rent free in his paternal grandmother's home. Because she has Alzheimer's disease, she has been living for the past year in an assisted-living facility. David reports that he visits his grandmother every few weeks and says that prior to her illness she would talk with him about his grandfather's brother who had died of alcohol dependence at a relatively young age "surrounded by empty bottles."

David is the youngest of four children, three of whom live nearby. Both of David's parents also live in close proximity and have been married for over 40 years. David describes his family upbringing as being "religious." No alcohol was served in the home. He says that when his parents first noticed his binge drinking patterns, they suggested that he speak with their minister about it. This resulted in David feeling alienated from his family as the minister spoke about his behaviors in terms "sin and redemption," which seems to have left David with more intense feelings of shame and guilt regarding his behaviors while drinking and drugging. Additionally, one of David's older brothers who drank alcohol heavily in his 20s and had a religious conversion that resulted in his staying sober tried to talk with David about "how to kick the habit" through "getting right with God." After David debated his brother about questioning the existence of God, he remembers the conversation ending with his brother saying "I guess you'll get it when you get it."

David relayed a story about the time period when he dropped out of college that is highly descriptive about his family relationships. Initially, he left school without calling his parents to let them know what he was planning to do. When they tried to reach David at college, his roommates told them that they had not seen him for a week or so after spring break. This left David's family in a panic and when he showed up at his parent's home a week later, his mother was sitting in a chair with a blanket over her shoulders unable to speak with him about her anger and fear for his safety. David said that his father's comment was: "I don't know whether to choke you or hug you," and his brothers and sisters all surrounded him and were "just looking at me with dismay, like what happened to you?" During this time, his family was supportive of him getting help and his father suggested that David talk with one of his friends that he knew had gotten sober through twelve-step meetings. David met with the "man from AA" and left feeling that he was too young to be an alcoholic, as he had not had a lifetime of "losing a wife and kids and jobs ..."

In terms of social relationships, David has a group of male friends with whom he drinks often, but no close friendships. He reports that he has had a series of girlfriends since high school, each relationship lasting approximately three to six months. He is sexually active and often will have unprotected sex with his girlfriends. He reports that his sister has had "many talks with me about AIDS and other crap like that."

Legal Status

David has had one charge of "public intoxication" in the past year that resulted in an overnight stay in the local police station and a fine of $300. He has no other legal issues other than having gotten a few speeding tickets. He says that he often drives home from his friend's house or from bars intoxicated and wonders how he has avoided getting a drunk driving charge. David lives in a relatively rural area, and he reports that he will often wake up sitting behind the wheel of his car having pulled the car over into a field to "sleep off the alcohol." On several occasions he has had to have his car jump started by passers-by because he "passed out with the lights still on" which had drained the car battery.

Psychiatric Status

Scores on a screen for depression indicate that David may be moderately depressed. He reluctantly reports that he has periods where he will find himself "tearing up," particularly when he is alone at home and "thinking about the last 5 years of my life and how much I have screwed things up for myself."

A Developmentally-Informed, Gender-Responsive Approach with David

Understanding Brain-States and Self-Traits

One of the things that baffled David when he entered treatment was the question of how he had gone from growing up in a "stable, religious home" with parents who "stayed together through tough times," and had success in high school and great potential in college, to being a "25-year-old guy living in an old farmhouse, working in a dead-end job at the paper mill." He described his current state of mind as being "disgusted with myself" and "feeling like a royal screw-up."

Although David was only minimally engaged and participating in the Twelve-Step group process in the local community (which was a requirement of the outpatient treatment setting), he was working diligently within the counseling process to grapple with his religious upbringing, the notion of spirituality that was central to the Twelve-Step process, and the work that was involved in making "a fearless and thorough moral inventory" of himself (Alcoholics Anonymous, 1976, pp. 59). To supplement this work in counseling, a family genogram (McGoldrick, 1985) was completed that opened up the discussion related to potential substance abuse patterns in the family, his family's religion, his ideas about spirituality, and the family relationships that had been important to him growing up. Additionally, he completed the exercise in Appendix C, "Looking Back to Plan Ahead: Setting Personal Goals" in order to get some sense of bearing on "where he had been and where he was going" in his life from a developmental standpoint.

Discussions in counseling that integrated insights from these exercises focused on his social and emotional development, and specifically on how he had come to this current place of being "disgusted with himself." Part of this discussion in counseling included a psycho-educational piece explaining neurobiological and developmental processes, e.g., how states of mind become traits of mine, the stamping in processes of repeated substance abuse, and the role of the middle prefrontal cortices in recovery. Understanding these underlying neurobiological processes helped David to make sense of (and reduce the shame about) how he had progressed at such a rapid rate from not drinking at all at age eighteen to having a diagnosis of Alcohol Dependence at age 25.

Several key issues became apparent when David was doing a review of his individual developmental socialization processes related to "brain-states and self-traits" using the exercise in Appendix C. First, he remembered several emotionally laden incidents from his life (one of which is described in a separate section below) that represented places where he recognized that he had been hurt, shamed, and or embarrassed by his loved ones (whether intentionally or not). These feelings were never processed with anyone because there was an overall pattern in his family of "sweeping all things emotional under the rug," i.e., there was an intergenerational family legacy of not talking about feelings. Similarly, he remembers his "failures" at attempting to try to meet gender role norms of masculinity, based on gender role stereotypes in his culture. For example, the emotionally restrictive process that was engendered in his family was reinforced by the notions of how "real men" were portrayed in the realm of David's cultural heritage. He was a Caucasian American whose ideals about real men came from the world of sports, and popular movies and television shows, where championships were celebrated by popping open champagne bottles or cases of beer, and where women were seduced by suave police detectives in locals bars after work or in a more sophisticated fashion drinking martinis in high stakes casinos. David remembers a specific time when he left a particularly arousing action-packed movie where the images were reverberating in his consciousness. Ironically, he felt emotionally moved by the portrayal of an emotionally stoic action hero, to the point that he found himself imitating the mannerisms and the stoic affectations of the leading man in the movie. Because movies are fiction (and life is not), David rarely felt like he could live up to the portrayal of his on-screen role models, and as a consequence, these cultural expectations that left him emotionally charged up about being a man also left him feeling like he never measured up to this idea of how a real man was depicted in American culture.

Second, David realized in completing the exercise of "Looking Back to Plan Ahead" that even though he carried an overall conceptual picture in his mind of his upbringing in a stable home (which was true from the standpoint that there was no apparent abuse or trauma), he realized that there was no single person from his childhood to whom he felt securely attached. Because his mother had suffered from what appeared to be undiagnosed depression, and she was trying to care for and nurture four children, David felt that he had been left looking for a sense of attachment security in multiple people (an older sister, an older brother, his grandmother, etc.). Therefore, he felt that he had different early attachment patterns with different people in his life (e.g., somewhat secure with his sister until she went off to college, somewhat anxious-ambivalent with his mother, somewhat anxious-avoidant with his father and older brother). None of these relationships left him with the feeling of a long-term secure base. Therefore, when he sat with his feelings about his early attachment history, he had implicit memories of a felt sense of anxiousness, sadness, and impending loss that did not seem to have a basis in reality. David realized that this socialization process as a boy had left him with both a sense of "never measuring up" and the feeling that he had no one to really talk with about his inner life.

Educating Males about Emotions

In terms of his emotional self, David said that he had known people that "got mean" when they drank alcohol, but that he felt like a "happy drunk" around his friends. He felt less inhibited both socially and emotionally when he drank. In a cost-benefit analysis, these points were included as the "benefits" of drinking. In a nutshell, he said that he "drank to feel good."

Yet David also reported that he had long periods of time where he would drink at home by himself, and that he "got lost in TV shows or movies" in these intoxicated states, and he "wouldn't answer the phone when it rang," and that overall he "felt like 'my life is crap'." He described this as "the cost of drinking alcoholically." Although these were painful feelings for David to relay, they represented a starting point for discussions in counseling about how emotions are information that come up from our bodies into our awareness to let us know that there are things that we need to attend to that are not being addressed in our day-to-day lives (or that may not have been addressed in an emotionally integrated way in our earlier life). If "emotions are information" for David, then what emotions was he having (or trying not to have), and what were they trying to tell him?

Conceptual and Embodied Self-Awareness: Monitoring Me-States of Mind

David was taught in counseling how to do a mindfulness-based body scan from head-to-toe and back again (Kabat-Zinn, 1990). He focused on the sensations that were in his body and the images that came into his mind (as he scanned through various parts of his body), as well as the feelings and thoughts that arose during this process. As mentioned in chapter 3, this process of mindful awareness broadens our consciousness so that we can notice what is happening in our experience as we pause and reflect on the *sensations*, images, *feelings*, and *thoughts* (Siegel, 2010) in our body and mind. Siegel used the acronym SIFT to help us remember this process, so that we can "sift through" our experiences (e.g., our emotions) to see what is going on for us in different relational and situational contexts. Building this type of emotional awareness can work in tandem with and strengthen the cognitive-behavioral strategies that are used in relapse prevention (Marlatt & Donovan, 2005).

For example, David noticed as he scanned his awareness in his body that his "feeling" was primarily a general sense of sadness. However, he was not able to pinpoint what the sadness might be telling him about what he needed, other than the surface issues of "getting out of a crummy job," "not having a girlfriend right now," etc. Although David did see the value of practicing mindful awareness, i.e., he felt relaxed after doing the meditation practices, it also took some time before he started to notice patterns in his thought processes when he meditated that related to his awareness of his sense of self. For example, he was amazed at how difficult it was just to pay attention to his breathing patterns without getting swept away by his thoughts.

Similarly, David was stunned by how he was emotionally swept away by one particular memory that came into his awareness that related to his male socialization process, specifically his developing sense of self as a young boy. In a journal entry, he relayed the following story about how a random comment from a family member provoked a surprisingly intense emotional reaction in him:

I am shocked at how much emotion I have right now around what someone said in passing at a family get together last night. We were all sitting around telling family stories, and someone mentioned a prank that
had been played on me by a family friend when I was a young boy. I
think that my reaction is so intense because I had so much admiration
and respect as a young boy for the guy who played the prank on me. He
represented what it meant for me at that age to "be a man." That prank
just encapsulated how it was for me as a young boy, who was looking for
a solid male role model to look up to, and to be humiliated and shamed
in front of my family and friends (who were all in on the "joke"). The
feelings of intense shame and humiliation that I felt were so great that I
locked myself in the bathroom after I realized that people were laughing
at me. It is one of the most difficult memories from my childhood. I can
still see the people trying to grab me before I locked myself in the bathroom, and coddle me like a little girl, saying, "What's the matter?" while
still laughing at me. Even though when my family has brought this up
as a "joke that we all remember" before, I have kind of blown them off.
But last night when it came up again and the laughter started, I felt these
intense emotions welling up in me, and it was pure shame and humiliation. I just sat there and acted like it wasn't bothering me. But I was really
pissed off. I am sick and tired of that "joke" continuing to be retold. I am
sad, angry, and ashamed about the whole thing, and yet I feel relieved
that it is finally coming out.

As David was growing more adept at getting in touch with his
embodied self-awareness by doing meditation, body scans, and journaling, he was starting to notice a valuable change happening in his overall
sense of self in recovery. If you remember, David reported that he was
feeling "disgusted with himself" when he entered treatment. When
reminded of this, David said that in hindsight, he was really "thinking
disgusted with himself." What this turn of phrase indicated was that
David was learning how to differentiate between his conceptual self-
awareness (e.g., how he saw himself conceptually, i.e., thinking of himself as a "disgusting person") and his embodied self-awareness, which
provided a more in-depth feeling of sadness and understanding of the
"feeling states of being" of his youth that had contributed to his negative conceptual view of himself all the way into his present life.

Educating Males about "Others": Modulating
Me-, You-, and We-States of Mind

As David sat with his feelings of shame about the joking comments
from family members that related to the prank incident that occurred
when he was an 8-year-old boy, he questioned the value "at this point"
of "being with" these difficult memories. However, one of his developmental tasks as a 25-year-old male in young adulthood is to deepen
the intimacy that he has with his loved ones through gaining a greater
sense of social and emotional awareness and communicating with
others in a personal way. Without paying attention to his me-state of

being directly after the prank comment, he would have undoubtedly had a sub-cortical reaction that may have led him to want to escape by a process that he had stamped in to his neural circuitry over the last 7 years; namely, he would very likely have wanted to leave the family situation and drink alcohol in order to deal with his family and interpersonal problems.

However, in recovery he had noticed the intensity of his feelings, and he was able to process the past reactivity in a presently responsive way, i.e., through the self-reflective processes of the middle prefrontal cortices. The next step is communicating his experiences with his loved ones. This may mean talking with his family the next time that this "prank joke" is being remembered, and how he was affected by the experience. He may request that they not revisit it as if it were a harmless joke. Second, he may need to talk with the man who played the prank on him in order to have some resolution, especially if he still has a relationship with the family friend. These are the choices that can be made when one takes the time to pause and reflect on the process of modulating me-, you-, and we-states of being in treatment and recovery, which is particularly important as one navigates relationships with family and significant others.

Learning to Check-In (Not Out)

David said that he used the Check-In system to hold the experience of the "prank joke" in his awareness before he started to write the journal entry above. By doing this, he was able to see how his state of mind in the past was affecting his "me-state of mind" in the present. This awareness allowed him to move through the feelings and process the experience in counseling with only a slight urge to drink alcohol to deal with the uncomfortable feelings that he was experiencing.

David also has some additional choices about who in his environment he feels safe with in terms of doing a reality check about his needs and what he should do in the present moment in terms of the next right thing in recovery. Perhaps there is someone in his family that he is beginning to trust enough to talk about his family's intergenerational legacy of not sharing feelings. David's behaviors in recovery could be a catalyst for his family in terms of making a break from the unhealthy family patterns of not communicating on an emotional level in the past. His counselor or his outpatient substance abuse counseling group would be a good resource for him to process these choices. He may also find that self-help group participation, including sponsorship, can be a place to connect with others who have experiences similar to his own and have asked for support in comparable situations. Any and all of these outlets could be considered as potential resources for David to build a recovery support network to which he can turn when he needs someone to talk with about his emotional life and his efforts at maintaining his integrity and his relationships in recovery.

SONNY (AGE 31): A DEVELOPMENTAL
CASE STUDY

Imagine that you are a substance abuse professional in private practice as part of a group of licensed associates that includes psychologists, marriage and family therapists, and mental health counselors. As you are the only professional in your practice that is trained specifically in substance abuse and addiction counseling, you often get client referrals from your associates where the mental health challenges and/or marital and relational difficulties are unable to be sufficiently treated without addressing the substance-related issues as well. In these instances, you and the referring associate work essentially as a treatment team to address the substance abuse, mental health, and relational challenges of the individual, couple, or family members involved in the treatment process.

In this clinical setting you have been asked by one of your marriage and family counseling associates to do a substance abuse assessment on, and possibly work with, Sonny, a 31-year-old African American of Caribbean descent. Sonny's wife, with whom your associate is working, is concerned about how his substance abuse is going to affect his ability to provide for the family (i.e., he has the potential to lose his employment) and to be a father for their children.

The information provided in the psychosocial case presentation that follows was gathered in a structured clinical interview with Sonny using the Addiction Severity Index (ASI). Sonny stated that he is coming in for counseling because his wife has threatened to leave him and his boss is complaining about his work performance. Sonny's response is: "I just need to get these people off my back ... and if I need to settle down for awhile, then I will." All quotes (such as the previous one) come directly from Sonny during his intake interview.

Psychosocial Case Presentation of Sonny

Medical Status

Sonny is 5'8" and 190 lbs. and reports that he is not currently taking any medications and has no medical concerns at the time of intake. As a substance abuse professional, you know that clients will often deny any medical issues, and particularly male clients, therefore, you have asked Sonny to have a physical examination to verify that he is in good health; however, it is uncertain whether he will (a) follow through with the referral or (b) provide you with a reliable report about the status of his physical health.

Employment/Support Status

Sonny reported that he "was held back" in kindergarten, which made him slightly older than his classmates. He believes that he was held back because he was less prepared after his family moved from Jamaica to the United States when he was 5 years old. When Sonny entered the 11th grade, he was enrolled in a technical high school where he learned metal working and automobile repair. During this time in his adolescence, he worked odd jobs, e.g., washing dishes in the local diner and helping with a landscaping business.

After he graduated from high school at age 18, through family contacts he was offered a job working as a steelworker through a local union. He has been working "on and off" as a steelworker for the past 13 years, having been laid off on occasion when the economy has slowed. He also has a part-time lawn-mowing business to supplement his income.

Alcohol/Drugs

Sonny said that he started smoking cigarettes at age 12 and marijuana at age 13. He also began drinking alcohol at 13 with co-workers at the diner where he washed dishes part-time. At age 15, he began experimenting with hallucinogens (LSD and psilocybin mushrooms). Sonny reported that he used marijuana and alcohol every weekend and every day during the summer months. He said that he was able to hide his use from his parents until he was arrested for under-age drinking at age 16, and as part of his sentencing, had to attend psycho-educational counseling classes.

Sonny said that he began selling cocaine at age 17 and ended up "in some pretty scary situations, which led me to get out of that business right away." While intoxicated, he was placed on in-school suspension at the high school for "fighting and insubordination," and after cutting classes and getting into a fight with a gym teacher Sonny was suspended from high school and transferred to a technical school. He has never had formal substance abuse treatment in the past, although he has participated in mandatory drunk driving groups because of several charges of Driving Under the Influence (DUIs).

Sonny's first DUI happened at the age of 19, which he blamed "on the cops who used to just wait around outside the bar and bust people when they were leaving." At age 21, he was given a second DUI and became a habitual offender, resulting in the loss of his driver's license for 8 years. During this time he had to take public transportation and "stopped drinking for a while ... at least while I was in the drunk driving classes."

Even though he had lost his driver's license, at age 23, Sonny was arrested again for driving under the influence. He was intoxicated on marijuana and he was immediately sentenced to 90 days in the county jail. It was after this incident that he "got serious" with his girlfriend, and she became pregnant with their son. Sonny's girlfriend also smoked marijuana at that time, and when his son was a young child, they "limited their partying" to the evening hours after their son had gone to bed; although Sonny confided that he would also "smoke a joint on breaks" at work with his coworker.

At age 28, Sonny married his wife when she became pregnant with a second child. He reported that he "started to get restless" when she was pregnant because she could no longer smoke marijuana with him in the evenings. Instead of coming home, he began going to bars after work with his co-workers. It was during this time that he started doing cocaine on a regular basis, which rapidly progressed to daily use. Sonny stated that he liked to have sex while he was on cocaine and that he was hiding his cocaine use from his wife. He began to steal money from her purse and from their savings account to pay for drugs.

When the local economy went into a recession, he was laid-off from his job as a steelworker, and he began a part-time lawn-mowing service. He used this business as a way to hide the amount of drugs that he was using by paying for them with cash from his business, while lying to his wife about the amount of money he was making. During this period, his wife had to reduce her work hours due to the pregnancy, and after a year of his being laid-off and using monies from his part-time job for drugs, they declared bankruptcy. During the period they were filing for bankruptcy, his wife learned the truth about his cocaine use, and after her protestations, he vowed to stop drinking and drugging in order to stay in the relationship. Additionally, Sonny sold his truck and his lawn equipment in order to pay off several bills and to remain in their apartment. Because they had a newborn girl and a 5-year-old son, they "made a pact" with each other to stop smoking cigarettes and "to only smoke pot at night in the bathroom with an exhaust fan."

As fortune would have it, Sonny was able to return to his job as a steelworker and things began to look up for the family. However, Sonny was smoking pot at work with his co-workers. He began to get into arguments with his wife, and on several occasions would storm out of their home and go to the local bar and drink to intoxication. Additionally, Sonny has been reprimanded for poor work performance on several occasions, which his boss has suspected is due to substance abuse. Sonny is periodically called in for drug screens; however, to date, he has been able to use another person's urine to successfully escape getting caught with a positive urine screen for marijuana.

Family/Social Relationships

In light of Sonny's past behaviors related to substance abuse, his wife has decided that she does not trust him any longer and has stated that if he does not get help to control his anger and alcohol and drug abuse, then she will choose to divorce him. Sonny explained that she has threatened to move in with her sister who is also divorced.

Sonny is the fourth of five children. He has two older brothers and an older sister, and one younger brother. After his father died of alcoholism, his mother remarried; however, Sonny does not have a relationship with her new husband. Sonny's relationship with his siblings has been strained for most of his adult life, primarily because Sonny has asked to borrow money from them "time and time again to support my family" and then has failed to pay them back. Sonny's father would take trips to Jamaica to visit his grandparents, however, Sonny has not returned to Jamaica since he left there at age 5.

Legal Status

As mentioned in the "Alcohol/Drugs" domain area above, Sonny has had three DUI's and he lost his license for 8 years from age 21 to 29. At the time of the initial assessment, he has no legal issues pending.

Psychiatric Status

Sonny has not been diagnosed with any mental disorder in the past. He currently has diagnoses of Alcohol and Cannabis Dependence. Further assessments will be provided if there is an indication that a co-occurring disorder may be contributing to Sonny's substance use and mental health challenges.

A Developmentally-Informed, Gender-Responsive Approach with Sonny

Understanding Brain-States and Self-Traits

Sonny's intrinsic motivation to abstain from alcohol and marijuana use was minimal. He was motivated to some extent to keep his family intact. However, as the assessment interview revealed, there had been periods of time where he had tried on his own to reduce his substance use at home to appease his wife, only to return to abusing substances with her in relatively short order. Because he had never received outpatient substance abuse counseling services beyond mandated psycho-educational drunk driving groups, attempting to address the issue through a general outpatient model was seen as the next step-up in the treatment continuum. However, it was conveyed to both Sonny and his wife after the assessment that a referral for a more intensive outpatient level of care may be needed if Sonny's behavior related to his substance use disorders did not change as a result of the general outpatient counseling intervention processes that the associates' practice could offer.

An additional key clinical complication remained, namely that Sonny's wife, Beth, was continuing to smoke marijuana in their home even though she was saying that it was a "problem at times" for their relationship. Because Sonny and Beth had expressed in couples counseling that they felt that they did not need to stop smoking marijuana completely in order to make their relationship work, it was a professional decision in the associates' staff meeting that the substance abuse professional and the marriage and family therapist could work with Sonny and Beth only under certain circumstances. Specifically, in order to address their substance abuse issues, both Sonny and Beth would need to agree to meet with them for 6 weeks of bi-weekly conjoint sessions in order to do a psycho-educational counseling process that would use family genograms (McGoldrick, 1985) and other assessment and feedback processes (like the one's found in the Appendices of this book) to focus on the neurobiological, developmental, and familial affects of substance abuse on individuals, couples, and families. Through this process, the hope was that this information that would be presented in a personally relevant way (using genograms and self-assessments) would raise their consciousness about how their lives had been affected by their decisions to continue to use substances of abuse. For the 6 weeks of meetings, both Sonny and Beth were asked to abstain from substance use. If they were unwilling to try to abstain, then they would need to attempt to keep their substance use to a minimum and complete a daily use chart that recorded when they used, what and how much they used, what they were thinking and feeling prior to their use, and what they were thinking and feeling after their use. This process was designed to (a) educate them about brain-states and self-traits, (b) raise their conscious awareness before they make the serious commitment to work through their individual and relational challenges that they faced, and (c) reduce their substance use significantly (if not completely) for at least the period of time in which they were trying to process their thoughts and feelings about changing their substance use behaviors.

From a neurobiological perspective, this process was an attempt to shift from the bottom up neural circuitry related to addictive processes that are dominated by the limbic region to a top down engagement of the recovery processes that activate the middle prefrontal, executive functioning areas (described in chapter 2). Additionally, the hope was that these processes would build the capacity for Sonny and Beth to be more responsive and empathetic with one another, rather than to continue with the reactive stances that represented their current mode of functioning together.

As expected, both Sonny and Beth agreed to this 6-week treatment process, however rather than abstaining, they each opted for trying to keep their use to a minimum, and to keep a record of this process in the manner described above. The substance abuse professional and the marriage and family therapist expressed together to Sonny and Beth that they reserved the option to refer either of them for a higher level of care for their substance abuse issues if they felt that the process described above was not achieving a level of stability that was appropriate for a general outpatient level of care.

Educating Males about Emotions

This conjoint treatment modality offered the opportunity for Sonny and Beth to be educated about the central role of emotions and emotional development in substance abuse and recovery, as well as in healthy relationships from two different (but congruent) theoretical and practice perspectives. Specifically, the substance abuse professional talked with Sonny and Beth about the Brain in the Palm of Your Hand model and the relationship of the emotional and executive centers of the brain (and other neurobiological information found in chapter 2 of this book). To compliment this discussion, the marriage and family therapist discussed relational dynamics and attachment-related issues from a theoretical and practice perspective that was informed by Emotionally Focused Couples Therapy (Johnson, 2004). Additionally, as their family genogram was completed, the specific aspects of their intergenerational family dynamics in relation to substance abuse, emotions, and relationship patterns were discussed.

One important revelation evolved out of the family genogram discussion. The eye-opening insight occurred through the identification of people in their families who they felt were emotionally available for them, as well as other family members that they could identify as key attachment-type figures. These individuals were able to bond with their loved ones in an emotionally attuned and resonant way. Interestingly, when asked about the levels of substance abuse among specific family members, they both agreed that the people that they had identified as being emotionally attuned to others did not have the level of substance abuse as those who were identified as having struggled with both substance abuse issues and interpersonal relationships. This was true despite the fact that Sonny and Beth came together from very different ethno-cultural backgrounds. Among Beth's ethno-cultural family heritage, which was primarily Irish decent, alcohol use was seen as relatively normal, but alcohol dependence and drug *use* was "frowned upon." While among Sonny's ethno-cultural heritage that originated in the Caribbean Islands, specifically Jamaica, marijuana use was seen as less problematic than alcohol abuse. Yet no matter which ethno-cultural background that they were looking at in their family lineages, the higher levels of substance abuse (whether alcohol or marijuana) showed a positive correlation with the interpersonal challenges and issues across generations. This validated the basic brain science that had been discussed related to repetitive substance abusing behaviors and an individual's social and emotional development.

Conceptual and Embodied Self-Awareness:
Monitoring Me-States of Mind

Because Sonny and Beth chose to limit their substance use for the 6-week period rather than abstain, they were given monitoring cards that had the days of the week and specific ways to monitor their states of being related to their choices on a daily basis about whether to use marijuana, alcohol, or any other substances. This process provided immediate data about, and an educational opportunity to discuss, their me-states of mind and how they were affected by various situational and relational contexts.

Surprisingly, both Sonny and Beth stated that they felt the other was being honest about their substance using behaviors in the first few weeks of counseling. However, Sonny's process of keeping up with the monitoring cards began to drop off by the third week, and Beth's behavior indicated that she was suspicious about his honesty related to his marijuana use. By the fourth week, it appeared that Sonny had arrived for the counseling session having smoked an undetermined amount of marijuana, as evidenced by his inability to attend to and stay with the process of counseling. He appeared distant, lethargic, and unengaged in the process, which was very different from the way that he had been participating in the earlier sessions.

Educating Males about "Others": Modulating
Me-, You-, and We-States of Mind

This return to heavy marijuana use for Sonny despite having intentions of cutting back was not surprising to the substance abuse professional. In fact, it is a characteristic feature for some individuals with substance use disorders who are faced with the challenge of reducing their substance use. It was determined by the associates in a subsequent staff meeting that their general outpatient practice was not sufficient to treat the level of substance use disorder that Sonny was manifesting. However, rather than discontinue the couples bi-weekly sessions, the associates' referred Sonny to a higher level of outpatient care that included random drug screens, and a combination of individual and group counseling sessions.

In the last few couples counseling sessions remaining, the focus was placed on helping Sonny to grasp the impact of his behaviors, specifically on Beth and their children. This was a difficult task because Sonny was still in the stabilization and relapse prevention phase at his increased level of care. That is, he was still trying to monitor and modulate his me-states of mind without the influence of substances, and so it was an emotional stretch for him to extend this reflective ability to understand and have empathy for others (Beth and the children) while he was trying to understand and have empathy for and acceptance of his own emotional states. As he remained abstinent for 1, and then 2 weeks, Sonny was able to begin to grasp the impact of the "cloud of smoke" that had hovered over his life for years.

Learning to Check-In (Not Out)

The conjoint couples' psycho-educational intervention for Sonny and Beth led to some positive and healthy developments for both of them, even though it did not lead to abstinence and recovery in the traditional sense. As Beth was continuing to participate in her own individual counseling within the associates' practice, she decided that she would remain abstinent while Sonny was in treatment to support his recovery, although she did not want to commit to "a lifetime" of not smoking marijuana.

Checking-in for Beth meant that she was accountable to her individual therapist and that she spent time exercising in the park while Sonny played with the children on the play sets. For Sonny, checking-in meant that he was engaged in his intensive outpatient treatment process and the subsequent aftercare plans that included becoming more involved in a local Twelve-Step group. Within his participation in the Twelve-Step process, he checked-in by utilizing prayer and meditation, as well as the process of taking an inventory of his behaviors on a daily basis (Alcoholics Anonymous, 1976), particularly in his relationships with Beth and their children. As his treatment and recovery progressed, it was recommended that he and Beth resume emotionally focused couples counseling with the marriage and family therapist to deepen their intimacy and the experiences in their roles of spouses and parents.

7

Substance Abuse Counseling with Males in Middle Adulthood (Ages 34 to 60)

From their training, mental health professionals will have a basic understanding about what are considered to be normal psychosocial developmental challenges of middle adulthood for both women and men, e.g., managing one's career and work life, nurturing an intimate relationship while expanding other caring relationships, and managing one's household, home, and family life (Newman & Newman, 2012). The reality for men in this age group is that male gender role norms and expectations continue to affect how they will coordinate work and home life, how they will act in close, intimate relationships (e.g., in terms of self-disclosure and expressing vulnerability in relationships), and how they will handle either expected or unexpected events in their lives, such as the emotional and legal implications of a possible separation or divorce, the sudden change that comes from losing one's steady employment (and sense of masculinity that may accompany a job), or even the unexpected consequences of a planned career change or transition in middle adulthood that has repercussions related to status, meaning, and assumptions about one's self (O'Neil & Egan, 1992).

Moreover, in middle adulthood, as the ages of 40 and 50 pass by, and 60 looms on the horizon, the realization begins to settle in that one is aging. With the changes in a man's physical appearance and health that come with age, e.g., from possible balding and/or graying of one's hair, to the probable lessening of one's stamina and strength, to the potential for sexual dysfunction or challenges in urination because of changes in prostate health, there are implications related to one's self-concept that may change how a male in middle adulthood will visualize himself as becoming an older man (O'Neil & Egan, 1992). Include in this picture the wreckage that may be left behind after years of substance abusing and addictive behaviors and we will find that each of these developmental challenges is amplified. And it can be sobering (pun intended) to emerge from the haze of years of substance abuse to see one's self more clearly, only to find that there is an aging man looking back at you in the mirror whom you can hardly recognize.

Of course, not all men who seek help in middle adulthood have years of substance abuse behind then. However, given the statistics that "addictive disorders identified in adults most commonly have onset in adolescence or young adulthood" (Chambers, Taylor, & Potenza, 2003, p. 1041), the chances are good that there will be an accumulation of years of social, emotional, and career-related issues to face in substance abuse treatment, including high levels of shame and guilt related to one's behavior in significant relationships with partners, spouses, and children. Additionally, it has been found that the earlier the onset of substance use, the greater the severity and morbidity of the addiction, including the use of multiple substances and associated substance use disorders (Chambers et al., 2003). This finding paints a picture of a client who will have multiple physical, mental, and emotional challenges that will extend well beyond the drugs of abuse leaving the biological systems of the body (i.e., the detoxification process).

Interestingly, with men in middle adulthood, it is oftentimes the threat or actual loss of employment that is the main motivating factor for seeking help to address substance abuse issues. For example, a man may be 50 years old and facing job termination because of his alcohol abuse. And yet, it is only now that he is considering getting help, even though he lost his marriage 10 years ago, he lost contact with his children 5 years ago, and he lost his last friend 1 year ago. In this example, there are at least two possible reasons why the job is the last thing to go and the one thing that will motivate him to get help. First, so much of this man's identity is wrapped up in his work and career life. When this last realm of self-worth is threatened, he feels that he has no choice. And second, quite simply, he needs to have a job in order to have money to buy alcohol and other drugs. He may be able to survive through cashing in his savings and/or retirement accounts for a period of time if he has these resources, however the next level down would be homelessness and having to beg or steal in order to obtain one's drug of choice (the borrowing option having expired when he lost his relationships with his family and friends).

Obviously, this is a bleak example of where substance abuse and addiction can take a man in middle adulthood. However, the point is that gender role norms and one's notions about masculinity play an important role in a man's decision to seek help in treatment, e.g., in this latter case, his sense of identity as a man was closely tied to his employment, as opposed to his roles as husband and father that were lost earlier on in his life. A gender-responsive assessment related to male socialization processes will give us an understanding of how a client's motivation for treatment may be wrapped up in the powerful influences of "male-ness" that are based on factors associated with culture, race, ethnicity, religion, and socioeconomic status, as well as sexual orientation and the geographic region in which a man was raised.

Chances are good that as a man's head begins to clear after detoxification he will be faced with feelings that are associated with how he has lived out the gender role conflict (O'Neil, Good, & Holmes, 1995; O'Neil, Helm, Gable, & Wrightsman, 1986) and gender role strain (Pleck, 1981) in his life. For example, if we take the case above where the job was the last thing to go, as he examines his life, he may begin to realize that the gender role patterns of having an emphasis on success, power, and competition, restrictive emotionality, and conflicts between work and family relations (O'Neil et al., 1986; as cited in Englar-Carlson, 2006) have all played a role in his abandoning his wife and children, and all of his close friends. And even though the combination of the traditional male value of intense self-reliance and/or the mandated status of losing one's job may have propelled him into treatment, he is now having to face an emotional and relational history that may trigger conflict with his traditional male role norms, e.g., avoidance of anything feminine, such as having and expressing feelings (Levant et al., 1992).

Therefore, when feelings of anger, self-loathing, disgust, and/or shame begin to emerge, there may be layers of psychological defenses related to gender role norms that will need to be addressed openly and with compassion in treatment. For example, the impact of his emotional life (e.g., his mood and general affective states) on his relationships, specifically his choices about emotional expression around others may emerge as he learns the cognitive-behavioral skills of relapse prevention. Additionally, as he begins to make sense of his life in recovery, examining how he has attempted to live up to the gender role expectations (stereotypes, rigid standards, and norms) of his ethno-cultural background will be important in terms of his creating a coherent life narrative that allows him to move forward and talk with others about the behavioral, cognitive, and emotional challenges in his life that were (and still are) related to his history of substance abuse and addiction.

The two case studies that follow illustrate how these male-specific challenges can have an impact on the counseling process at various phases of treatment. For example, we will examine how these males may have struggled with deviating from or violating the gender role norms of their family and culture, or tried to meet their gender role norms of masculinity, or experienced personal devaluing of themselves as men if they feel that they have failed to live out gender role stereotypes (Englar-Carlson, 2006). As the cases demonstrate, these factors are often deeply interwoven with their past histories of substance abuse and addiction and their current struggles with finding a sense of stability and serenity in recovery.

LUIS (AGE 43): A DEVELOPMENTAL CASE STUDY

Imagine that you are working as a mental health counselor in a long-term residential treatment program designed for males who are suffering from chronic addiction and co-occurring mental health conditions. This structured, sober living environment provides the opportunity for men to find full-time employment and to live in a therapeutic community for up to six months in order to find a sense of stability in recovery that may have eluded them in an outpatient counseling setting or after brief periods in inpatient treatment that did not include substantial aftercare services. Oftentimes, clients are being referred to this facility directly from a detoxification center or a residential treatment facility. Individual and group counseling, as well as a case management services, are include in the treatment protocol in order to provide integrated treatment for addiction and co-occurring disorders. Counseling approaches in this facility include (but are not limited to) psycho-educational groups related to managing co-occurring disorders, career counseling, Twelve-Step facilitation, and cognitive-behavioral relapse prevention strategies.

You have a caseload of 15 to 18 clients, and your newest client is a 43-year-old divorced male of Puerto Rican descent named Luis. Luis is a self-referral who enters treatment saying that he wants to "turn my life around." However, there are issues of legal charges and upcoming court dates that may also be playing a significant role in Luis' motivation to enter treatment at this time in his life. Luis stated that he had come to realize that his substance abuse issues have kept him from maintaining steady employment, have caused "numerous problems with the law" and his family relationships, and have begun to have a noticeable effect on his physical and emotional health.

The information provided in the psychosocial case presentation that follows was gathered upon admission into the program in a structured clinical interview with Luis using the Addiction Severity Index (ASI; McLellan, Luborsky, O'Brien, & Woody, 1980). He appeared to be a reliable informant during the interview. All quotes below come directly from Luis during his intake interview.

Psychosocial Case Presentation of Luis

Medical Status

Luis is 5'9" and 165 lbs. He is taking anti-inflammatory medication for pain in his knees and shoulders due to an injury while doing carpentry work. He reports that he fell through a floor and damaged his knees to the point that he "will need surgery at some point." A full medical examination revealed no other physical health conditions at the time of intake.

Employment/Support Status

Luis is employed full-time as a retail salesperson for a clothing store. He applied for disability benefits because of his injured knees, however his claim was denied. He said that he has not appealed because he has found retail sales to be rewarding and a possible career opportunity as his manager has indicated to him that he might be considered for more of a management-type role in the future. At present, Luis has a high school education, but he would like to go to community college to learn more about business management or merchandising to further his career in retail sales.

Alcohol/Drugs

Luis reported that he had his first drink of alcohol when he was 12 years old with his older brothers. He says that he drank small quantities of beer when he was around his brothers "to fit in," but that he hated the taste at that early age. However, at 14, a traumatic event (described below) left him in a state of anxiety and confusion, and he soon learned that drinking large amounts of alcohol and smoking marijuana helped to soothe his emotional and psychic pain from the incident. At age 18, Luis left home to be a musician in a rock band and began experimenting with other drugs, such as cocaine and heroin. Today, Luis reported that he "would use anything that was available," but that his primary pattern of drug and alcohol use would be to begin a binge episode with cocaine, and then drink alcohol in combination with smoking marijuana or snorting heroin to "level out" and "take the edge off" of the stimulant high.

Luis reports that he entered treatment because of numerous relapses to alcohol, cocaine, and heroin. He has a diagnosis or Polysubstance Dependence, and he stated that he needed a long-term residential treatment program to provide a stable, structured, sober environment because outpatient counseling has not proved to be effective for him. Previous attempts at recovery include seven detoxifications and four outpatient treatment episodes.

Family/Social Relationships

Luis has four children. From his first marriage, he is the stepfather to two girls, ages 5 and 6, and the biological father to a 3-year-old boy and a 2-year-old girl. Luis reports that his children are living with their mother who is "battling addiction to crack." He has a great deal of emotion (e.g., guilt, fear, and anger) surrounding the fact that he cannot help to take care of his children at this time. Luis stated that he is currently dating a former police officer who now works with troubled adolescent girls. He was engaged to be married to her 2 months prior to entering treatment; however, the engagement has been cancelled, and she was apparently very instrumental in getting him into treatment. She supports his staying sober at this time and says that she will only consider being his fiancée again if he stays clean and sober.

Luis' family history includes several generations of family members whom he describes as having been alcoholic (grandfather, aunts, uncles, and brothers). His father has apparently suffered from alcohol dependence for most of his life and is currently dealing with the onset of Alzheimer's disease in a retirement community. Two of Luis' brothers are reportedly in recovery from alcohol and other drug dependence. One other younger brother was murdered in a shooting at a neighborhood party when Luis was in his 20s.

Legal Status

Luis has Driving Under the Influence (DUI) and drug possession charges pending with an upcoming court date. He was pulled over for drunken driving 2 weeks prior to entering treatment and the police found small amounts of heroin and marijuana hidden in his car. As was previously stated, the legal issues are a major motivating factor for Luis entering treatment at this time in his life.

Psychiatric Status

On admission, Luis reported "mood swings" and was just beginning to take antidepressant medications prescribed by a family physician. One traumatic event of note related to Luis' mental health occurred when he was 14 years of age. As he describes it:

> I was asked to report to a painting job for the first time that was about a fifteen-minute walk from my home. When I arrived on the supposed job site, four guys jumped me, raped me, and left me suffering and bleeding. It took me about an hour and a half to get home. I was ashamed ... my brothers found out, cleaned me up, and took me back to identify these guys. They will literally never be the same people again. Neither will I.

Luis said that he began talking about the incident with a counselor in outpatient treatment and that it was his first time "sharing this with anybody because of the shame of it." He said that he has not discussed this event with his brothers since the day that it happened. Apparently, he has dealt with family history and trauma by leaving home directly after high school to play guitar in a rock band, abusing alcohol and drugs, and practicing extensively with martial arts for self-defense.

In addition to his diagnosis of Polysubstance Abuse, Luis has a co-occurring diagnosis of Post Traumatic Stress Disorder (PTSD). He is very charismatic, personable, and well-spoken. He cares deeply for his family. He also presents as very put together; however, this behavior also has a tone of perfectionism, e.g., his wardrobe and grooming habits are paramount to him and he often wears an amount of cologne that is almost stifling to others when he enters a room.

A Developmentally-Informed, Gender-Responsive Approach with Luis

Understanding Brain-States and Self-Traits

Like Tony in chapter 5, Luis has a significant traumatic event that occurred when he was an adolescent that was never processed from an emotionally integrative standpoint. He has a treatment history that includes four prior outpatient treatment attempts. In each of these settings, he was introduced to the Twelve-Step recovery group process, and he tried to learn about how to prevent relapse (e.g., cognitive-behavioral strategies of "surfing" urges and managing thoughts of using) (Marlatt & Donovan, 2005). However, in each setting he left treatment early and relapsed because he was unable to tolerate the feelings that were associated with his being raped as a 14-year-old that surfaced when he stopped using alcohol and other drugs of abuse. In the last outpatient setting, he had opened up for the first time and tried to talk about the rape, but the feelings of shame and humiliation were too much for him to tolerate and he again relapsed.

From the perspective outlined in this book, Luis was developmentally stuck, specifically in his ability to process his emotions related to the trauma. From a brain-state standpoint, the intense affective traumatic symptoms that he was experiencing were "subcortically initiated rather than cortically controlled" (Ogden, Minton, & Pain, 2006, p. 155). As he was becoming more aware of his "emotional states of being" in treatment, he was using traditional relapse prevention techniques to attempt to "think his way through" the emotional arousal that was intensifying as he tried to express verbally what had happened to him. In his last treatment attempt, this process had escalated his subcortically mediated autonomic responses and this level of hyperarousal had proven to be too much for him to tolerate. He could not understand why he "couldn't hang in there like the other guys who were trying to stay sober," and he was framing his failure in treatment as a manifestation of a "lack of strength" as a man. Educating Luis about the "basic mechanics" of trauma and substance abuse in the brain reduced his feelings of inadequacy and shame that accompanied his "failures at getting sober."

Educating Males about Emotions

Luis had figured out in his first few attempts at treatment that restricting his emotional expression was not healthy. And he was able to talk about his feelings in almost all areas of his life. He said that this was true because his family had always been "very emotionally expressive, even the guys."

The challenge for Luis centered on the rape incident. He and his brothers had never talked about the incident. Furthermore, Luis had almost immediately begun using alcohol and other drugs to cope with the intense feelings of shame and humiliation that he was unable to share with anyone. Therefore, in a sense, the emotions that were associated with the rape were trapped. It would take a particular type of approach and therapeutic environment for Luis to deal with the trauma and the subsequent urges to medicate the symptoms of the trauma with alcohol and other drugs.

Conceptual and Embodied Self-Awareness: Monitoring Me-States of Mind

Throughout the book, we have talked about the importance of learning how to monitor me-states of mind by SIFTing through our experiences of the *sensations* in the body, the *images* in the mind, and the *feelings* and *thoughts* that arise into our awareness (Siegel, 2010). The same can be true for Luis, however, the sensorimotor approach to treating trauma proposed by Ogden and colleagues (2006) suggests that for Luis to be able to begin to integrate the intense emotions that are associated with his being raped, he would need to focus first primarily on the "sensate precursors to emotion" in order to expand his "window of tolerance," e.g., by "increasing mindfulness and focusing exclusively on body sensations" he "may paradoxically facilitate more integrated brain functioning," while helping to ensure that he does "not suffer the discomfort of activation with little integration or transformation of that distress" (p. 155). A full description of how this approach would unfold with a client like Luis is beyond the scope of this book. Readers are referred to the excellent resource that is Ogden et al.'s (2006) book, *Trauma in the Body: A Sensorimotor Approach to Psychotherapy*. In short, recovery for Luis will begin with slowly increasing his embodied self-awareness and his window of tolerance for the emotional pain that is being integrated. He will gradually build the capacity for his responsiveness to these feelings, rather than reactively reaching for substances to numb the pain.

Educating Males about "Others": Modulating Me-, You-, and We-States of Mind

As Luis steadily increased his ability to tolerate his intense emotional arousal from the trauma, he encountered another level of resistance within himself that related to sharing what had happened to him with others. The resistance centered on his fears about how people would perceive his "manhood" with the fact that he had been raped by other men. Because he was an open and a naturally expressive person, he wanted to be able to share himself fully with his girlfriend and his children.

In substance abuse treatment, significant others are often involved in the counseling process in one form or another. In this particular setting, there were two opportunities for families to be involved: (a) Select family members were invited for an hour and half psycho-educational group that was separate from the individuals in treatment, which consisted of a presentation and discussion about addiction and families; and (b) Conjoint sessions were included where possible to help integrate the treatment process within the family system in which the client would be returning. Because of the ages of his children, neither they (nor his ex-wife) were invited for treatment (even though Luis felt that his ex-wife who was struggling with her own addiction would have possibly benefitted from the presentation). Luis did invite his girlfriend, and even though she declined to attend the psycho-educational group session, she did agree to come in for a conjoint couples' session with him.

To prepare for this session, Luis completed the exercise "Looking Back to Plan Ahead: Setting Personal Goals" for males in middle adulthood (found in Appendix D). He wanted to be clear about where he had been, what he was working on in treatment, and what his wishes were for the future, particularly in relation to his long-term relationship with his girlfriend. He expressed that he was tremendously relieved to "have the monkey off my back" of the secret of his rape and he was eager to move on with his life. Members of Twelve-Step groups that he belonged to were saying that he was "in a pink cloud" state of mind, and that he would need to slow down and take his time in making life-changing long-term plans (e.g., Luis had considered proposing marriage again to his girlfriend in the conjoint session, but was advised against it by clinical staff and fellow clients alike). Luis knew that he admired his girlfriend tremendously for her career and volunteer work with troubled youth, and he felt a sense of urgency about "not wanting to lose her" because he was not emotionally stable enough for a long-term committed relationship.

Learning to Check-In (Not Out)

As Luis practiced the check-in system outlined in Appendix A in treatment and recovery, a significant pattern of insight about himself emerged. Luis realized that he was often troubled by a nagging feeling that he was not being authentic with people. Particularly at work, he "felt like a phony." In counseling, he was able to process the ways in which he had developed adaptive specialized selves that could survive in various situations (e.g., moving from being a very professional, "highly put together" clothing merchant in one moment to moving through "a crack infested neighborhood" to buy drugs in the next). Luis found that even though he was no longer drug-seeking in "seedy neighborhoods" he was stuck "without a sense of authenticity," and "filled with intense and unresolved conflicts across self-states" (Siegel, 2001, p. 231).

By repeatedly checking-in with himself when these self-states arose, he was able to create a coherent self-narrative that made sense of these disparate parts of himself as being adaptive coping mechanisms for surviving the aftermath of both his history of trauma and his substance abusing and addictive behaviors. Additionally, although drinking, drugging, and playing in a band were inextricably linked in his earlier life, he used the same process of understanding self-states in different contexts to begin to experiment with playing music in a band. This experiential process allowed him to find ways to deepen the enjoyment of his newfound recovery, as well as express himself through music in sobriety.

JB (AGE 54): A DEVELOPMENTAL CASE STUDY

Imagine that you are working as a mental health professional in an outpatient behavioral healthcare setting that is located in a mostly middle-class suburban area in close proximity to a major city. Your work is primarily in a partial hospitalization day program that is affiliated with the local hospital. You provide individual and group counseling services and have a caseload of approximately twelve to fifteen clients who have a range of moderate to severe substance use disorders in combination with some type of physical health issues. Additionally, some clients have mild symptoms of depression, anxiety, and other mental health challenges. You are part of a treatment team that includes a number of licensed mental health professionals. The team is supervised by a psychiatrist who is trained in managing addictive behaviors, and particularly addiction in individuals who are suffering from chronic pain.

You have recently been assigned a new client named JB, a 54-year-old divorced, Caucasian American male of German and Italian descent. JB stated that his admission was not prompted by the criminal justice system. However, he stated: "They highly recommended that I seek outpatient counseling ... and I just decided to do it all the way;" referring to his self-referral for partial hospitalization services having come directly from a detoxification center after being assessed as having Polysubstance Dependence (alcohol, benzodiazepines, and opiates).

The information provided in the psychosocial case presentation below mirrors the domains of the Addiction Severity Index (ASI). During the intake interview, JB reported that he had "been to hundreds of treatment programs ... 50% having been detox only," and that "I've been doing this for a long time and I know what I need," meaning that he understands the treatment system well and that he feels that he needs a semi-structured environment to begin his recovery process "for the last time." All quotes below come directly from JB.

Psychosocial Case Presentation of JB

Medical Status

JB is 5'8" and 140 lbs. In addition to the chemical dependency issues, JB has been diagnosed with Peripheral Neuropathy and Degenerative Bone Disease. At times, he uses a cane and is limited in terms of the amount of physical activity in which he is able to participate. JB also suffers from seizures and is currently taking anti-seizure medications. He minimizes the seriousness of the threat of seizures. JB also tends to minimize his disability with such statements as: "My physical health really isn't that bad when you consider what I've subjected my body to in 30 plus years ... the neuropathy in my legs and the degenerative bone disease in my hip are a direct consequence of my addiction and are unfortunate, but I accept these with no self-pity whatsoever." Additionally, JB reports that he was in a coma "for several days" as a result of his substance abuse, and reports having trouble remembering because of this event.

Employment/Support Status

JB is receiving a monthly check from the government for a medical disability. He has not had stable, full-time employment in his life with the exception of having been a case manager for the chronically mentally ill during the 3-year period that he was sober. JB dropped out of college after one semester, and sees himself as a creative writer and musician. He also feels that he will need to be dependent upon disability checks for the remainder of his life. JB stated with a smile that "if I had only worked longer, then I would have been able to collect more disability." He currently has a fiancée who collects alimony from her ex-husband. Because of these two incomes, JB does not appear to be motivated to seek part-time employment. He describes his life prior to entering treatment as "writing, playing the guitar, watching TV, and hanging out at the ocean." During the intake session, JB made a joke about himself saying that he seems to have a "lack an understanding of the potential connection between my idealizing 'free time' and my chronic relapsing behaviors ... and you can quote me on that in your assessment."

Alcohol/Drugs

JB began using alcohol and marijuana at age 16. He reported that as he entered his senior year in high school, his alcohol and marijuana use increased along with his experimentation with hallucinogens such as LSD and psilocybin mushrooms. In addition to heavy drinking episodes, JB continued a pattern of polysubstance abuse well into his late 30s, and as he began to experience physical pain and anxiety, he began abusing prescription drugs (benzodiazepines and opiate-based pain medications). Lastly, he began using heroin, which in combination with other drugs, resulted in a drug-related comatose state.

JB reported that he had approximately three years of recovery that ended several years ago, and that he has been "struggling to put together 2–3 weeks of sobriety ever since." He reports that "I have been abusing my body for the last 32 years," and he is showing serious signs of physical deterioration as a consequence. JB describes his drug of choice as "everything," and that his "initiation to an addict lifestyle happened in the counter culture of the 70s."

Family/Social Relationships

JB has been divorced for 20 years. He reports that he lives with his fiancée who has several months of sobriety from alcohol abuse. They have not set a date for their wedding. JB states that he has very little family support: "My father has been through the wringer with me ... he sends me money occasionally." JB says that he has no problems with his mother and spoke very little about her in the intake. He reports having minimal contact with his 24-year-old son and his two grandchildren. JB has one sister with whom he reports getting along "OK most of the time"; however, he does not contact her because "my brother-in-law is an asshole."

Legal Status

JB is currently on probation for assaulting his fiancée, which he minimizes, saying that "the cops exaggerated what happened." He reports: "The legal issues I have whether warranted or unwarranted are a consequence of my drinking, and that is something I have to accept. Case closed on that one. The only time we've ever had disagreements or harsh words is when we were both intoxicated."

Psychiatric Status

JB reports no past treatment for any psychiatric disorder. He states that "my biggest problem is that I intellectualize everything." JB says that he has "been to hundreds and thousands of meetings," and he refers to his knowledge of and experience with Alcoholics Anonymous (AA) and Narcotics Anonymous (NA) as "extensive." However, he reports that he "went AWOL as a home group leader and sponsor" for others in the Twelve-Step programs. JB discussed his "character defects" in abstract terms without saying specifically what they are. Because of his Twelve-Step experiences and his understanding about addiction and mental health treatment modalities from his work as a case manager, JB appears to use this knowledge and his intellectual ability to move away from the self-reflective processes that can help him to take responsibility for his behaviors in recovery.

A Developmentally-Informed, Gender-Responsive Approach with JB

Understanding Brain-States and Self-Traits

JB's self-described traits were that he was "lazy, obnoxious, and too smart for my own good." He had 3 years of experience as a mental health case manager and he knew the Twelve-Step model "inside and out," having sponsored multiple people over years of trying to maintain sobriety. Interestingly, he assigned a grade of "B+" to his intake counselor for "the way that he kept re-directing me back to the strict structure of the assessment." Although JB presented himself as "an expert" on addiction and mental illness, the information related to neurobiology (see chapter 2, this volume) was "new to him" and what piqued his interest about it was the capacity of parts of the nervous system to be able to regenerate connections given the right circumstances. Specifically, he was intrigued by "the hope of neuroplasticity" in the brain.

When JB dropped his "expert" stance in individual counseling and began to share about his life experiences of dealing with addiction, he revealed that he was feeling like he had damaged his body "beyond repair," and at age 54, he was resigned to coping with the damage by self-medicating his pain. He described himself as having the "progressive, fatal disease of addiction," and that after his last relapse, he had decided to "start my own self-medicated hospice care," even though he did not have an incurable, fatal illness. In short, he had lost hope and had resigned himself to "dying as the addict that I am."

When JB had maintained sobriety through the fellowships of AA and NA for a 3-year period, he had experienced a sense of stability for the first time in his life. During this time, he had secured a steady job, met his fiancée, and had planned to get married. However, when he relapsed and was in a comatose state for several days, he awakened with a sense of shame and hopelessness that he "wasn't able to shake." The domestic violence incident with his fiancée stemmed from her remaining in recovery and challenging him while he was intoxicated. JB stated that: "She basically said that I should get my shit together, or I was going to be bounced to the curb."

With the new information about neuroplasticity, JB could see how he had been on "a course of repairing myself" when he was sober. He had not heard about the physiological reality of how the structures of the brain can change as clusters of neurons fire together and trigger gene activation and protein production, which in turn creates new synaptic connections, and/or strengthens those that already exist (Siegel, 2010). He could see on a practical level that when he was sober, he was repeating positive experiences that were very likely changing the neural structure and function of his brain in positive ways.

JB talked about "what had worked before" for him, e.g., he had developed an intimate relationship with his fiancée and had a support network with individuals in AA and NA, and he was going for walks on the beach on a regular basis, and "really getting into" helping other people who were struggling with mental illness in his job. All of these activities provided a basic framework for talking about long- and short-term goals and objectives while putting together a treatment plan with him in a collaborative fashion, a plan that he was intrinsically motivated to follow.

Educating Males about Emotions

Like Ben in chapter 5, JB's intelligence was a hindrance for his ability to attend to his emotional states of being. Unlike Ben who rather by unconscious default always thought before feeling, JB knew on a conscious level that he had "the ability to intellectualize practically anything." For JB, intellectualizing was a defense mechanism against feeling emotional stress and pain. Once again, the new information about the neuroscience of addiction opened a window for JB to reframe his personal approach to having an emotional life.

JB admitted that he had always felt superior to people ("especially women") who were not able to "control their emotions." He said that his mother, who was a first generation Italian American, "was an emotional woman who was incredibly hard to live with ... my Dad and I just rolled our eyes every time she would go off." At the start of treatment, he saw emotions as being in the realm of femininity and he did not see the value of expressing them as a man. He later stated that: "I probably got this from my Germanic ancestry" (his father's heritage). Descartes' famous saying, "I think, therefore I am" was used by JB as a rationalization for taking a purely cognitive, intellectual stance in counseling.

However, seeing emotions as information for surviving and thriving, particularly from the viewpoint that the structures in the brain related to emotion were literally at the crossroads of the energy and information flow in the brain, shifted JB's perspective on the importance of emotion. He was intrigued by the idea that emotions were integral to making meaning out of one's life, which opened the door for him to begin to more intentionally experience embodied (i.e., emotions in his body) states of being.

Conceptual and Embodied Self-Awareness: Monitoring Me-States of Mind

In the late 1970s, JB was deeply involved in the "counter-culture" that was coming to a head in the United States. Part of this experience for him, as a later adolescent male, included experimentation with psyche-delic drugs and transcendental meditation. JB said that these experi-ences were confusing for him because he had no control over "what kind of trip he was going to have on any given day," and that as an adolescent there were several times when he felt extremely uncomfort-able in his body and he had used a mantra of repeating a word or say-ing over and over again in his mind until he was able to ride out the experience. These experiences strengthened his intellectual stance of "I think, therefore I am." Because he had connected "bad trips on LSD" with meditation, he had always avoided the idea of "prayer and medita-tion" in the Twelve Steps (Alcoholics Anonymous, 1976). And with the exception of how he felt connected "to something transcendent when I'm at the beach," he did not feel that he had a concept of a Higher Power that he could "use to stay sober."

Mindfulness-Based Relapse Prevention (MBSP) (Bowen, Chawla, & Marlatt, 2011) was introduced to JB in treatment as a way to capitalize on the processes that were described in chapter 2 related to developing mindful awareness (processes that JB was "buying into"). Specifically, from the perspective of neuroscience, mindfulness effectively con-nects the energy and information flow between the upper and lower parts of the brain and the central nervous system in the body. MBSP teaches clients how to do body scans and intentionally focus on the sensations and feelings in the body (embodied self-awareness) and the thoughts and images that are coming into the mind (conceptual self-awareness). Framing this process as "watching the mind" and "seeing what's happening in the gut" worked for JB to move beyond his sticking point related to "doing meditation" and helped him to create a sense of embodied self-awareness.

Educating Males about Others: Modulating Me-, You-, and We-States of Mind

Not without a feigned struggle, JB completed both a family genogram (McGoldrick, 1985) and the "Looking Back to Plan Ahead: Setting Per-sonal Goals" exercise for males in middle adulthood (found in Appen-dix D). In these activities, JB was able to see and acknowledge that as a child he did not have a secure attachment figure to which he felt close and could approach if he were upset, feeling rejected, alone, or threat-ened. As an adult, he could see that this earlier experience had created in him an attachment style that was primarily avoidant, and that the challenges that he had faced in maintaining an intimate relationship with other people, particularly his fiancée, were obviously affected by his relational style. For example, JB realized that the longer he had been engaged to be married to his fiancée during his 3 years of sobriety, the more "moody" he got around her. He had blamed her for the difficulties that they were experiencing, and in fact, had gone as far as to say that she had "pushed him" so much that he had relapsed, which in effect, was blaming her for his return to alcohol and drug use.

In treatment, JB was able to see how his avoidant attachment style had shaped the way that he saw himself (me-state), how he perceived his fiancée (you-state), and how he grew increasingly uncomfortable as their relationship became more intimate (we-state). Mikulincer and Shaver (2007) describe the ways that people with a tendency towards avoidant styles of attachment will "defensively inflate self-conceptions, presumably to feel less vulnerable and less interested in relying on deficient relationship partners," and "flee if a relationship becomes too intimate or demanding" (p. 42). JB reluctantly admitted that this relational pattern was true for him (e.g., "going AWOL from AA") and that in order for him to move forward in recovery and re-establish a relationship with his fiancée and the AA community, he would need to be able to monitor and modulate the residual negative emotions that were embedded in his implicit memory from his childhood.

Learning to Check-In (Not Out)

As treatment progressed, JB became an "expert" at spotting when others needed to "go do a check-in" on whatever issue they were struggling with in treatment. Importantly, he was able to do this because he himself had benefitted from understanding and practicing this process of checking in that opens up communication of energy and information between structures in the brain related to conceptual self-awareness (i.e., the dorsomedial prefrontal cortex) and embodied self-awareness (i.e., the ventromedial prefrontal cortex).

In treatment, JB was becoming increasingly aware of his "old pattern of thinking things to death." Therefore, when he noticed that "something was amiss with him," he would hold whatever activating event that was bothering him in his conceptually-guided, thinking form of self-awareness temporarily, and then make a shift to "feel his way through" the same situation with embodied-guided self-awareness. He was able to do this because he had practiced mindful awareness enough to understand the importance of taking the time to breathe down into (and do a Gut Check of) his experience of the event from an emotional perspective. In this way, JB was learning to listen to and trust the information that his physiology (i.e., his "gut") was trying to tell him. Additionally, he was able to benefit from bringing mindful awareness to the physical pain in his hip in much the same way that is described in the work of Jon Kabat-Zinn in *Full Catastrophe Living* (1990). As a consequence, JB was surprised at how he was able to hold a level of acceptance about his pain and live with it in a more embodied way in recovery.

8

Substance Abuse Counseling with Older Adult Males (Ages 60 and Above)

The unfortunate truth about older adult males who are entering substance abuse treatment at age 60 or above is that if they have had a lifetime of chemical abuse, then there is a high likelihood that there will be physical health issues that will need to be addressed immediately, even before discussing the psychological, emotional, and relational aspects of their lives that will be central to their treatment. Years of saturating their bodies and brains with alcohol and/or other drugs have serious implications for their neurophysiology and for the health of their major organs (brain, heart, liver, etc.). Some of the apparent psychological and emotional challenges that we will see in the beginning of treatment may stem directly from biological causes, e.g., the physical health issues related to substance abuse and poor nutrition like thiamine deficiency, which can be addressed through a change in diet and nutritional supplements that will aid in the recovery of mental capacities. Therefore, as it should be with every client that enters substance abuse treatment, it is imperative to have a full physical check-up to begin to address the physical health challenges of older adult males.

Once the physical health issues are stabilized, we can start to examine how he is facing the normal developmental challenges of his current life, while looking back over his lifespan with a goal of bringing compassionate understanding and acceptance to the social and emotional consequences of his substance abuse and addictive behaviors. This process can be increasingly challenging with age as depression and grief issues are a common occurrence among this population of older men.

One potential barrier that may surface related to male socialization processes are the internal prohibitions that these older adult males may have related to having feelings of sadness (Lynch & Kilmartin, 1999), grief (Rabinowitz & Cochran, 2002), or shame and fear (Park, 2006). If they are of a generation, or have a cultural background, that defined strong men as being stoic and women as being the bearers of emotion, then they may try to "convince themselves that they are not experiencing feelings and therefore do not express them" (Wong & Rochlen, 2005, p. 63).

As a gender-responsive professional, we can recognize when these older adult males may be essentially putting the cap on their emotional experiences. When we see this process happening, we can explore what it may mean for them as a male to begin to talk about the normal developmental challenges of this stage of life. We can expect that there will be an emotional component to the discussion because "normal development" at this psychosocial stage includes gaining a sense of acceptance of one's life and developing a point of view about death (Newman & Newman, 2012). Although this type of discussion can be difficult as it brings up the often intense emotional responses associated with death and dying, it may also help to increase a sense of urgency to redirect newfound energies in recovery towards discovering new activities and new (or renewed) roles related to work (paid or volunteer), family, and leisure.

In addition to coping with the physical changes of aging and the potential end of life issues, this process of exploring one's life from an autobiographical perspective (using visual developmental timelines, pictures, self-descriptions at various life stages, etc.) to create coherent narratives of one's life can give these older males a "psychohistorical perspective" in both looking back and moving forward as they "travel through uncharted terrain" (Newman & Newman, 2012). Creating this birds-eye point of view on their life can help give them the vision to see ways in recovery to deepen the enjoyment of their life in the present moment. It can also provide them with a balanced viewpoint on how they can measure the "progress" of their life in treatment and into recovery. A long-term developmental perspective that spans their lifetime can adjust the measuring stick against which they view "achievement" in their lives, i.e., how they defined success in the past versus how they view it in the present (or will view it in the future).

Lastly, even in the face of the major gender role transitions that are related to being an older adult male, i.e., the decision to withdraw from one's primary occupation, work, or career (retirement), experiencing decreasing levels of energy (loss of stamina), and dealing with the end of life and giving up ultimate control (facing death) (O'Neil & Egan, 1992), there is the encouraging notion of the neuroplasticity of the brain (Siegel, 2007). From a neurobiological perspective, people of all ages can benefit from repeating positive experiences, such as having secure nurturing relationships, doing aerobic exercise or exercising the mind with intellectually vigorous material, enjoying novel experiences, or simply focusing our attention, and/or being emotionally and passionately aroused by people or places that have significance and meaning to them. Even after a lifetime of substance abuse, if these types of experiences are repeated in recovery, then there is hope for improving mental and emotional capacity as the neural structure and function of our brains can continue to change in positive ways throughout our lives.

In short, describing this process can provide a sense of hope for change. The simple message that can be conveyed about the hope of neuroplasticity for older adult males is this: No matter what your age, the more that you stimulate healthy neural pathways in the brain and body (through the intrapersonal and interpersonal skills of recovery) the more that you will feel a general sense of health, wholeness, and integrity.

JOE (AGE 62): A DEVELOPMENTAL CASE STUDY

Imagine that you are a substance abuse counselor working for the Veterans Administration (VA) in an outpatient addiction and co-occurring treatment facility. You use a combination of motivational enhancement strategies, Twelve-Step facilitation, pharmacotherapy and cognitive-behavioral therapy. The following information was gathered after a first assessment session with Joe using the Addiction Severity Index (ASI; McLellan, Luborsky, O'Brien, & Woody, 1980). All quotes below are Joe's unless otherwise indicated.

Joe is a 62-year-old African American male, and a decorated Vietnam War veteran, who is self-referred because he is afraid that he is about to lose his third wife and his business because of his alcoholic drinking patterns and gambling behaviors. He reports that he was addicted to heroin in Vietnam, but promptly quit without treatment when he returned to the United States after the war. His was hoping to retire at age 62, but he is no longer in a financial position to do so. He has eight children from three wives, ranging in age from 15 to 40. He has five grandchildren.

Joe says that he has to "take care of business," stating: "All I have to do is stop drinking the way that I quite heroin when I was 25. The problem is that my wife doesn't think I can do it by myself." He added: "Losing my health, my business, and my wife are my main concerns ... and not necessarily in that order."

Psychosocial Case Presentation of Joe

Medical Status

Joe is 5'11" and 240 lbs. He had a complete physical at the VA hospital prior to entering treatment which revealed that he has high blood pressure (145 over 95) and esophageal hemorrhaging, as well as elevated blood sugar and liver enzymes. Additionally, his cholesterol and tri-glyceride levels were higher than normal for a male of his age. Joe was wounded in combat and has a limp that has gotten progressively worse over time for which he often uses a cane. He reports having some pain; however, he refuses to take any pain medication because of his prior addiction to heroin.

Employment/Support Status

After his service in the military, Joe found that he was unable to find work in his mid-20s, which he blames on "people's racism, and igno-rance about combat veterans." Subsequently, he decided to take advan-tage of the GI bill and went to the local community college to study business management. During this time, he worked as a short-order cook in a local restaurant. When he completed his associate's degree, with the support of family and a business loan, he opened a diner that, over time, became a success. It was Joe's personality, i.e., his charm and sense of humor that apparently played a large role in his success in busi-ness. At one point, Joe had three diners that were thriving, however, his substance abuse and gambling behaviors resulted in mismanagement of the business, and he now only has one diner remaining.

Alcohol/Drugs

Joe was an avid athlete as an adolescent, which served as a protective factor against substance abuse in the urban environment of his youth. However, at the age of 17 he began drinking alcohol moderately with his friends on the weekends. He did not smoke cigarettes or try any of the drugs that were available (primarily marijuana) and being used by his peer adolescent group. After high school, he was drafted into the war, and began drinking more heavily with his buddies in his army unit. In Vietnam, he was wounded in a battle that left him with an injured leg and hip joint. It was during this time that he became dependent on opiates, beginning with morphine, which he used to relieve his physical pain, and progressing to daily heroin use once he rejoined his unit and the morphine use was discontinued.

Joe reports that when he returned to the states he saw the extent of his heroin addiction "through the eyes of my family," meaning that in returning to the context of his youth, he did not recognize himself and "made the decision to just go cold turkey." He said that he asked his wife and parents to "lock me in a room until I came out straight." His family did not hide the fact that they were doing this for Joe, and apparently, it was this relatively public detoxification process that helped to keep him accountable after the heroin had left his system.

Joe's intake of alcohol increased as he got a license to serve beer and wine in his diners. Additionally, he was working long hours "on my feet," and with increased weight gain from overeating, and a lack of exercise, the pain in his hip increased. Over time, he reports that he began to drink daily as part of a routine to deal with stress from work and family life, as well as the pain in his hip. In the months leading up to his intake at the VA, his alcohol consumption peaked at a fifth of alcohol during the morning and afternoon hours (which he hid from public view) and approximately six to eight beers in the evening hours with patrons at his diner.

At admission, Joe showed signs of tolerance and withdrawal and required a medically supervised detoxification process through the VA medical system. Additionally, Joe has a pattern of engaging in sports betting in a bingeing fashion that sporadically has resulted in his owing large debts to several bookies in the area. In fearing for his life and the safety of his family, he has sold-off business assets and personal items in order to pay off these gambling debts.

Family/Social Relationships

Joe was raised in an urban area "in a tough neighborhood," the second oldest of four boys. He was a star athlete at his high school and had hoped to play baseball in college. However, his family did not have the resources to pay for higher education and, as he was drafted into the army at age 18, he was never able to pursue this dream.

Joe's father worked in an automobile manufacturing plant and was laid off when Joe was a teenager. He reports that his father moved to another city for work and was "an alcoholic womanizer" but never home after he was laid off from the local plant. Joe feels that his father abandoned his family and stated that "this is why I have always supported my kids financially, even though my wives didn't want me around them all that often."

Joe married his first wife prior to leaving for Vietnam, which he said was a "hasty decision based on the fact that she was pregnant" with his first daughter. When he returned from the war, they had a second child, a boy, who is Joe's namesake. As Joe's business ventures began to succeed, he repeatedly began to stay out late at night. He reports that his first wife "cheated on me" with another man during this period. Given Joe's fathers' history of infidelity, he quickly decided that he could never trust her again and divorced her, but did not pursue custody of his two children.

Several years later, he decided to marry a woman that worked as a waitress in one of his diners. Over a 5-year period, they had three children, two daughters and a son. When Joe began drinking heavily and gambling, his second wife filed for divorce. Joe stated that she "nearly took the shirt off my back," i.e., in order to pay his gambling debts, and pay child support and alimony for two wives, he had to sell one of his diners. He was able to stop gambling and reduce his drinking to some extent after this second divorce.

Subsequently, he met his third wife who was also a waitress at one of his remaining two diners and they had two twin boys who are now 15 years old. Joe states that his sons are "starting to run with the wrong crowd." Increased drinking and a return to gambling behaviors have resulted in Joe having to sell his second diner. Additionally, his third wife is threatening to divorce him "if things don't change." Joe feels that he is at a crossroads both physically and spiritually in his life, and that most importantly to him, he is concerned about losing the important roles of husband "to the woman of my dreams" and a father "to my twin boys."

Legal Status

Joe has one charge of Driving Under the Influence (DUI) pending. He reports having several "close calls" over the years in which he was pulled over by the police, but was able to "talk them out of giving me a ticket" because they were regular patrons at his diners. His popularity as a colorful local personality was beginning to wane because he was often intoxicated in public, and the police were apparently no longer tolerating his drinking and driving behaviors.

Psychiatric Status

Joe has never been diagnosed with a mental disorder; however, he reports that "there are times when I just don't want to get up out of the bed in the morning" and "if it weren't for my wife and boys, I don't think that I would want to go on." An assessment for suicidal ideation revealed that Joe was not a threat to himself or others at the time of intake. Further evaluation for depression will continue as treatment for Alcohol Dependence progresses.

A Developmentally-Informed, Gender-Responsive Approach with Joe

Understanding Brain-States and Self-Traits

Joe's motivations for being in substance abuse treatment at age 62 were complicated. He felt like he could "kick the alcohol habit" the same way that he had "kicked the heroin habit" years before. Speaking to the admissions counselor, he said: "Just get the alcohol completely out of my system, and I'll be fine." His wife, who was over 20 years younger than him, felt differently. She had seen Joe try to cut back only to return to drinking heavily in a matter of days. Joe knew from experiencing the loss of his first two wives to divorce, and from losing two out of three of his businesses, that he was "at the end of his rope." So in doing a decisional balance worksheet (SAMHSA, 2002) to look at the costs and benefits of stopping drinking versus not stopping, Joe was able to see that he was facing major losses of "practically everything that I have worked for in my life – my business, my family, and my dignity."

Even though these were major psychosocial concerns for Joe, treatment started with addressing his physical health issues. The reason for this primary initial focus was that years of alcohol dependence had taken a toll on Joe's physical health, and he seemed to be unaware of how serious these challenges were, not only for his quality of life, but also his longevity. First, he was downplaying the impact of the combination of high blood pressure and higher than normal cholesterol and triglyceride levels on his risk for heart disease and stroke. Second, he had elevated blood sugar levels that indicated that he may be at risk for Type II diabetes. Third, he had elevated liver enzymes and esophageal hemorrhaging, which are signs that he had cirrhosis of the liver. Lastly, he had physical pain in his body from war wounds that were only exacerbated by all of the aforementioned physical health challenges.

In light of these physical consequences alone, it became apparent to Joe that even though heroin was a dangerous drug to be addicted to, and difficult to quit when he returned from Vietnam, he was "facing a whole different animal" with chronic alcohol dependence at his age. The medical doctor on staff at the VA had explained these high risk areas to him, and he was left with an even greater reason to abstain from alcohol than losing his wife and business—he was possibly facing the loss of his life.

Joe described his state of mind after hearing the news about his physical health problems as "being all over the place." He said that one minute he was feeling better physically after detoxification and convincing himself that he could go home and "just deal with it on his own," and the next he was "feeling depressed" because he knew that he needed professional help to mend the damage to his body and his mind.

Joe had entered the VA to get through the detoxification process and "just go home." Instead, he was confronted with the possibility of his own death if he "slipped up again." In reality, he was also facing the normal psychosocial developmental tasks of his age group, i.e., the challenge of gaining a sense of acceptance of his life and developing a point of view about his own death (Newman & Newman, 2012). The combination of drinking heavily, working long hours, gambling, marrying women much younger than him, and having children in his 50s, had left him with the false sense that he would "easily live well into my 80s." Although the discussion was difficult, reality was setting in that he was aging and that death and dying issues were creating a sense of urgency in Joe to see this treatment process as "a final wake-up call."

Educating Males about Emotions

In outpatient group counseling, when the idea that human emotions were part of a system that provides information that helps us to survive and thrive was discussed, Joe laughed out loud, saying: "That is the absolute truth! I can tell you from experience that I did not pay attention to my emotions, and I nearly died." Joe was also able to identify in individual counseling specific incidents in the past 5 years where he had ignored feelings in his body that would have given him a clue that he needed to address his physical health issues.

Even though Joe was intrinsically motivated to pay attention to his feelings in treatment, he admitted that with years of only allowing himself to feel anger or pride, having and moving through feelings of fear, sadness, shame, and vulnerability were a challenge to his notion's about what a man should both feel and express to his peers. Because the group composition was all male veterans, there was a camaraderie that helped the individual members of the group to feel safe enough to move beyond the gender role restrictions that they were able to identify and discuss in the group process related to emotional restrictiveness and its consequences on men's physical and mental health.

Conceptual and Embodied Self-Awareness: Monitoring Me-States of Mind

Joe claimed after he found out how serious his health issues were that his "compulsion to drink had completely lifted." Rather than challenge this viewpoint in order to insist that his treatment focus on relapse prevention skills (e.g., managing cravings, urges, and thoughts of using substances) (Daley & Marlatt, 2006), the staff instead honored this revelation and sought to direct his newfound energies in recovery towards helping Joe to deepen this feeling of stability in recovery *in his body*, which he had been neglecting for such a long time.

Efforts to teach Joe mindful breathing and body scan activities resulted in him falling quickly to sleep. This result was not a wasted effort, however, because prior to coming into treatment, Joe was having difficulties both falling and staying asleep—situations to which he responded by drinking alcohol to "settle my nerves." Therefore, Joe used the focused breathing and body scans to help him to fall asleep each night.

Being more active athletically (to the extent that it was possible) seemed to be the answer to finding ways to increase Joe's embodied self-awareness. He had loved to play baseball when he was an adolescent. Since he had twin teenage sons who were interested in sports, Joe took advantage of this opportunity and began going to the ballpark and batting cage with them on a regular basis. He also used his connections in the community and was able to occasionally "take the field" at the local semi-pro baseball arena, which his sons were thrilled to be able to do. Additionally, given his war injuries, Joe decided that swimming on a regular basis would be the best activity for him to do "long-term to me keep fit." After a follow-up physical, the medical staff cleared Joe to get into the pool several times a week and begin to slowly rebuild his stamina.

Interestingly, even though Joe was feeling confident that he would abstain from alcohol, the trips to the local baseball arena had triggered thoughts and cravings in him to try to gamble again "just for fun." Fortunately, because of Joe's trust in his counselor and his deep feeling of integrity and connection that had developed in relation to the men in the group counseling process, he was able to talk about these urges. He responded well to suggestions to attend Gamblers Anonymous (GA) in his local community. Although the gambling process felt very different to Joe than his alcohol abuse, he was able to transfer some of the skills that he had learned in substance abuse counseling to his urges to gamble (e.g., managing emotions). Additionally, psycho-educational processes in the outpatient counseling setting demonstrated the similarities in terms of the neurobiology of addiction between chemical and process addictions, specifically the "sight of action" in the mesolimbic dopamine system in the brain.

Educating Males about "Others": Modulating Me-, You-, and We-States of Mind

Joe said that he felt "really out of touch" with his friends and extended family. Over the years, he had simply placed "drinking, work, and gambling" before these relationships that had been important to him earlier in his life. Therefore, in addition to learning how to cope with the physical changes of aging and the potential end of life issues that he was facing, he also used the exercise in Appendix E, "Looking Back to Plan Ahead: Setting Personal Goals" (for older adult males) to explore his life from an autobiographical perspective.

Joe used the questions in the exercise to write a narrative description of his life. He hoped to put together something from his writings that he could pass on to his wife and children, because he realized that "they don't know the half of my story." This process helped Joe to create a coherent narrative of his life, i.e., it helped him to "put things into perspective," and gave him an emotional sense of who he would like to try to reconnect with in his life. For example, there were some people with whom he identified as having harmed in some way (e.g., people that he knew that he needed to make amends to in his Twelve-Step work in AA and GA). And there were some people with whom he had simply lost touch over the years. Discussing the process of deciding who to contact, and who to make amends to, flowed naturally into an educational piece about the differences between me-, you-, and we-states of mind. Each of these states provided different viewpoints on the reasons for connecting or making amends. Joe realized that the ultimate decision to contact someone or not would be best decided after considering each viewpoint carefully and doing a reality check, i.e., by discussing his decision with people that he trusted in recovery.

Learning to Check-In (Not Out)

Being a former soldier, Joe typically followed orders. And in the case of his treatment and recovery processes, he tried with the same due diligence to follow the suggestions that his counselors made related to developing a personalized Check-In System. Joe practiced the system outlined in Appendix A and used the process in combination with AA's Tenth Step that states: "Continued to take personal inventory and when we were wrong promptly admitted it" (Alcoholics Anonymous, 1976, p. 60). Joe said that he found as he did this check-in process on a daily basis that it helped to supplement his Twelve-Step recovery process, i.e., that it was "keeping me honest," and "helping to keep me focused on what matters" in treatment and recovery.

GRAY (AGE 67): A DEVELOPMENTAL CASE STUDY

Imagine that you are a licensed mental health professional in private practice that sees individuals with primarily adjustment disorders, developmental transition issues, and/or mild to moderate mental disorders. You had a modest level of training in substance abuse and addiction counseling during your graduate program (i.e., two courses and a number of supervised cases during your clinical training sequence). Even though you are not licensed or certified specifically as a substance abuse professional, you do feel that providing individual counseling as part of a treatment and discharge aftercare plan for individuals with a history of substance abuse is within the scope of practice of your mental health license.

You have recently received a call from a woman named Betsy. She is in her early 50s and would like you to see her uncle who is apparently suffering from Major Depression. His name is Gray, and he is a 67-year-old Caucasian American of Scottish decent. He is a divorced male whose mood has been stabilized after a brief stay in an inpatient mental health facility. Gray has been prescribed and is taking an antidepressant medication that has been found both to elevate depressed moods and alleviate cravings for nicotine.

Gray describes himself as a recovering alcoholic whose chief complaint is that he has "a niece that should mind her own business." The information that follows was gathered in an initial consultation session with both Betsy and Gray in a conjoint family session. In this initial interview, Gray appeared to be guarded during the session and provided only minimal personal information. However, by the end of the consultation session, there was mutual agreement that Gray would begin individual counseling twice a week, take his medication as prescribed, and continue to attend Twelve-Step meetings as often as he would like, which he had been doing continuously for a number of years.

Psychosocial Case Presentation of Gray

Medical Status

Gray is approximately 5'10" and 180 lbs. He reports that he suffers from emphysema. His breathing is visibly labored and he appears to be motivated to "try to quit smoking again." He reports that he has been hospitalized multiple times in the past for either "a brief stay in detox because of the shakes" or pain from a swollen liver and pancreatitis.

Employment/Support Status

Gray is a retired English professor who receives monthly checks from a retirement pension and has access to both Medicare and retirement benefits. He received both his undergraduate and graduate education at a well-known and highly respected university in the United States. He currently volunteers to teach adults who are learning how to read for the first time.

Alcohol/Drugs

Gray appears to have a history of polysubstance abuse. However, he says that his primary drug of choice "has always been alcohol." He openly disclosed that he has been sober for the last 5 years ("one of many 3- to 5-year stints in AA") and has been attending AA and "working the program regularly," which was defined by him as "sponsoring people and attending meetings" on a regular basis at his AA "home group." He currently does not have a sponsor of his own, but does report sponsoring "several young men in the program." Gray also reports that he has smoked cigarettes for "the last 50 years on and off" and that he was addicted to prescription medications (i.e., primarily benzodiazepines, such as Xanax and Valium) "for about 20 years," having stopped using prescription drugs at the same time that he quit drinking alcohol 5 years ago. Additionally, he says that he tried "everything under the sun in the 70s" (e.g., marijuana, LSD, psilocybin mushrooms) and that he "had a brief period where cocaine was all the rage in my social circles in the 80s." Gray said that "cocaine was the worst for me" because it left him depressed for days after a binge-type using pattern. He states: "Alcohol was always the thing that I turned to the most to settle down after one of my weekend binges on coke."

Family/Social Relationships

Gray says that he has an older sister in her mid-70s (Betsy's mother) with whom his is very close. He reports that he was "married once, but that was a big mistake." He has no children from this marriage that lasted for approximately 2 years when he was in his mid-20s. His social support system is his AA home group, and he says that he "mentors" young men in AA. With this disclosure in the initial consultation session, his niece appeared to be visibly upset. She said that she thinks that part of the reason that Gray had a recent "set-back" and had to be hospitalized for depression and suicidal ideation was the fact that one of Gray's sponsees, with whom Gray was very close, relapsed and "ran off with one of the young girls in the program." Gray admitted that this was troubling for him, but said that his niece was "making too much out of this." Betsy stated emphatically that her uncle needed to "talk to somebody about these relationships with these young men." The implication of her statement seemed to be that Gray was a closeted homosexual who was not being honest about his sexuality, and in particular about his relationships with his male sponsees in AA. When asked if she would consider commenting further about her concerns, Betsy said: "No ... that is something that Uncle Gray will need to get into with you." Gray stated again that "my niece worries too much about me," and "if we need to talk about my sexuality at my age, then so be it. But I have not behaved inappropriately with anyone in AA."

Legal Status

Gray has had a number of arrests for public intoxication. He has had one Driving While Intoxicated (DWI) charge that occurred when he was in his early 30s. He also added that he has several arrests for "civil disobedience ... it was the 60s for God's sake."

Psychiatric Status

As indicated above, Gray has been suffering from Major Depression (for which he is taking an anti-depressant medication), has a history of Alcohol Dependence (which appears to be in remission at present), and has abused other illicit and prescription drugs to varying degrees depending on the context at different points throughout his life. The documentation that was requested from Gray's most recent inpatient stay included statements by the referring psychologist about Gray's "narcissistic tendencies," and his "ability to rationalize away any feedback about the antecedents of his latest Major Depressive episode."

A Developmentally-Informed, Gender-Responsive Approach with Gray

Understanding Brain-States and Self-Traits

Gray began his first individual counseling session by stating that he was only there to appease his niece: "I guess I should be grateful that I have someone looking in after me ... but I'm not." Gray presented as "the old curmudgeon"; however, he also had a look in his eyes that was more of a combination of sadness and cunning rather than bitterness. Because of his "mandated" status, the initial conversation focused on some of the highlighted areas from the consultation session, e.g., his participation in AA, his career as a professor, and his choice to move back to his home-town when he retired. Gray was obviously feeling out the counseling relationship and deciding whether he would return. In this initial session, some of the questions from the "Looking Back to Plan Ahead: Setting Personal Goals" exercise for older adult males (Appendix E) were being asked in reverse order to engage Gray about his life.

Gray did return to counseling, and it took several sessions to work backward in time to gather some information about his earlier life experiences. He admitted that he was homosexual and that as a young man he had "tried to marry a woman to hide this fact," because his parents "held deep religious convictions" and "would have never accepted the fact that I was gay." Gray felt that he had hurt his ex-wife deeply and that, as a consequence, he had "decided long ago to give up trying to live up to other people's expectations."

Gray expressed that his most recent 5-year period of recovery had been relatively stable until he "fell into" the major depressive state. He was able to admit that he had felt intense love for his sponsee who had relapsed and "ran off with the young maiden." However, Gray insisted that he did not consider these relationships with his sponsees "to be of a sexual nature," and he was obviously disturbed and embarrassed that his niece had thought that he might be "that dishonest and deceptive." Importantly, he was able to identify the intense feelings of sadness, loneliness, and abandonment that came from this event as being the triggers for his recent major depressive episode. Also of significance was the fact that he did not relapse to alcohol and/or other drug abuse in response to his intense emotional pain. This was considered a "success" for his recovery efforts, particularly when he thought about the number of times that he had been able to maintain sobriety for a 3- to 5-year period only to have an emotionally charged event "send me spinning right back to the bottle."

Because most of the emotionally laden events that Gray spoke about that had led to his relapses in his past were centered on romantic relationships, several assessment instruments related to adult attachment styles were provided for Gray. They were the "Attachment Style Questionnaire" (ASQ) (Feeney, Noller, & Hanrahan, 1994) and the Experiences in Close Relationships Scale (ECR) (Brennan, Clark, & Shaver, 1998). Additionally, when the therapeutic relationship progressed to the point where Gray was engaged in the process enough to complete a homework assignment, he was given the "Looking Back to Plan Ahead: Setting Personal Goals" exercise for older adult males (Appendix E). In addition to providing attachment and relational history for Gray, the assessments and the developmental questionnaire also helped to get a sense of how he had struggled with his sexuality throughout his life.

The picture that emerged from the assessments showed a mixed attachment strategy, i.e., Gray scored relatively high on both anxious and avoidant dimensions of the assessments. In the literature, this pattern of scoring suggests a fearful avoidant style of attachment that derives from "a failure to achieve any of the goals of the major attachment strategies: safety and security following proximity seeking (the primary, secure strategy), defensive deactivation of the attachment system (the avoidant strategy), or intense and chronic activation of the attachment system until security-enhancing proximity is attained (the anxious strategy)" (Mikulincer & Shaver, 2007, p. 43). Research also indicates that this style of attachment is associated with "especially negative representations of their romantic partners," being "cognitively closed and rigid," and exhibiting "the least empathy for people who are distressed" (p. 43).

The "Looking Back to Plan Ahead" exercise also revealed a family history that may have set the stage for this adult attachment style. For example, Gray's parents were upper-middle class, highly educated and prominent adults in their community. They sent Gray and his older sister to private boarding schools as adolescents, which Gray reported "was a blessing" because his father was verbally and physically abusive at home and his mother would often vacillate between being "a social butterfly" in the community and "locking herself away in her room" with apparent depression and alcohol dependence. Gray said that his older sister had met "a wonderful man and found her own Shangri-La," but that he had not been able to have a long-term stable relationship in his life. Furthermore, Gray described his father as a "very traditional man who loathed homosexuals" and who wanted a son that would carry on the family business (real estate development). Instead, Gray said that "he got a son who loved poetry and other boys." Despite the fact that these socialization experiences had happened long ago, Gray realized that they were repeated states of being that had resulted in his developing a depressive affect and a residual sense of self-loathing.

Educating Males about Emotions

It was obvious to a man of Gray's intelligence and life-experiences that his emotional states were central to his mental health and recovery. However, because Gray had consciously chosen to live as a closeted homosexual for his entire life, he had created an outward persona that would be considered by many to be that of a highly traditional man. He did not want to be seen as what he described as a "stereotypical gay man." Instead, he presented as an intellectual stoic who allowed his emotional self to show in public only when he was reciting poetry. Even when he did this, he avoided sounding effeminate and would instead speak in a slow, measured tone with a deep voice. He remembered bristling at critiques of his poetry readings that implied that he was "stiff" and "dry," because he felt anything but that on the inside.

Educating Gray about the centrality of the structures in the brain related to emotion fell on deaf ears. He was not interested in understanding brain structures and function. However, he did have a passion for poetry. And so as the therapeutic relationship progressed, Gray began to share his poetry in sessions and allowed himself to express intense emotions as he read and discussed the feelings that he was conveying in his poetry. From a neurobiological perspective, the space was being created in the therapy room, and within the person-to-person counseling relationship, for Gray to integrate emotion and logic through using language and the arts (which in terms of brain science represents both right- and left-hemisphere modes of processing and involves the "top to bottom" neural integration of the circuitry related to self-regulation). In this process, a responsive therapeutic relationship was helping him to amend a painful attachment history and to create a more coherent and integrated narrative of his life.

Conceptual and Embodied Self-Awareness: Monitoring Me-States of Mind

Reciting poetry in front of another human being that touched on a great emotional depth within Gray was a fully embodied experience for him. He reported feeling "truly alive" for the first time in his life. The persona that he had presented to the world felt "like a lie" and represented Gray's conceptual sense of self that he had created that was not congruent with his embodied self-awareness. In essence, he had been living as a "false self," which was contributing to his chronic feeling of self-loathing. Gray was experiencing what Siegel (2001) described in his seminal work, *The Developing Mind*: "If people become stuck and disabled, if they are filled with adaptive specialized selves without a sense of authenticity, or if they are filled with intense and unresolved conflicts across self-states, then the development of a specific process that integrates the selves across time may become important" (p. 231). As shocking as it was for Gray as a 67-year-old man to experience, the interpersonal relationship of "being seen" reading poetry in counseling started a process of transformation in terms of his self-organization. Whether he wanted to move this emotionally expressive process into other social realms became the question.

Educating Males about "Others": Modulating
Me-, You-, and We-States of Mind

The challenge in the months following Gray's realization (i.e., that he had lacked embodied self-awareness for most of his life) was to "come out" into public as a fully embodied homosexual man. Discussions focused on the merits of doing this "at my age." How would this affect his professional reputation and legacy as a poet? How might this change his relationship with his niece and his ability to participate in AA? Would he really act any differently? Over the course of time, Gray tried "experiments in being himself" in public. He found that his niece was delighted. In AA, he was met with mixed reactions. Some were happy that he was able to be himself. Others exhibited homophobia and became more standoffish towards him.

However, through this process Gray realized that he was feeling increasingly comfortable in his body, and that he had fewer days of depressive feelings and fewer thoughts of using substances. Importantly, he felt that his relationships in recovery were no longer remaining on a superficial level and that people really knew and appreciated him for who he was becoming.

Learning to Check-In (Not Out)

Prior to the start of counseling, Gray rarely left the confines of his home, except to go to AA meetings and the grocery store. As he deepened his relationship with himself and others, he found that he was accepting more invitations for coffee, lunch, and other social engagements. Gray also found that his way of checking-in was to take a walk in the park and to write poetry outdoors by the lake or in the woods. In this way, Gray found a sense of spirituality and a deepening, embodied feeling of enjoyment in his life.

References

Alcoholics Anonymous. (1976). *Alcoholics anonymous: The story of how many thousands of men and women have recovered from alcoholism* (3rd ed.). New York City: Alcoholics Anonymous World Services, Inc.

American Psychiatric Association. (2000). *Diagnostic and statistical manual of mental disorders* (4th ed., text rev.). Washington, DC: Author.

Bachman, J. G., O'Malley, P. M., Schulenberg, J. E., Johnston, L. D., Bryant, A. L., & Merline, A. C. (2002). *The decline of substance use in young adulthood: Changes in social activities, roles, and beliefs. Research monographs in adolescence.* Mahwah, NJ: Erlbaum.

Badenoch, B. (2008). *Being a brain-wise therapist: A practical guide to interpersonal neurobiology.* New York: Norton.

Berger, S. B. (2010). *Invitation to the lifespan.* New York: Worth Publishers.

Brady, K. T., Back, S. E., & Greenfield, S. F. (Eds.). (2009). *Women and addiction: A comprehensive handbook.* New York: Guilford Press.

Bowen, S., Chawla, N., & Marlatt, G. A. (2011). *Mindfulness-based relapse prevention for addictive behaviors: A clinician's guide.* New York: Guilford.

Brennan, K. A. Clark, C. L., & Shaver, P. R. (1998). Self-report measurement of adult romantic attachment: An integrative overview. In J. A. Simpson & W. S. Rholes (Eds.), *Attachment theory and close relationships* (pp. 46–76). New York: Guilford Press.

Brooks, G. R. (2010). *Beyond the crisis of masculinity: A transtheoretical model of male-friendly therapy.* Washington, DC: American Psychological Association.

Brooks, G. R., & Good, G. E. (Eds.). (2001a). *The new handbook of psychotherapy and counseling men: A comprehensive guide to settings, problems, and treatment approaches* (Vol. 1). San Francisco: Jossey-Bass.

Brooks, G. R., & Good, G. E. (Eds.). (2001b). *The new handbook of psychotherapy and counseling men: A comprehensive guide to settings, problems, and treatment approaches* (Vol. 2). San Francisco: Jossey-Bass.

Casey, B. J., & Jones, R. M. (2010). Neurobiology of the adolescent brain and behavior: Implications for substance use disorders. *Journal of the American Academy of Child and Adolescent Psychiatry, 49*(12), 1189–1201.

Chambers, R. A., Taylor, J. R., & Potenza, M. N. (2003). Developmental neuro-circuitry of motivation in adolescence: A critical period of addiction vul-nerability. *American Journal of Psychiatry, 160*(6), 1041–1052.

Childress, A. R. (2006). What can human brain imaging tell us about vulner-ability to addiction and to relapse? In W. R. Miller & K. M. Carroll (Eds.), *Rethinking substance abuse: What the science shows, and what we should do about it* (pp. 46–60). New York: Guilford.

Cochran, S. V. (2005). Evidence-based assessment with men. *Journal of Clinical Psychology, 61*(6), 649–660.

Conway, M. A., & Holmes, A. (2004). Psychosocial stages and the accessibil-ity of autobiographical memories across the life cycle. *Journal of Personality, 72*(3), 461–480.

Cozolino, L. (2006). *The human science of human relationships: Attachment and the developing social brain.* New York: Norton.

Crews, F., He, J., & Hodge, C. (2007). Adolescent cortical development: A criti-cal period of vulnerability for addiction. *Pharmacology, Biochemistry and Behavior, 86,* 189–199.

Daley, D. V., & Marlatt, G. A. (2006). *Overcoming your alcohol and drug problem: Effective recovery strategies: therapist guide* (2nd ed.). New York: Oxford Uni-versity Press.

DiClemente, C. C. (2003). *Addiction and change: How addictions develop and addicted people recover.* New York: Guilford Press.

Dimeff, L. A., & Koerner, K. (Eds.). (2007). *Dialetical behavior therapy in clinical practice: Applications across disorders and settings.* New York: Guilford Press.

Doweiko, H. E. (2009). *Concepts of chemical dependency* (7th ed.). Pacific Grove, CA: Brooks/Cole.

Eliot, L. (2009). *Pink brains, blue brains: How small differences grow into trou-blesome gaps – and what we can do about it.* New York: Houghton Mifflin Harcourt.

Englar-Carlson, M. (2006). Masculine norms and the therapy process. In M. Englar-Carlson & M. Stevens (Eds.), *In the room with men: A casebook of therapeutic change* (pp. 13–47). Washington, DC: American Psychological Association.

Erikson, E. H. (1963). *Childhood and society.* New York: Norton.

Erickson, C. K. (2007). *The science of addiction: From neurobiology to treatment.* New York: Norton.

Feeney, J. A., Noller, P., & Hanrahan, M. (1994). Assessing adult attachment. In M. B. Sperling & W. H. Berman (Eds.), *Attachment in adults: Clinical and developmental perspectives* (pp. 128–152). New York: Guilford Press.

Flores, P. J. (2004). *Addiction as an attachment disorder.* New York: Jason Aronson.

Fogel, A. (2009). *The psychophysiology of self-awareness: Rediscovering the lost art of body sense.* New York: Norton.

Fosha, D., Siegel, D. J., & Solomon, M. F. (Eds.). (2009). *The healing power of emotion: Affective neuroscience, development, & clinical practice.* New York: Norton.

Grossman, P., Niemann, L., Schmidt, S., & Walach, H. (2006). Mindfulness-based stress reduction and health benefits: A meta-analysis. *Journal of Psychosomatic Research, 57,* 35–43.

Haley, J. (1976). *Problem-solving therapy: New strategies for effective family therapy.* San Franscisco: Jossey-Bass.

Hasin, D, Hatzenbuehler, M., & Waxman, R. (2006). Genetics of substance use disorders. In W. R. Miller & K. M. Carroll (Eds.), *Rethinking substance abuse: What the science shows, and what we should do about it* (pp. 61–77). New York: Guilford Press.

Hayes, S. C., Luoma, J. B., Bond, F. W., Masuda, A., & Lillis, J. (2006). Acceptance and commitment therapy: model, processes and outcomes. *Behaviour Research and Therapy, 44,* 1–25.

Hayes, S. C., Strodahl, K. D., & Wilson, K. G. (2003). *Acceptance and commitment therapy: An experiential approach to behavior change.* New York: Guilford Press.

Hesselbeck, V. M., & Hesselbeck, M. N. (2006). Developmental perspectives on the risk for developing substance abuse problems. In W. R. Miller & K. M. Carroll (Eds.), *Rethinking substance abuse: What the science shows, and what we should do about it* (pp. 97–114). New York: Guilford Press.

Hogan, J. A., Gabrielsen, K. R., Luna, N., & Grothaus, D., (2003). *Substance abuse prevention: The intersection of science and practice.* Upper Saddle River, NJ: Pearson Education.

Horne, A. M., & Kiselica, M. S. (Eds.). (1999). *Handbook of counseling boys and adolescent males: A practitioner's guide.* Thousand Oaks, CA: Sage.

Hughes, D. (2009). The communication of emotions and the growth of autonomy and intimacy within family therapy. In D. Fosha, D. J. Siegel, M. F. Solomon (Eds.), *The healing power of emotion: Affective neuroscience, development, and clinical practice* (pp. 280–303). New York: Norton.

Isenhart, C. (2001). Treating substance abuse in men. In G. R. Brooks & G. E. Good (Eds.), *The new handbook of psychotherapy and counseling with men: A comprehensive guide to settings, problems, and treatment approaches* (pp. 246–262). San Francisco: Jossey-Bass.

Johnson, S. M. (2004). *The practice of emotionally focused couples therapy: Creating connection.* New York: Brunner-Routledge.

Johnston, L. D., O'Malley, P. M., Bachman, J.G., & Schulenberg, J. E. (2006). *Monitoring the Future national survey results on drug use, 1975–2005: Volume 1, Secondary school students* (NIH Publication No. 06-5883). Bethesda, MD: National Institute on Drug Abuse.

Johnston, L. D., O'Malley, P. M., Bachman, J .G., & Schulenberg, J. E. (2010). *Monitoring the Future national survey results on drug use, 1975–2009: Volume 1, Secondary school students* (NIH Publication No. 10-7584). Bethesda, MD: National Institute on Drug Abuse.

Kabat-Zinn, J. (1990). *Full catastrophe living: Using the wisdom of your mind to face stress, pain and illness.* New York: Dell.

Kabat-Zinn, J. (2003). Mindfulness-based interventions in context: Past, present and future. *Clinical Psychology: Science and Practice, 10*(2), 144–156.

Kassel, J. D., & Veilleux, J. C. (2010). Introduction: The complex interplay between substance abuse and emotion. In J. D. Kassel (Ed.), *Substance abuse and emotion* (pp. 3–12). Washington, DC: American Psychological Association.

Kilmartin, C. (2007). *The masculine self* (3rd ed.). Cornwall-on-Hudson, NY: Sloan Publishing.

Kiselica, M. S., Englar-Carlson, & Horne, A. M. (Eds.). (2008). *Counseling troubled boys: A guidebook for professionals.* New York: Routledge.

Kiselica, M. S. (2011). Promoting positive masculinity while addressing gender role conflict: A balanced theoretical approach to clinical work with boys and men. In C. Blazina & D. S. Shen-Miller (Eds.), *An international psychology of men: Theoretical advances, case studies, and clinical interventions* (pp. 127–156). New York: Routledge.

Koob, G. F., & Le Moal, M. (2006). *Neurobiology of addiction.* London: Elsevier.

Levant, R. F., Hirsch, L., Celentano, E., Cozza, T., Hill, S., MacEachern, et al. (1992). The male role: An investigation of norms and stereotypes. *Journal of Mental Health Counseling, 14,* 325–337.

Levant, R. F., & Pollack, W. S. (Eds.). (1995). *A new psychology of men.* New York: Basic Books.

Linehan, M. (1993). *Skills training manual for treating borderline personality disorder.* New York: Guilford Press.

Lynch, J., & Kilmartin, C. T. (1999). *The pain behind the mask: Overcoming masculine depression.* Binghamton, NY: Haworth.

Marlatt, G. A., & Donovan, D. M. (2005). *Relapse prevention: Maintenance strategies in the treatment of addictive behaviors.* New York: Guilford Press.

McGoldrick, M. (1985). *Genograms in family assessment.* New York: W.W. Norton & Company.

McLellan, A. T., Luborsky, L., O'Brien, C. P., & Woody, G. E. (1980). An improved diagnostic instrument for substance abuse patients: The Addiction Severity Index. *Journal of Nervous & Mental Diseases, 168,* 26–33.

Meyers, K., Hagan, T. A., Zanis, D., Webb, A., Frantz, J., Ring-Kurtz, S., et al. (1999). Critical issues in adolescent substance use assessment. *Drug and Alcohol Dependence, 55,* 235–246.

Mikulincer, M., & Shaver, P. R. (2007). *Attachment in adulthood: Structures, dynamics, and change.* New York: Guilford Press.

Miller, P. M. (Ed.). (2009). *Evidence-based addiction treatment.* New York: Elsevier.

Miller, W. R., & Rollnick, S. (2002). *Motivational interviewing: Preparing people for change* (2nd ed.). New York: Guilford Press.

Minuchin, S. (1974). *Families and family therapy.* Cambridge, MA: Harvard University Press.

Monti, P. M., Barnett, N. P, O'Leary, T. A., & Colby, S. M. (2001). Motivational enhancement for alcohol-involved adolescents. In P. M. Monti, S. M. Colby, & T. A. O'Leary (Eds.), *Adolescents, alcohol, and substance abuse: Reaching teens through brief interventions* (pp. 145–182). New York: Guilford Press.

Monti, P. M, Kadden, R. M., Rohsenow, D. J., Cooney, N. L., & Abrams, D. B. (2002). *Treating alcohol dependence: A coping skills training guide.* New York: Guilford Press.

Moore, T. (1994). *Soul mates: Honoring the mysteries of love and relationships.* New York: HarperCollins.

Mortola, P., Hiton, H., & Grant, S. (2008). *BAM! boys advocacy and mentoring: A leader's guide to facilitating strengths-based groups for boys, helping boys making better contact by making better contact with them.* New York: Routledge.

Naar-King, S., & Suarez, Mariann. (2011). *Motivational interviewing with adolescents and young adults.* New York: Guilford Press.

Newman, B. M., & Newman, P. R. (2012). *Development through life: A psychosocial approach* (11th ed.). Belmont, CA: Wadsworth Cengage Learning.

Office of Applied Studies. (2004). Results from the 2003 National Drug Survey on Drug Use and Health: National findings (DHHS Publication No. SMA 04-3964, NSDUH Series H-25). Rockville, MD: Substance Abuse and Mental Health Services Administration.

Ogden, P., Minton, K., & Pain, C. (2006). *Trauma and the body: A sensorimotor approach to psychotherapy.* New York: Norton.

O'Neil, J. M. (1981). Patterns of gender role conflict and strain: Sexism and fear of femininity in men's lives. *Personnel and Guidance Journal, 60,* 203–210.

O'Neil, J. M. (2006). Helping Jack heal his emotional wounds: The gender role conflict diagnostic schema. In M. Englar-Carlson & M. Stevens (Eds.), *In the room with men: A casebook of therapeutic change* (pp. 259–284). Washington, DC: American Psychological Association.

O'Neil, J. M. (2008). Summarizing 25 years of research on men's gender role conflict using the gender role conflict scale: New research paradigms and clinical implications. *The Counseling Psychologist, 36*(3), 358–445.

O'Neil, J. M., & Egan, J. (1992). Men's gender role transitions over the lifespan: Transformations and fears of femininity. *Journal of Mental Health Counseling, 14*(3), 305–324.

O'Neil, J. M., Good, G. E., & Holmes, S. (1995). Fifteen years of theory and research on men's gender role conflict: New paradigms for empirical research. In R. Levant & W. Pollack (Eds.), *The new psychology of men* (pp. 164–206). New York: Basic Books.

O'Neil, J. M., Helm, B., Gable, R., David, L., & Wrightsman, L. (1986). Gender Role Conflict Scale (GRCS): College men's fear of femininity. *Sex Roles, 14,* 335–350.

Panksepp, J. (2009). Brain emotional systems and qualities of mental life: From animal models of affect to implications for psychotherapeutics. In D. Fosha, D. J. Siegel, & M. F. Solomon (Eds.), *The healing power of emotion: Affective neuroscience, development, and clinical practice* (pp. 1–126). New York: Norton.

Park, S. (2006). Facing fear without losing face: Working with Asian American men. In M. Englar-Carlson & M. Stevens (Eds.), *In the room with men: A casebook of therapeutic change* (pp. 151–173). Washington, DC: American Psychological Association.

Park, M. J., Mulye, T. P., Adams, S. H., Brindis, C. D., & Irwin, C. E. (2006). The health status of young adults in the United States. *Journal of Adolescent Development, 39*, 305–317.

Pleck, J. H. (1981). *The myth of masculinity.* Cambridge, MA: MIT Press.

Pollack, W. S., & Levant, R. F. (1998). *New psychotherapy for men.* New York: Wiley.

Porges, S. W. (2009). Reciprocal influences between body and brain in the perception and expression of affect: A polyvagal perspective. In D. Fosha, D. Siegel, & M. Solomon, (Eds.), *The healing power of emotion: Affective neuroscience, development, and clinical practice* (pp. 27–54). New York: Norton.

Prochaska, J. O., & DiClemente, C. C. (1984). *The transtheoretical approach: Crossing the traditional boundaries of therapy.* Malabar, FL: Krieger.

Prochaska, J. O., DiClemente, C. C., & Norcross, J. C. (1992). In search of how people change: Applications to addictive behavior, *American Psychologist 47*(9), 1102–1114.

Rabinowitz, F. E., & Cochran, S. V. (2002). *Deepening psychotherapy with men.* Washington, DC: American Psychological Association.

Robert, T., & Kelly, V. A. (2010). Metaphor as an instrument for orchestrating change in counselor training and the counseling process. *Journal of Counseling and Development, 88*(2), 182–188.

Shore, A. N. (2003). *Affect regulation and disorders of the self.* New York: Norton.

Siegel, D. J. (1999). *The developing mind: Toward a neurobiology of interpersonal experience.* New York: Guilford Press.

Siegel, D. J. (2001). *The developing mind: How relationships and the brain interact to shape who we are.* New York: Guilford Press.

Siegel, D. J. (2006). An interpersonal neurobiology approach to psychotherapy: Awareness, mirror neurons, and neural plasticity in the development of well-being. *Psychiatric Annals, 36*(4), 247–258.

Siegel, D. J. (2007). *The mindful brain: Reflection and attunement in the cultivation of well-being.* New York: Norton.

Siegel, D. J. (2010). *Mindsight: The new science of personal transformation.* New York: Random House.

Siegel, D. J., & Hartzell, M. (2003). *Parenting from the inside out: How a deeper self-understanding can help you raise children who thrive.* New York: Tarcher/ Putnam.

Substance Abuse and Mental Health Services Administration (SAMHSA). (2002). Enhancing motivation for change in substance abuse treatment: Treatment improvement protocol (TIP) 35. U.S. Department of Health and Human Services. DHHS Publication No. (SMA) 08-4212.

Substance Abuse and Mental Health Services Administration (SAMHSA). (2009a). *Results from the 2008 National Survey on Drug Use and Health: National Findings* (Office of Applied Studies, NSDUH Series H-36, HHS Publication No. SMA 09-4434). Rockville, MD.

Substance Abuse and Mental Health Services Administration, Office of Applied Studies. (2009b). Treatment Episode Data Set (TEDS) Highlights — 2007 National Admissions to Substance Abuse Treatment Services. OAS Series #S-45, HHS Publication No. (SMA) 09-4360, Rockville, MD.

Substance Abuse and Mental Health Services Administration, Office of Applied Studies. (2009c). The TEDS Report: School System Referrals to Substance Abuse Treatment. Rockville, MD.

Sweet, H. (2006). Finding the person behind the persona: Engaging men as a female therapist. In M. Englar-Carlson & M. Stevens (Eds.), *In the room with men: A casebook of therapeutic change* (pp. 69–90). Washington, DC: American Psychological Association.

Tapert, S. F., & Schweinsburg, A. D. (2005). The human adolescent brain and alcohol use disorders. *Recent Developments in Alcoholism, 17,* 177–197.

Taylor, J. B. (2006). *My stroke of insight: A brain scientist's personal journey.* New York: Penguin Group.

Thatcher, D. L., & Clark, D. B. (2010). Neurobiological liability for adolescent substance use disorders. In L. M. Scheier (Ed.), *Handbook of drug use etiology: Theory, methods, and empirical findings* (pp. 209–224). Washington, DC: American Psychological Association.

Tronick, E. (2007). *The neurobehavioral and social-emotional development of infants and children.* New York: Norton.

Velasquez, M. M., Maurer, G. G., Crouch, C., & DiClemente, C. C. (2001). *Group treatment for substance abuse: A stages-of-change therapy manual.* New York: Guilford Press.

Vogel, D. L., Wade, N. G., Wester, S. R., Larson, L., & Hackler, A. H. (2007). Seeking help from a mental health professional: The influence of one's social network. *Journal of Clinical Psychology, 63*(3), 233–245.

Wallace, B. C. (2005). *Making mandated addiction treatment work.* New York: Jason Aronson.

Webster's New College Dictionary (3rd ed.). (2008). Boston: Houghton Mifflin.

Wills, T. A., & Ainette, M. G. (2010). Temperament, self-control, and adolescent substance use: A two-factor model of etiological processes. In L. M. Scheier (Ed.), *Handbook of drug use etiology: Theory, methods, and empirical findings.* (pp. 127–148). Washington, DC: American Psychological Association.

Wong, Y. J., & Rochlen, A. B. (2005). Demystifying men's emotional behavior: New directions and implications for counseling and research. *Psychology of Men and Masculinity, 6*(1), 62–72.

A

Check-In System

1. Check In

Hold _____ in your awareness and breathe down into your body. (You fill in the blank. It can be a difficult situation, a crisis event, an actual person's name, etc.)

Use your mind to scan yourself from head to toe for any sensations in your body.

Where are these sensations located physically in your body?

As you hold your attention on these bodily sensations, what images are coming to your mind (past memories, recent events, or future expectations)?

How do you feel about these images? What do you think about them?

2. Gut Check

Continue to hold these bodily sensations and images in your awareness.

If they are from the past, what does your gut tell you that you needed and valued the most at that time in your life?

If they are from the present, what does your gut tell you that you need and value the most right now?

If they are about the future, what does your gut tell you that you will need and value at that point in your life?

As you hold your needs and values in your awareness, what value-based actions can you take right now that will be your best efforts at *both*: (a) getting your needs met and (b) "doing the next right thing" in recovery?

3. Reality Check

What people and places do you trust as being safe to talk about what you need? Who can you speak openly with about what you value the most right now in your life?

Seek out those people and places that will respect your best efforts to act according to your emotional integrity. Talking with people that you trust and respect can help to give you some perspective and an objective viewpoint. It gives you a "reality check" on your needs and values.

If you are unable to identify or get in touch with specific people that you trust, then find a safe place where you can "come home to yourself" and gain a sense of stability and peace in the present moment. Journaling can be an excellent way to process through these sensations, images, feelings, and thoughts as they arise into your awareness.

B

Looking Back to Plan Ahead
Setting Personal Goals

AN EXERCISE FOR EARLY ADOLESCENT
MALES (AGES 12 TO 18)

The questions below are designed to start you thinking about setting personal goals for yourself. It asks you to look back over your life, so that you can see where you have come from, know where you are, and make plans for where you are going.

All you need is a pencil, paper, and the willingness to take a look at your life.

The questions are grouped together according to specific time periods in a person's life and should help you remember specific things that have happened in your life and get you thinking about your future and your personal goals.

As you read through the questions for a particular time period, write down your answers with as much detail as possible. For example, in writing down the descriptions of memories, make sure to include where you were at the time, what you were doing, who you were with, how you felt, and any other details that come to mind.

For the later time periods, write down at least three things that you hope to accomplish during that time in your life.

Take the time to really pause and think about your memories and about your future.

There is no time limit to complete this exercise.

Childhood (Ages 0–12)

Try to picture the home(s) of your childhood. If you are able, it can be helpful to find actual pictures of yourself as a young child.

What memories do you have of being, or wanting to be, helped, taught, or nurtured?

What were you doing when you were having fun? Where, when, and with whom did you play?

What memories do you have of encounters with your parents, family members, or teachers?
With whom did you feel the closest? When you were upset, feeling rejected, alone, or threatened in any way, to whom did you turn for help and support?

Did you experience any losses as a child?

Who from your childhood best represents what you thought it would mean to "be a man"?
This person(s) could be someone that you actually knew and/or someone from TV, movies, sports, comic books, etc.

Were there experiences in your childhood when you or your friends (or family members) were either being put down, or put someone else down, for being a "sissy," a "wimp," or "gay" (or some other derogatory name)?

Adolescence (Ages 13–19)

Think about your home and school life.

Who are your friends? Who would you say is your best friend?

What would you say have been your most important romantic or sexual experiences?

These could be brief encounters, fantasies, and/or relationships.

What have your dating experiences been like? If you haven't been on a date, where would you choose to go and who would you want to take?

When do you feel like you get recognition or acceptance from your friends and peers?

When have you felt disapproval or rejection from your friends and peers?

What experiences do you have of avoiding others or avoiding conflict?

When you think about the adults in your life, like your mother or your father, or other family members, or teachers, with whom who do you feel the closest?

When you are upset, feeling rejected, alone, or threatened in any way, to whom do you turn for help and support?

Have you experienced any losses as an adolescent?

If you could think of one person that you would say is a "real man," who would it be?
This person (or persons) could be someone that you actually know and/or someone from TV, movies, sports, comic books, etc.

Have you had experiences where you or your friends (or family members) were either put down, or put someone else down, for being a "sissy," a "wimp," or "gay" (or some other derogatory name)?

What are you noticing about the changes that are happening in your body, or the comments from others, that have to do with you physically becoming a young man?

What are your thoughts about getting work or having a career as an adult? Are there people in your life (or on TV or in movies) that you think have jobs that you would want as an adult?

How have alcohol and other drugs (and your expectations about them and their actual effects on you) played a role in shaping your "state of mind" about yourself and others, for example, with the physical changes in your body, your romantic or sexual experiences, and your sense of who you are in relationship to other people?

Young Adulthood (Ages 20–34)

What do you think your experiences might be like when you choose to leave home, go to school, get your first job, or find a sense of independence (or maybe not) from your family?

In young adulthood, being loved and giving love to others can become pretty important.
What qualities would you want in the person who you would choose to love and be loved by?
How would you want to show concern for that person? If you wanted them to show concern for you, how would you want them to do that?

Men in young adulthood may start to take on roles like being a "husband" or a "father."
What roles do you think you will find yourself in as a young man? What words would you use to describe yourself in these roles? Who might best represent someone with the qualities that you see as ideal in these roles? This person(s) could be someone that you actually know and/or someone from a TV show, a movie, a book, an historical figure, etc.

How do you think alcohol and other drugs might affect your decisions to leave home, go to school, or get a job? Do you think it will affect your close relationships and the possibility of marriage and parenthood?

Middle Adulthood (Ages 35–60)

Use your imagination to think about yourself as a middle-aged man (somewhere between the ages of 35 to 60 years old). Where do you think you will be living? Who do you think you will be living with? Try to picture this in your mind as clearly as you can.

How do you see yourself taking care of others who need it? Think about children, adults, employees, or animals.

How do you see yourself getting along with your loved ones, like your partner or wife, or your children or grandchildren? Do you think that they will have the opportunity to know who you are because you are able to let me know what you think and how you feel about things?

How do you see yourself being either concerned or unconcerned about the welfare of others (who are not your loved ones)?

Where will you be working? How do you think alcohol and other drugs might affect your "states of mind" as a middle age man who is trying to balance work and family life?

Later Adulthood (Ages 60 and above)

Imagine yourself as an older adult male who is over 60 years old. Where do you think that you will be living? Who do you think that you will be living with? Try to picture this in your mind as clearly as you can.

Will you still be working? Will you be retired?

How physically fit do you think you will be?

When you look back over your life as an older adult male, what do you think you will be feeling about how you chose to live your life?

How do you think you will be feeling about your own mortality (i.e., that you will die some day)?

How do you think alcohol and other drugs might affect your "state of mind" as an older adult male?

This exercise was developed based on materials from the following sources:

Conway, M. A., & Holmes, A. (2004). Psychosocial stages and the accessibility of autobiographical memories across the life cycle. *Journal of Personality, 72*(3), 461–480.

Mikulincer, M., & Shaver, P. R. (2007). *Attachment in adulthood: Structures, dynamics, and change.* New York: Guilford Press.

Newman, B. M., & Newman, P. R. (2012). *Development through life: A psychosocial approach* (11th ed.). Belmont, CA: Wadsworth Cengage Learning.

O'Neil, J. M. (2008). Summarizing 25 years of research on men's gender role conflict using the gender role conflict scale: New research paradigms and clinical implications. *The Counseling Psychologist, 36*(3), 358–445.

O'Neil, J. M., & Egan, J. (1992). Men's gender role transitions over the lifespan: Transformations and fears of femininity. *Journal of Mental Health Counseling, 14*(3), 305–324.

C

Looking Back to Plan Ahead

Setting Personal Goals

AN EXERCISE FOR LATE ADOLESCENT AND
YOUNG ADULT MALES
(AGES 18 TO 34)

The questions below are designed to facilitate a self-reflective process that will help you to set personal goals for yourself. It is often valuable to take a look back over your life, so that you can see where you have come from, know where you are, and make plans for where you are heading. All you need is a pencil, paper, and the willingness to take a look at your life.

The questions are grouped together according to specific time periods in a person's life and should serve as prompts for remembering specific events in your life. As you read through the questions for a particular time period, write down your answers with as much detail as possible.

For example, in writing down the descriptions of these memories, include where you were at the time, what you were doing, who you were with, how you felt, and any other details that come to mind. It is also helpful to separate how these memories produce sensations in the body, images in the mind, and feelings and thoughts that arise into your awareness.

For the later time periods, write down at least three things that you hope to accomplish during that time in your life.

Take the time to really pause and reflect on your memories and to think about the future.

There is no time limit to complete this exercise.

Childhood (Ages 0–12)

Try to picture the home(s) of your childhood. If you are able, it can be helpful to find actual pictures of yourself as a young child.

What memories do you have of being, or wanting to be, helped, taught, or nurtured?

What were you doing when you were having fun? Where, when, and with whom did you play?

What memories do you have of encounters with your parents, family members, or teachers?
With whom did you feel the closest? When you were upset, feeling rejected, alone, or threatened in any way, to whom did you turn for help and support?

Did you experience any losses as a child?

Who from your childhood best represents what you thought it would mean to "be a man"?
This person(s) could be someone that you actually knew and/or someone from TV, movies, sports, comic books, etc.

Were there experiences in your childhood where you remember when you or your friends (or family members) were either being put down, or put someone else down, for being a "sissy," a "wimp," or "gay" (or some other derogatory name)?

As you were approaching your teenage years, what memories do you have of changes that were beginning to happen in your body that prompted your thoughts, or comments from others, that you were becoming a young man?

Adolescence (Ages 13–19)

Think about your home(s) as a teenager and your time in middle school and high school. Pictures or other memorabilia may help to prompt your memories.

What memories do you have of encounters with friends or peers? With whom did you feel the closest?

What are your memories related to romantic and sexual experiences (e.g., fantasies and relationships)? What were your dating experiences like?

When did you feel like you got recognition, esteem, or acceptance from your friends and peers?

When did you feel disapproval or rejection from your friends and peers?

What memories do you have of avoiding others or avoiding conflict?

What experiences did you have of encounters with your parents, family members, or teachers? With whom did you feel the closest? When you were upset, feeling rejected, alone, or threatened in any way, to whom did you turn for help and support?
Did you experience any losses as an adolescent?

Who from your adolescence best represents what you thought it would mean to "be a man"? This person(s) could be someone that you actually knew and/or someone from TV, movies, sports, comic books, etc.

Were there experiences in your adolescent years where you remember you or your friends (or family members) either being put down, or putting someone else down, for being a "sissy," a "wimp," or "gay" (or some other derogatory name)?

What memories do you have of changes that were happening in your body that prompted your thoughts, or comments from others, that you were becoming a man?

What were your thoughts about who you would become in terms of your interests and aspirations related to getting work or having a career for yourself as an adult? Were there people in your life (or on TV or in movies, etc.) that you thought had jobs that you would want to do or careers that you would want to have as an adult?

How did alcohol and other drugs (and your expectations about and the actual effects of them) play a role in shaping your subjective experiences (i.e., your states of mind) around the challenges of being an adolescent male, e.g., the physical changes in your body, your romantic and sexual experiences, and your sense of self in relationship to other people?

Young Adulthood (Ages 20–34)

How did you choose where and with whom you live and work?

What have been your experiences with leaving home, going to school, getting your first job, or finding a sense of independence (or not) from your family?

What experiences have you had related to being loved and giving love to others (i.e., reciprocal or mutually-felt love)? Is there someone with whom you feel that you are achieving a sense of mutual connection or intimacy? If not, what would be the qualities of the person with whom you might achieve a sense of mutual connection or intimacy? What personal qualities do you "bring to the table"? For example, how would you show concern for your partner? If you wanted your partner to show concern for you, how would you want them to do that?

What roles do you find yourself in as a young man (e.g., husband, father, etc.)? What words would you use to describe yourself in these roles (e.g., protector, provider, nurturer, etc.?)
Who best represents someone with the qualities that you see as ideal in these roles?
This person(s) could be someone that you actually knew (or know) and/or someone from a TV show, a movie, a book, an historical figure, etc.

How do alcohol and other drugs (and your expectations about and the actual affects of them) play a role in shaping your subjective experiences (i.e., your states of mind) around the challenges of being a young adult male, e.g., leaving home, going to school, getting a job, and/or gaining independence from your family, developing a capacity for intimate relationships, and the possibility of marriage and parenthood?

Middle Adulthood (Ages 35–60)

Use your imagination to think about yourself as a middle-aged man (somewhere between the ages of 35 to 60 years old). Where do you think you will be living? With whom do you think you will be living? Try to picture this in your mind as clearly as you can.

How do you see yourself taking care of others who need it? Think about the possible adult responsibilities of childrearing, teaching, demonstrating, and supervising, etc., which you might have with children, adults, employees, or animals.

What might your encounters be like with your partner, children, or grandchildren? How do you see your level of intimacy in these relationships (i.e., your ability to share yourself and be vulnerable with them?)

How do you see yourself being either concerned or unconcerned about the welfare of others (who are not your loved ones)?

How might you manage to coordinate your work and home life?

What mid-life changes in your career and work life might you anticipate?

How do you see yourself becoming older (with the changes that come with age in terms of physical appearance and your self-concept)?

How do you see alcohol and other drugs affecting your subjective experiences (i.e., your states of mind) around the challenges of being a middle age man, e.g., balancing your work and family life, maintaining intimacy in committed relationships, dealing with career changes, transitions, or unemployment, and the aging processes that affect one's physical appearance and sense of self?

Later Adulthood (Ages 60 and above)

Imagine yourself as an older adult male who is over 60 years old. Where do you think that you will be living? Who do you think that you will be living with? Try to picture as clearly as possible your home life and your environment at work or in retirement.

How will you make your decisions about when to withdraw or retire from your primary occupation, work, or career?

What do you imagine your stamina will be like as an older man? How might you deal with decreasing levels of energy to work and live life? How physically fit do you think you will be?

When you look back over your life as an older adult male, what do you think you will be feeling about how you chose to live your life?

How are you becoming aware of your own mortality (i.e., that you will die some day)?
Is there an event(s) that you will have been a part of that might make you feel that things had been taken care of, that you had done your part?

How do you see alcohol and other drugs affecting your subjective experiences (i.e., your states of mind) around the challenges of being a male in later adulthood?

This exercise was developed based on materials from the following sources:

Conway, M. A., & Holmes, A. (2004). Psychosocial stages and the accessibility of autobiographical memories across the life cycle. *Journal of Personality, 72*(3), 461–480.

Mikulincer, M., & Shaver, P. R. (2007). *Attachment in adulthood: Structures, dynamics, and change.* New York: Guilford Press.

Newman, B. M., & Newman, P. R. (2012). *Development through life: A psychosocial approach* (11th ed.). Belmont, CA: Wadsworth Cengage Learning.

O'Neil, J. M. (2008). Summarizing 25 years of research on men's gender role conflict using the gender role conflict scale: New research paradigms and clinical implications. *The Counseling Psychologist, 36*(3), 358–445.

O'Neil, J. M., & Egan, J. (1992). Men's gender role transitions over the lifespan: Transformations and fears of femininity. *Journal of Mental Health Counseling, 14*(3), 305–324.

D

Looking Back to Plan Ahead
Setting Personal Goals

AN EXERCISE FOR MALES IN MIDDLE
ADULTHOOD (AGES 34 TO 60)

The questions below are designed to facilitate a self-reflective process that will help you to set personal goals for yourself. It is often valuable to take a look back over your life, so that you can see where you have come from, know where you are, and make plans for where you are heading. All you need is a pencil, paper, and the willingness to take a look at your life.

The questions are grouped together according to specific time periods in a person's life and should serve as prompts for remembering specific events in your life. As you read through the questions for a particular time period, write down your answers with as much detail as possible.

For example, in writing down the descriptions of these memories, include: where you were at the time, what you were doing, who you were with, how you felt, and any other details that come to mind. It is also helpful to separate how these memories produce sensations in your body, images in your mind, and feelings and thoughts that arise into your awareness.

For the "Later Adulthood" section, use the questions to consider at least three things that you hope to accomplish during that time in your life.

Take the time to really pause and reflect on your memories and to think about the future.

There is no time limit to complete this exercise.

Childhood (Ages 0–12)

Try to picture the home(s) of your childhood. If you have actual pictures of yourself as a child, this can be helpful to prompt memories.

What memories do you have of being, or wanting to be, helped, taught, or nurtured?

What were you doing when you were having fun? Where, when, and with whom did you play?

What memories do you have of encounters with your parents, family members, or teachers?
With whom did you feel the closest? When you were upset, feeling rejected, alone, or threatened in any way, to whom did you turn for help and support?

Did you experience any losses as a child?

Who from your childhood best represents what you thought it would mean to "be a man"?
This person(s) could be someone that you actually knew and/or someone from TV, movies, sports, comic books, etc.

Were there experiences in your childhood where you remember when you or your friends (or family members) were either being put down, or put someone else down, for being a "sissy," a "wimp," or "gay" (or some other derogatory name)?

As you were approaching your teenage years, what memories do you have of changes that were beginning to happen in your body that prompted your thoughts, or comments from others, that you were becoming a young man?

Adolescence (Ages 13–19)

Try to picture the home(s) and school(s) of your adolescent years. Pictures or other memorabilia may help to prompt your memories.

What memories do you have of encounters with friends or peers? With whom did you feel the closest?

What are your memories related to romantic and sexual experiences (e.g., fantasies and relationships)? What were your dating experiences like?

When did you feel like you got recognition, esteem, or acceptance from your friends and peers?

When did you feel disapproval or rejection from your friends and peers?

What memories do you have of avoiding others or avoiding conflict?

What experiences did you have of encounters with your parents, family members, or teachers? With whom did you feel the closest? When you were upset, feeling rejected, alone, or threatened in any way, to whom did you turn for help and support?
Did you experience any losses as an adolescent?

Who from your adolescence best represents what you thought it would mean to "be a man"? This person(s) could be someone that you actually knew and/or someone from TV, movies, sports, comic books, etc.

Were there experiences in your adolescent years where you remember you or your friends (or family members) either being put down, or putting someone else down, for being a "sissy," a "wimp," or "gay" (or some other derogatory name)?

What memories do you have of changes that were happening in your body that prompted your thoughts, or comments from others, that you were becoming a man?

What were your thoughts about who you would become in terms of your interests and aspirations related to getting work or having a career for yourself as an adult? Were there people in your life (or on TV or in movies, etc.) that you thought had jobs that you would want to do or careers that you would want to have as an adult?

How did alcohol and other drugs (and your expectations about and the actual effects of them) play a role in shaping your subjective experiences (i.e., your states of mind) around the challenges of being an adolescent male, e.g., the physical changes in your body, your romantic and sexual experiences, and your sense of self in relationship to other people?

Young Adulthood (Ages 20–34)

Remember your life in your twenties and early thirties. Where and with whom did you live? Try to picture as clearly as possible your home and work environment.

What were your experiences with leaving home, going to school, getting your first job, or finding a sense of independence from your family?

What experiences did you have related to being loved and giving love to others (i.e., reciprocal or mutually-felt love)? With whom did you feel that you achieved a sense of mutual connection or intimacy?

What memories do you have of being concerned or unconcerned for your partner? What memories do you have of being concerned or unconcerned for yourself?

What roles did you find yourself playing as a young man (e.g., husband, father, etc.)? What words would you use to describe yourself in these roles (e.g., protector, provider, nurturer, etc.)? Who best represented someone with the qualities that you saw as being ideal in these roles? This person(s) could have been someone that you actually knew and/ or someone from a TV show, a movie, a book, an historical figure, etc.

How did alcohol and other drugs (and your expectations about and the actual affects of them) play a role in shaping your subjective experiences (i.e., your states of mind) around the challenges of being a young adult male, e.g., leaving home, going to school, getting a job, and/or gaining independence from your family, developing a capacity for intimate relationships, and the possibility of marriage and parenthood?

Middle Adulthood (Ages 35–60)

Consider your current life as a middle-aged man.

How did you choose where and with whom you live and work?

What are your experiences of taking care of others who need it? Think about the adult responsibilities of childrearing, teaching, demonstrating, and supervising, etc., which could be with children, adults, employees, or animals.

What are your encounters like with your partner, children, or grandchildren? Do you feel a level of intimacy in these relationships (i.e., you are able to share yourself and be vulnerable with them)?

How do you see yourself being either concerned or unconcerned about the welfare of others (who are not your loved ones)?

What experiences do you have with divorce or separation, or the dissolving of another significant relationship or union?

How do you manage to coordinate your work and home life?
What events and nonevents have occurred in your life that have caused (or might cause) changes in your work status (e.g., loss of employment or job changes), and/or the meaning of your career or work life?

How do you see yourself becoming older (with the changes that come with age in terms of physical appearance and your self-concept)?

How do alcohol and other drugs (and your expectations about and the actual effects of them) play a role in shaping your subjective experiences (i.e., your states of mind) around the challenges of being a middle age man, e.g., balancing your work and family life, maintaining intimacy in committed relationships, dealing with career changes, transitions, or unemployment, and the aging processes that affect one's physical appearance and sense of self?

Later Adulthood (Ages 60 and above)

Imagine yourself as an older adult male. Where and with whom will you be living? Try to picture as clearly as possible your home life and your environment at work or in retirement.

How will you make your decisions about when to withdraw or retire from your primary occupation, work, or career?

What do you imagine your stamina will be like as an older man? How might you deal with decreasing levels of energy to work and live life? How physically fit do you think you will be?

When you look back over your life as an older adult male, what do you think you will be feeling about how you chose to live your life?

How are you becoming aware of your own mortality (i.e., that you will die some day)?

Is there an event(s) that might make you feel that things had been taken care of, that you had done your part?

How did alcohol and other drugs (and your expectations about and the actual affects of them) play a role in shaping your subjective experiences (i.e., your states of mind) around the challenges of being a male in later adulthood?

This exercise was developed based on materials from the following sources:

Conway, M. A., & Holmes, A. (2004). Psychosocial stages and the accessibility of autobiographical memories across the life cycle. *Journal of Personality, 72*(3), 461–480.

Mikulincer, M., & Shaver, P. R. (2007). *Attachment in adulthood: Structures, dynamics, and change*. New York: Guilford Press.

Newman, B. M., & Newman, P. R. (2012). *Development through life: A psychosocial approach* (11th ed.). Belmont, CA: Wadsworth Cengage Learning.

O'Neil, J. M. (2008). Summarizing 25 years of research on men's gender role conflict using the gender role conflict scale: New research paradigms and clinical implications. *The Counseling Psychologist, 36*(3), 358–445.

O'Neil, J. M., & Egan, J. (1992). Men's gender role transitions over the lifespan: Transformations and fears of femininity. *Journal of Mental Health Counseling, 14*(3), 305–324.

E

Looking Back to Plan Ahead
Setting Personal Goals

AN EXERCISE FOR OLDER ADULT
MALES (AGES 60 AND ABOVE)

The questions below are designed to facilitate a self-reflective process that will help you to set personal goals for yourself. It is often valuable to take a look back over your life, so that you can see where you have come from, know where you are, and make plans for where you are heading. All you need is a pencil, paper, and the willingness to take a look at your life.

The questions are grouped together according to specific time periods in a person's life and should serve as prompts for remembering specific events in your life. As you read through the questions for a particular time period, write down your answers with as much detail as possible.

For example, in writing down the descriptions of these memories, include: where you were at the time, what you were doing, who you were with, how you felt, and any other details that come to mind. It is also helpful to separate how these memories produce sensations in your body, images in your mind, and feelings and thoughts that arise into your awareness.

Take the time to really pause and reflect on your memories and to think about the future.

There is no time limit to complete this exercise.

Childhood (Ages 0–12)

Try to picture the home(s) of your childhood. If you have actual pictures of yourself as a child, this can be helpful to prompt memories.

What memories do you have of being, or wanting to be, helped, taught, or nurtured?

What were you doing when you were having fun? Where, when, and with whom did you play?

What memories do you have of encounters with your parents, family members, or teachers?
With whom did you feel the closest? When you were upset, feeling rejected, alone, or threatened in any way, to whom did you turn for help and support?

Did you experience any losses as a child?

Who from your childhood best represents what you thought it would mean to "be a man"?
This person(s) could be someone that you actually knew and/or someone from TV, movies, sports, comic books, etc.

Were there experiences in your childhood where you remember when you or your friends (or family members) were either being put down, or put someone else down, for being a "sissy," a "wimp," or "gay" (or some other derogatory name)?

As you were approaching your teenage years, what memories do you have of changes that were beginning to happen in your body that prompted your thoughts, or comments from others, that you were becoming a young man?

Adolescence (Ages 13–19)

Try to picture the home(s) and school(s) of your adolescent years. Pictures or other memorabilia may help to prompt your memories.

What memories do you have of encounters with friends or peers? With whom did you feel the closest?

What are your memories related to romantic and sexual experiences (e.g., fantasies and relationships)? What were your dating experiences like?

When did you feel like you got recognition, esteem, or acceptance from your friends and peers?

When did you feel disapproval or rejection from your friends and peers?

What memories do you have of avoiding others or avoiding conflict?

What experiences did you have of encounters with your parents, family members, or teachers? With whom did you feel the closest? When you were upset, feeling rejected, alone, or threatened in any way, to whom did you turn for help and support?

Did you experience any losses as an adolescent?

Who from your adolescence best represents what you thought it would mean to "be a man"? This person(s) could be someone that you actually knew and/or someone from TV, movies, sports, comic books, etc.

Were there experiences in your adolescent years where you remember you or your friends (or family members) either being put down, or putting someone else down, for being a "sissy," a "wimp," or "gay" (or some other derogatory name)?

What memories do you have of changes that were happening in your body that prompted your thoughts, or comments from others, that you were becoming a man?

What were your thoughts about who you would become in terms of your interests and aspirations related to getting work or having a career for yourself as an adult? Were there people in your life (or on TV or in movies, etc.) that you thought had jobs that you would want to do or careers that you would want to have as an adult?

How did alcohol and other drugs (and your expectations about and the actual effects of them) play a role in shaping your subjective experiences (i.e., your states of mind) around the challenges of being an adolescent male, e.g., the physical changes in your body, your romantic and sexual experiences, and your sense of self in relationship to other people?

Young Adulthood (Ages 20–34)

Remember your life in your twenties and early thirties. Where and with whom did you live? Try to picture as clearly as possible your home and work environment.

What were your experiences with leaving home, going to school, getting your first job, or finding a sense of independence from your family?

What experiences did you have related to being loved and giving love to others (i.e., reciprocal or mutually-felt love)? With whom did you feel that you achieved a sense of mutual connection or intimacy?

What memories do you have of being concerned or unconcerned for your partner? What memories do you have of being concerned or unconcerned for yourself?

What roles did you find yourself playing as a young man (e.g., husband, father, etc.)? What words would you use to describe yourself in these roles (e.g., protector, provider, nurturer, etc.)? Who best represented someone with the qualities that you saw as being ideal in these roles? This person(s) could have been someone that you actually knew and/ or someone from a TV show, a movie, a book, an historical figure, etc.

How did alcohol and other drugs (and your expectations about and the actual affects of them) play a role in shaping your subjective experiences (i.e., your states of mind) around the challenges of being a young adult male, e.g., leaving home, going to school, getting a job, and/or gaining independence from your family, developing a capacity for intimate relationships, and the possibility of marriage and parenthood?

Middle Adulthood (Ages 35–60)

Consider your life as a middle-aged man.

How did you choose where and with whom you lived and worked?

What were your experiences of taking care of others who needed it? Think about the adult responsibilities of childrearing, teaching, demonstrating, and supervising, etc., which could be with children, adults, employees, or animals.

What were your encounters like with your partner, children, or grandchildren? Did you feel a level of intimacy in these relationships (i.e., you were able to share yourself and be vulnerable with them)?

How did you see yourself being either concerned or unconcerned about the welfare of others (who were not your loved ones)?

What experiences did you have with divorce or separation, or the dissolving of another significant relationship or union?

How did you manage to coordinate your work and home life?

What events and nonevents occurred in your life that caused changes in your work status (e.g., loss of employment or job changes), and/or the meaning of your career or work life?

How did you see yourself becoming older (with the changes that come with age in terms of physical appearance and your self-concept)?

How did alcohol and other drugs (and your expectations about and the actual effects of them) play a role in shaping your subjective experiences (i.e., your states of mind) around the challenges of being a middle age man, e.g., balancing your work and family life, maintaining intimacy in committed relationships, dealing with career changes, transitions, or unemployment, and the aging processes that affect one's physical appearance and sense of self?

Later Adulthood (Ages 60 and above)

How will you make (or have you made) your decisions about when to withdraw or retire from your primary occupation, work, or career? Are you pursuing a new avocation or pastime, i.e., something that you once did and want to continue doing now that you have some free time?

Are you keeping physically fit? How is your stamina? How might you deal with decreasing levels of energy to work and live life?

When you look back over your life, how do you feel about how you chose to live your life?

How are you becoming aware of your own mortality (i.e., that you will die some day)?

Is there an event(s) that might make you feel that things had been taken care of, that you had done your part?

How did alcohol and other drugs play a role in shaping your subjective experiences (i.e., your states of mind) around the challenges of being a male in later adulthood?

This exercise was developed based on materials from the following sources:

Conway, M. A., & Holmes, A. (2004). Psychosocial stages and the accessibility of autobiographical memories across the life cycle. *Journal of Personality, 72*(3), 461–480.

Mikulincer, M., & Shaver, P. R. (2007). *Attachment in adulthood: Structures, dynamics, and change.* New York: Guilford Press.

Newman, B. M., & Newman, P. R. (2012). *Development through life: A psychosocial approach* (11th ed.). Belmont, CA: Wadsworth Cengage Learning.

O'Neil, J. M. (2008). Summarizing 25 years of research on men's gender role conflict using the gender role conflict scale: New research paradigms and clinical implications. *The Counseling Psychologist, 36*(3), 358–445.

O'Neil, J. M., & Egan, J. (1992). Men's gender role transitions over the lifespan: Transformations and fears of femininity. *Journal of Mental Health Counseling, 14*(3), 305–324.

Index